FROM FORMAL TO MATERIAL EQUALITY

European Contract Law and Theory Series, Volume 6

FROM FORMAL TO MATERIAL EQUALITY

Comparative Perspectives from History, Plurality of Disciplines and Theory

Edited by
Stefan GRUNDMANN
Jan THIESSEN

INTERSENTIA
Cambridge – Antwerp – Chicago

Intersentia Ltd
8 Wellington Mews
Wellington Street | Cambridge
CB1 1HW | United Kingdom
Tel: +44 1223 736 170
Email: mail@intersentia.co.uk
www.intersentia.com | www.intersentia.co.uk

Distribution for the UK and
Rest of the World (incl. Eastern Europe)
NBN International
1 Deltic Avenue, Rooksley
Milton Keynes MK13 8LD
United Kingdom
Tel: +44 1752 202 301 | Fax: +44 1752 202 331
Email: orders@nbninternational.com

Distribution for Europe
Lefebvre Sarrut Belgium NV
Hoogstraat 139/6
1000 Brussels
Belgium
Tel: +32 (0)800 39 067
Email: mail@intersentia.be

Distribution for the USA and Canada
Independent Publishers Group
Order Department
814 North Franklin Street
Chicago, IL 60610
USA
Tel: +1 800 888 4741 (toll free) | Fax: +1 312 337 5985
Email: orders@ipgbook.com

From Formal to Material Equality. Comparative Perspectives from History, Plurality of Disciplines and Theory

Artwork on cover: Composition with figures (detail), Hendrik Nicolaas Werkman, 1944 - Rijksmuseum, Amsterdam

ISBN 978-1-83970-277-8
D/2023/7849/3
NUR 822

British Library Cataloguing in Publication Data. A catalogue record for this book is available from the British Library.

CONTENTS

LIST OF AUTHORS

Marietta Auer
Director at the Max Planck Institute of Legal History and Legal Theory in Frankfurt, Germany; Professor of Private Law and Interdisciplinary Foundations of Law at the University of Giessen, Germany.

Andreas Engert
Professor of Private Law, Commercial, Company and Capital Markets Law, and Foundations of Law at Freie Universität Berlin, Germany; research member of the European Corporate Governance Institute (ECGI).

Muriel Fabre-Magnan
Professor at the University of Paris 1 (Panthéon-Sorbonne).

Stefan Grundmann
Professor of Transnational Law & Theory at the European University Institute in Florence, Italy; Professor of Private and Business Law at Humboldt-University in Berlin, Germany.

Tilman Repgen
Professor of Civil Law, History of German Law, Private Law in Modernity; Dean of the Faculty of Law at Universität Hamburg, Germany.

Dan Wielsch
Professor of Private Law and Legal Theory, University of Cologne.

FROM FORMAL TO MATERIAL EQUALITY

Key Insights from History and in a Multidisciplinary Perspective

Stefan GRUNDMANN

1. INTRODUCTION TO EQUALITY, HISTORY AND SOCIAL THEORY

Equality – the principle of equality, including principles of anti-discrimination that in many jurisdictions and/or languages are seen as specific principles of equality – appears in at least three manifestations in law. It comes in the form of legal norms (for example, Art. 3 of the German Constitution – Grundgesetz; Title III (Arts. 20–26) of the EU Charter of Fundamental Rights). It also comes – according to the understanding of fundamental rights – as an overarching legal principle.[1] Finally, over a good two millennia, equality has even been perceived as the ultimate *ratio* and goal of law itself – if, with Aristotle, one sees equality as the essence of justice.[2] Yet, despite this multilayered, comprehensive meaning of equality – the principle of equality, the principles of equality – in and for law, and despite the overarching character of the concept, two paradoxical main trends need to be seen for equality and the principles of equality. They

---

1 Globally, probably the most prominent author for the distinction between "rules" and "principles" – in his concept both are legally binding, but principles are more open-textured and contain overarching value judgements of the whole legal system and thus guiding adjudication, as well rule-setting – is R. Dworkin, *Taking Rights Seriously*, Harvard Univ. Press, Cambridge, MA., 1977, esp. pp. 81–130 *et passim*; in German literature very early, J. Esser, *Grundsatz und Norm in der richterlichen Fortbildung des Privatrechts*, Mohr-Siebeck, Tübingen 1956 (4th edn. 1990); today, for instance, T. Möllers, 'Working with Legal Principles – demonstrated using Private Autonomy and Freedom of Contract as Examples' (2018) 14(2) *European Review of Contract Law* 101, taking as its main example party autonomy and freedom of contract; on the characterisation of fundamental rights as "principles", see the so-called *"Prinzipientheorie"* (theory of principles), which is seen as an alternative to the German Constitutional Court's approach of weighing fundamental rights and the interests embodied in them (in a so-called "practical alignment" – '*praktische Konkordanz*': R. Alexy, *Theorie der Grundrechte*, Suhrkamp, Frankfurt 1986, esp. pp. 77–87 (based on Dworkin's distinction, but specifying that the concretisation and concrete decision on the clash of interests is possible only in each individual case, and that there is no absolute rule of precedence of one principle over another); R. Poscher, 'Theorie eines Phantoms – die erfolglose Suche der Prinzipientheorie nach ihrem Gegenstand' (2010) 1(4) *Rechtswissenschaft (ReWiss)* 349; J. Klement, 'Vom Nutzen einer Theorie, die alles erklärt – Robert Alexys Prinzipientheorie aus der Sicht der Grundrechtsdogmatik' (2008) 63 *Juristen-Zeitung (JZ)* 756.

2 On Artistotle's concept of equality as the essence of justice, see K. Röhl, *Die Gerechtigkeitstheorie des Aristoteles aus der Sicht sozialpsychologischer Gerechtigkeitsforschung*, Baden-Baden, Nomos 1992, p. 11 *et seq*. The key treatise is the *Nicomachean Ethics*, esp. pp. 1129–33. On the concept of justice constituting the core aim of law creation (for millennia), see B. Rüthers, C. Fischer and A. Birk, *Rechtstheorie*, 12th ed., C.H. Beck, Munich 2021, §9 pp. 214–57; paradigmatic for the equality principle as the concept of justice: German Constitutional Court, Official Reports (BVerfGE) 3, 58 (135): "The equality principle implies for the legislature a general guideline in the quest for justice, namely to treat equal things equally and unequal things (considering their characteristics) unequally." [translation by the author]; G. Robbers, *Gerechtigkeit als Rechtsprinzip – über den Begriff der Gerechtigkeit in der Rechtsprechung des Bundesverfassungsgerichts*, Nomos, Baden-Baden 1980, p. 163 gives a list of all decisions taken by the German Constitutional Court (until vol. 48) that invoke justice as the main guiding principle. Most prominent after, and in reference to, the NS regime of terror and injustice: G. Radbruch, 'Gesetzliches Unrecht und übergesetzliches Recht' (1946) 1 *Süddeutsche Juristen-Zeitung (SJZ)* 105 ("Radbruch's Formula") (law that does not even pertain to achieve equality loses its character as law). Of minor importance in this context is the question whether consequentialist theories and descriptions of benchmarks did not lead to a change in this respect, as of the 1960s. See K. Mathis, 'Consequentialism in Law', in K. Mathis (ed), *Efficiency, Sustainability and Justice to Future Generations*, Springer, Holland 2011, p. 3 *et seq*. (and also the whole book); C. Kirchner, 'Zur konsequentialistischen Interpretationsmethode – Der Beitrag der Rechtswissenschaft zur reziproken methodischen Annäherung von Ökonomik und Rechtswissenschaft' in *Festschrift für (Essays in Honour of) H-B. Schäfer*, Springer/Gabler, Wiesbaden 2008, p. 37; still worth reading: M. Deckert, *Folgenorientierung in der Rechtsanwendung*, C.H. Beck, Munich 1995.

have meant radically different things at different times in historical development (see below, section 2) and they are seen very differently in the circle of disciplines (see, paradigmatically, below, section 3).

Probably no other general legal concept – or, at best, freedom – has moved the history of the good and the right in society in a comparable and similarly controversial way as equality and the principle or principles of equality. Fraternity (*fraternité*) – later *solidarité*, and later in the nineteenth century, and in the twentieth century, social justice – had, and have, a much more recent history, at least if one does not want to understand the Christian, fundamentally non-legalised "charity" as a largely similar precursor.[3] As a lived political and legal postulate, solidarity had a comparably powerful effect only in the second half of the nineteenth century, and fully only in the twentieth century.[4] Equality and freedom, proclaimed as the two great (early) postulates of the two pioneering human rights declarations at the beginning of the "present", are undoubtedly

---

3 Today, this is probably the clearly prevailing view: see, for instance, J. Habermas, 'Why the Necessary Cooperation Does Not Happen: Introduction To A Conversation Between Emmanuel Macron and Sigmar Gabriel on Europe's Future' (*Social Europe*, 20.03.2017): "Solidarity is not the same thing as charity." (available at <https://www.socialeurope.eu/pulling-cart-mire-renewed-case-european-solidarity>).

4 On solidarity as a societal and as a legal concept, namely in France and Germany, see, e.g. K. Bayertz (ed), *Solidarität: Begriff und Problem*, 3rd ed., Suhrkamp, Frankfurt, 2020 (1st ed. 1998); H. Bude, *Solidarität: Die Zukunft einer großen Idee*, Hanser, Munich 2019; E. Carigiet, *Gesellschaftliche Solidarität: Prinzipien, Perspektiven und Weiterentwicklung der sozialen Sicherheit*, Helbing & Lichtenhahn, Basle 2001; J. Gerhards, H. Lengfeld, Z. Ignácz, F. Kley and M. Priem, *European Solidarity in Times of Crisis – Insights from a Thirteen-Country Survey*, Routledge, London 2019 (development of criteria and empirical inquiry); K-O. Hondrich and C. Koch-Arzberger, *Solidarität in der modernen Gesellschaft*, Fischer, Frankfurt 1992; C. Lahusen and M. Grasso (eds), *Solidarity in Europe – Citizens' Responses in Times of Crisis*, Springer, Cham 2018; G. Reisz, 'Solidarität in Deutschland und Frankreich: Eine politische Deutungsanalyse' (2006) 47 *Politische Vierteljahresschrift* 704. On social justice as a societal, and legal, concept, see the path-breaking R. Pound, 'Social Justice and Legal Justice (Social Justice and Legal Justice (address before the Allegheny County Bar Ass'n at Pittsburg, April 5, 1912)' (1912) 75 *Central Law Journal* 455; and today, for instance, A.B. Atkinson, *Social Justice and Public Policy*, MIT Press, Cambridge, MA., 1983; D. Damjanovic, 'The EU market rules as social market rules: why the EU can be a social market economy' (2013) 50 *Common Market Law Review* 1685; W. Droel, *What is Social Justice?*, Blackwell, Oxford 2011; L. Frederking, *Reconstructing Social Justice*, Routledge, London 2014; C. Pérez-Garzón, 'What is social justice? A new history of its meaning in the transnational legal discourse' (2019) 43 *Revista Derecho del Estado* 67; from the recent EU legislative agenda, see, for instance, Communication from the Commission – Europe 2020, COM(2010) 2020 final; Communication from the Commission to the European Parliament, the Council, the European Economic and Social Committee and the Committee of Regions: Social Business Initiative: Creating a favourable climate for social enterprises, key stakeholders in the social economy and innovation, COM(2011) 682 final; EU Commission, The European Pillar of Social Rights Action Plan, 12/2020; see also proposal for an EU directive on minimum wages: COM(2020) 682 final; but also Art. 3, para. 3 TEU (Treaty of the European Union) and Title IV of the EU Charter on Fundamental Rights ("Solidarity"); general survey (also on development in time) in U. Mückenberger, 'Eine europäische Sozialverfassung?' (2014) 49(4) *Europarecht (EuR)* 369.

in a relationship of tension with each other, and are, therefore, also considered together selectively or more broadly in the following, and in many of the other contributions to this volume.[5]

As it has been stated that probably no other general legal concept (except perhaps freedom) has moved the history of the good and the right in society in a comparable way to equality and equality principles, the test, in this contribution, for this claim is twofold. On the one hand, reference should be made to the core of central disciplines, and, on the other, to the staggering truth and rawness of history. With regard to the philosophical–ethical foundation as the one core discipline, the big question arises as to how two so fundamentally different (from today's point of view) standpoints as equality and freedom could come together. On the one hand, at the beginning of ethics and the consideration of justice, in Aristotle, there is an understanding of justice as the realisation of equality, i.e. the understanding that all justice must manifest itself in the equality of the members of a community of rights and duties (below, section 2.1). Conversely, slavery and the disenfranchisement of women and all foreigners, were not seen even remotely as ethical or justice problems (below, section 2.2). The relationship to equality in economics is similarly fraught with tension, or even conflict, as was the philosophical strand in at least the first two millennia – and the latter is even the outstanding strand of the normativity of the morally good. Economics is, after all, the strand of social sciences that many observers today see as the dominant one in the consideration of the reality of life. For it is not equal treatment but maximisation of overall welfare as an efficiency goal that is conventionally and (despite critical or differentiating voices) predominantly seen today as the ultimate yardstick in economics.[6] In economics, attempts are made to understand both goals as (partly) concurrent. In the final analysis,

---

5 This tension seems most intense in the contributions to this volume by M. Auer, 'Two Centuries of Private Law Theory on Formal and Material Equality'; and by A. Engert, 'Equality between Efficiency and Distribution: Perspectives in Law & Economics'.

6 For the classical orientation of economics, namely of market relations, towards the objective of total welfare and its most efficient pursuit, see, for instance, A. Kronmann and A. Posner, *The Economics of Contract Law*, Little, Brown & Company, Boston 1979, introduction pp. 1–2 (topmost evaluation standard: "wealth of society"); A. Posner, 'Wealth Maximization Revisited' (1985) 2(1) *Notre Dame Journal of Law, Ethics & Public Policy* 85. Of quintessential importance, redistribution is seen as irrelevant to this equation, e.g. J. Hirshleifer, *Price Theory and Applications*, Prentice-Hall, New Jersey 1976, p. 287; O.E. Williamson, 'Peak-load pricing and optimal capacity under indivisibility constraints' (1966) 56(4) *The American Economic Review* 810, esp. 813 ("society is indifferent to the income redistribution effects"); in detail, F. Gómez-Pomar, 'European Contract Law and Economic Welfare: A View from Law and Economics' in S. Grundmann (ed), *Constitutional Values and European Contract Law*, Wolters-Kluwer, Hürth 2008, p. 215, esp. pp. 228–36; and, very sharp, L. Kaplow and S. Shavell, 'Why the Legal System Is Less Efficient than the Income Tax in Redistributing Income' (1994) 23 (2) *The Journal of Legal Studies* 667; discussion by S. Grundmann in S. Grundmann, H-W. Micklitz and M. Renner, *New Private Law Theory: A Pluralist Approach*, CUP, Cambridge 2021, ch. 11.

however, the priority of the overall welfare goal is postulated (and considerations aimed at demonstrating a parallelism of the two goals appear, in part, rather artificial, in order to avoid an all-too-open fundamental discrepancy with socially strongly consensual developments in questions of concepts of equality). Two leading disciplines have, thus, for a very long time had their difficulties with equality as it is seen today, as a normative model in Western democratic societies based on the rule of law.

The truth and the rawness of history present themselves just as forcefully, or even more so, in opposition to what this truth is today. One is almost inclined to state that the fundamental violation of principles of equality over millennia characterises the darkest pages of history. Such violation runs from: (i) slavery and, later, serfdom to; (ii) more or less far-reaching disenfranchisement, or "only" disadvantage, of a whole sex – widespread, openly and directly – or, in other cases, "only" subtly systemically mediated; this continues (iii) with the attacks on, up to the extermination of, the foreigner (from foreigners to other ethnic groups designated as "races", often linked to the criterion of having a different religion). These three encroachments on the idea of equality and justice could hardly be more profound. At the same time, they have consistently marked centuries and millennia of history, with worldwide wars, genocide and daily cruelty. Hardly any other ethical postulates have been subject to such mass, systematic, and sometimes even conviction-based, violation as equality and the principle of equality. Therefore, probably no other general legal concept has (as has been said) moved the history of the good and the right in society in a comparable way to equality and the principle of equality. Moreover, the same applies to true core disciplines of their consideration; perhaps less immediately shocking, but no less important for scientific – including jurisprudential – discourse.

For this reason, it is important to assure oneself of central determinants both in the historical development *and* in the disciplinary survey, even though this can only be in a highly condensed and concise way. This is the aim of the present volume and the introduction to the core lines – historical and multi-disciplinary – because it would be inappropriate to see the concept from the perspective(s) of only one, or even two, disciplines.[7] Despite the breadth of the disciplines consulted, whose comparison is also combined with a comparison across the historical stages, some form of limitation is unavoidable. The editors and authors of this volume could have compared social theory or legal

[7] On my understanding of a modern (pluralistic) legal theory that is grounded in such a rich array of disciplines, and for heuristic, normative and ontological reasons must necessarily be grounded in them, see for more detail, S. Grundmann, H-W. Micklitz and M. Renner, above n. 6 (and also German version 2015) (esp. introduction); and in still more detail, S. Grundmann, 'Pluralistische Privatrechtstheorie – Prolegomena zu einer pluralistisch-gesellschaftswissenschaftlichen Rechtstheorie als normatives Desiderat' ("normativer Pluralismus"), *RabelsZ* 85 (2022) 364.

history (also) with doctrinal thinking related to the principle of equality, and then we would have noticed how radically different the fault lines are.[8] This would also be indispensable and important for concretisation: the question of suitability in practical cases. Nevertheless, doctrinal thinking is left out of this chapter to a large extent, for simplicity's sake. Complementary, as it were, to doctrinal thinking, a sketch of the core developments over the millennia – primarily some central moments of upheaval – should be sketched from a bird's-eye view, and this perspective should be combined with what society as a whole – in the mirror of its central scientific disciplines – thinks of equality. All this is related – as in a burning-glass – to the central question: is equality only formally, or more materially, guaranteed? In this context, "material" equality – in confrontation with "formal" equality – is understood as a more far-reaching actual realisation of equality (between those classified as equal). By focusing on this core criterion, we test the general intuition,[9] especially in German literature, where this distinction has been developed particularly intensively, and a trend towards an increase in materialisation has often been sensed.[10]

2. HISTORICAL STAGES OF MATERIALISATION

2.1. FRAMEWORK AND STARTING POINT

After what has been said, the brief outline of the history of equality (in this volume, and even more so in the introduction) can only take the form of a bird's-eye view of a few core moments. The focus, in each case, is on the question

---

8 S. Grundmann, 'Gleichheit zwischen Dogmatik und Sozialtheorie' in *Festschrift für Singer*, Berliner Wissenschaftsverlag, Berlin 2021, p. 225. Important insights and passages that this article develops on the tension between the factual structure of the equality principle, on the one hand, and the doctrinal understanding of it, on the other hand, are integrated into the present text, albeit now in a different context, namely that of both vertical and horizontal comparison.

9 E.g., in this volume, M. Auer; for more general quotations, see C-W. Canaris; M. Grünberger; M. Renner, below n. 10.

10 See powerful narrative in F. Wieacker, *Privatrechtsgeschichte der Neuzeit – unter besonderer Berücksichtigung der deutschen Entwicklung*, Vandenhoeck & Ruprecht, Göttingen 2016, pp. 586 *et seq.*; C-W Canaris, 'Wandlungen des Schuldvertragsrechts – Tendenzen zu seiner "Materialisierung"' (2000) 200 *Archiv für die civilistische Praxis (AcP)* 273; critical of both: J. Rückert in *Historisch-Kritischer Kommentar-BGB* (Band I) Mohr Siebeck, Tübingen 2003, before §1: "Das BGB und seine Prinzipien", paras. 93 *et seq.* and 105. In recent literature, coming back to Wieacker's and Canaris's narratives: M. Grünberger, *Personale Gleichheit – der Grundsatz der Gleichbehandlung im Zivilrecht*, Nomos, Baden-Baden 2013, esp. pp. 52–57 and pp. 106–15; and, in this volume, M. Auer; on the larger socio-theoretical context, see M. Renner, in S. Grundmann, H-W. Micklitz and M. Renner (above n. 6), ch. 10: Formalism, Material and Procedural Justice; from a philosophical–sociological perspective, see the concise thesis and summary by J. Habermas, 'Paradigms of Law' (1995–1996) 17 *Cardozo Law Review* 771.

of where transitions from a more formal, and at the same time narrower, understanding of equality to a more material guarantee, or vice versa, can be observed. From this perspective, the three core moments are described below.

The first core moment of development is addressed only implicitly, as an approach in the presentation of "equal human nature" (Repgen). In other contributions, it serves as a basis or background when discussing the last "two centuries of private law theory on formal and material equality" (Auer) and "equal dignity of human beings" ("*égale dignité des êtres humains*") (Fabre-Magnan), both contributions being strongly based on intellectual history, and partly on philosophy. This first moment has to be seen in the development of Aristotle's first pioneering concept of equality, which shaped antiquity and the Middle Ages like no other, and still seems very influential today. While Aristotle understood justice, in relation to the person, as an individual virtue, he saw the striving for equal treatment and its realisation as the core of justice itself and equated both (equal treatment and justice) – objectified, and at least in principle – with each other.[11] In doing so, he coined the formula – for the general principle of equality, although in his case it was formulated in general terms anyway – that what is equal should be treated equally, while what is unequal should be treated unequally. For Aristotle, the yardstick for equality and inequality lies in the (measure of) merit(s) for society (geometric or proportional equality). In the present context (the volume as a whole, as well as the introduction), Aristotle's doctrine of equality and justice is not in the foreground, for two reasons, and does not need to be explored further with its (important) further distinctions. Firstly, as Repgen points out, Aristotle (and, more generally, the ancient world) contributed nothing or little to equality in status. Equality in status, however, was to be at the centre of the political and legal development towards the principle of equality over the most recent centuries, whereas Aristotle viewed disenfranchisement of slaves, women and strangers as being in accordance with his concept of equality, because all were unequal in merit to men of their own polis or kingdom.[12] On the other hand – and related to the first aspect – the problem does not appear to be central, to Aristotle, that equality principles partly have only a formal effect; that for the reality of life it must be stated that this lags behind actual equal treatment; and that, therefore, a materialisation should be discussed. He does not discuss one aspect – so important for a perspective of materialisation – and this is the question of which means can be used to enhance

---

11 On this, and on the following, see references in n. 2 above (on Aristotle and his philosophy of equality and justice).

12 The key passage is *Nikomachische Ethik*, esp. pp. 1129–33; critical on this: C.A. MacKinnon, *Sexual Harassment of Working Women: A Case of Sex Discrimination*, Yale University Press, New Haven 1979, esp. pp. 106–141; C.A. MacKinnon, 'Auf dem Weg zu einer neuen Theorie der Gleichheit' (1994) *KritV* 363, 364 *et seq.*; For the other – important – distinctions in Aristotle's concept of equality and justice, see references in n. 2 above.

the effect and actual guarantee of equality. The latter, however, is the main topic of this paper and collection (see sections 3.1 and 4 below).

The most important developments in the history of the principle of equality beyond Aristotle, then, concern two aspects. These are, on the one hand, "personal equality" (Grünberger) or – probably identical in content – "equality in status" (Repgen); and, on the other hand, the struggle for the source of legitimacy for the principle of equality as a legal principle and fundamental right, not only a virtue and moral principle (as with Aristotle). The latter question refers, namely, to the legitimisation as a legal principle grounded in nature – namely human nature – or grounded in law. Both developments, closely related to each other, nevertheless fall into two key moments in time. These are, respectively, the beginning of the modern era (the first half of the sixteenth century – see section 2.2 below) and the time of the beginning of the present era ("*Gegenwart*"), in the years around 1800 (see section 2.3 below).[13]

2.2. EQUALITY AS HUMAN BEINGS – EARLY MODERN TIMES (REPGEN)

From today's perspective, the equality and justice gap in the work of the father of ethics, justice and equality thinking, Aristotle, could hardly be more dramatic than in the case of personal equality, equality in status, or (probably most precisely) equality by virtue of being human. The postulate that people are to be treated equally, even in their personal status, by virtue of their humanity, has a completely different, much more recent, root and history than Aristotle's ethics. It is precisely in this respect that the beginning of the modern era reaches aeons beyond even the most enlightened Attic-Hellenic ethics and philosophy. While in primitive Christianity (in Paul), predispositions to equal treatment can already be found for status (equal treatment and "brotherhood" in faith,

[13] This latter period is vividly described by Koselleck as the "saddle period" of human history (with, among other things, the American Declaration of Independence and Constitution, and the French Declaration of Human Rights). The core consideration is that the three or four decades before, and around, 1800 saw such fundamental reorientations conceptually (namely in political philosophy), but also in social developments, that they – and not a single point in time – marked the entry into the present day: see R. Koselleck, Introduction ("*Einleitung*") in *Geschichtliche Grundbegriffe-Historisches Lexikon zur politisch-sozialen Sprache in Deutschland Bd. 1*, Klett-Cotta, Stuttgart 1972, pp. XIII–XXIII; R. Koselleck (ed), *Historische Semantik und Begriffsgeschichte*, Klett-Cotta, Stuttgart 1979; e.g. G. Motzkin, 'On the Notion of Historical (Dis)continuity: Reinhart Koselleck's Construction of the Sattelzeit' (2005) 1 *Contributions to the History of Concepts* 145. In any case, such a fundamental re-evaluation can indeed be found with respect to the topic discussed, namely in the question of what has to be seen as the key reason for a universal principle of equality (see section 2.3 below).

but not yet in civic and civil life), equality in personal status becomes a legal postulate only much later. Grounded in the character of man, shared by all as human beings, such rule is first really established and championed as a political and legal postulate in the School of Salamanca, in the first half of the sixteenth century. The postulate is grounded here in a Christian-motivated human-related image of equality, developed, above all, in the sermons and writings of Antón Montesino and Francisco de Vitoria.[14]

This is a perhaps surprising, but very largely developed, early form of personal equality, and thus ultimately even the basis of modern anti-discrimination law. As an object, the line of argumentation in the concrete case primarily aims at foreignness, alienage or ethnicity (all too often (mis)defined as race, in history). The reasoning could, however, easily be applied to gender as well; and, of course, to serfdom and slavery. In the case of the South and Central American populations, the latter features are de facto added in the so-called encomienda system (despite an underlying rhetoric to the contrary).

As obvious as this source is, in retrospect, for modern anti-discrimination law – as well as the fact that this line of thinking does not start in natural law and Enlightenment thought only, as Repgen points out – central differences to the modern understanding of equality in status are also important. It seems less important that the basis of legitimation is biblical – the equality of man with God, of all men – because, as Repgen also points out, this consideration becomes a legal principle, and one that is also legally sanctioned. Discriminatory acts against indigenous peoples (especially expropriation, disenfranchisement and enslavement) are seen as mortal sins and secular injustices. From this ensues rights and obligations. Indeed, because mortal sin (according to the late scholastic doctrine of restitution) can only be redeemed through active repentance, legal obligations and claims for restitution arise from the violation of (formerly) indigenous property.

As important as this construction may be, it has a central limitation that I consider to be a particularly important difference, especially from the perspective of the twentieth century. This limitation results from the concrete design of the argument. In fact, in this line of arguments, the human nature of the indigenous population had to be positively proven, namely that the creature in question was created in the image of God. This creation in the image

---

14 On this development in more detail, see T. Repgen in this volume (with sharp juxtaposition, on the one hand, of the Christian-inspired lines of argumentation that base equality on the idea that all human beings derive their nature from a similarity with God, including development of this idea into a legal norm, and on the other hand of those that remained inspired by antiquity, e.g. in the *usus modernus*). The core idea is that the "person is [no longer] degraded to a mere thing". For a parallel line of arguments in the intellectual history, see L. Siedentop, *Die Erfindung des Individuums: Der Liberalismus und die westliche Welt*, Klett-Cotta, Stuttgart 2015.

of God was seen in the fact that the person had to be able to create society, and shape his or her environment in a meaningful way (which was obviously the case in South American empires such as those of the Aztecs or the Incas). This was the line of argumentation and evidence in the sermons and writings of Antón Montesino and Francisco de Vitoria. Consequently, in this concept, human nature is not established by human descent alone (the concept was already revolutionary enough without this further step and was, after all, only applied to a particularly blatant case – anything more would hardly have been conceivable). One point is still important: Christian faith was not demanded, i.e. not postulated as constituting humanity. While Jewish life in the Nazi era could also have been understood as obviously resistant to discrimination, in this line of thinking (i.e. easily subsumed under Montesino's and Vitoria's verdicts), this would not have been so self-evident in the case of so-called life-unworthy (human) life, which was also extinguished en masse. Moreover, in the case of less obvious complete disenfranchisement – for example in the relationship between the sexes – it would not necessarily have been argued that, here, a creature was not being treated as 'equal' according to its nature – created in the image of God. In this respect, modern anti-discrimination law – in the universal assumption of humanity as the basis of equality in status, but arguably also in the threshold above which discrimination is sanctioned – still significantly exceeds the truly groundbreaking considerations of Montesino and Vitoria. This applies, above all, to the conceptual foundation, namely the foundation in human descent alone, which, probably only since Rousseau, has guaranteed the right to equal treatment as such.[15] Moreover, the idea that discrimination between the sexes also appears incompatible with this argumentation approach was not taken up for centuries. Finally, the question of the extent to which a tendency towards the materialisation of the principle of equality is to be seen in this development remains to be addressed as well – indeed, it appears to be hotly disputed in recent times (see section 3.2 below). In summary, while the birth of a legal postulate of personal equality can be traced back to the sixteenth century, important steps – conceptual and practical, also in the ambit of application – were still to come.

---

15 Rousseau contrasts the state of nature with that of socialisation: the natural equality of man is not a legal category, since law only plays a role in the state of socialisation, but rather symmetrical independence. See J-J. ROUSSEAU, *Discours sur l'origine et les fondements de l'inégalité parmi les hommes*, Marc-Michel Ray, Amsterdam 1755; finally, the legal equality to be established by social contract can also remedy the natural mental and physical inequality between people: *Du Contrat Social*, Marc-Michel Ray, Amsterdam 1762 (esp. ch. IX). The temporal proximity of these powerful texts suggests an influence on the Declaration of the Rights of Man and of the Citizen of 1789, which is still formally part of the French Constitution today, and whose first article reads, "*Les hommes naissent et demeurent libres et égaux en droits. Les distinctions sociales ne peuvent être fondées que sur l'utilité commune.*" – more on this in the following.

2.3. EQUALITY IN LAW – TWO CENTURIES OF AN EQUALITY CONCEPT (AUER, JOUANJAN)

As important and groundbreaking as the thoughts of the School of Salamanca and the question of the treatment of the indigenous original populations of Latin America may have been, in hindsight they still appear as mere isolated appeals, albeit very intellectually powerful ones. The postulate of equality in status, and indeed as a legal-political issue, did not grasp the masses until two-and-a-half centuries later. Only with the human rights declarations in the US Constitution of 1786, and above all – particularly clearly and unconditionally – in the French Declaration of Human Rights of 1789, i.e. (in the saddle period) at the beginning of the present era, does it broadly become the lived postulate of a new age. Two further historical papers have been devoted to the developments of the two centuries following this prelude – which were also widely lived and enforced in legal terms; one more from a constitutional law perspective, the other from a private law and strongly intellectual-historical-philosophical perspective.

Jouanjan, according to his own statements, focused his contribution solely on the general principle of equality under constitutional law.[16] The formulation of this principle in the legal acts relevant to Jouanjan appears, however, mainly to be driven by the concern of guaranteeing equality in status (traditionally with the focus on the so-called 'specific', non-general equality principles). In this perspective, the considerations of the author concern both the general principle of equality and the specific principles of equality. At the core of the discussions was the transition from a concept in which the principle of equality was derived from human nature, to one in which the focus was on equality before the law and conferral by the law. While for Montesino and Vitoria, the word of the Bible formed the ultimate benchmark and ground for legitimacy, creation as a human being remained central in the Age of Enlightenment, and in the natural law approach, irrespective of these religious foundations. This applies up to the times of the Declarations of Human Rights (in the US and in France), especially Article 1 of the Déclaration des Droits de l'Homme et du Citoyen of August 1789, according to which human beings are born and remain free and equal (*"Les hommes naissent et demeurent libres et égaux"*) (in the individual enumeration in Article 2, the principle is not listed again, solely because of shortcomings in the editorial process). The creation as a human being – here

---

[16] The written contribution, unfortunately, failed to materialise. In Jouanjan's publications on the principle of equality, see esp. O. Jouanjan, 'Logiques de l'égalité' (2020) *Conseil constitutionnel* (ed), Titre VII, n° 4; O. Jouanjan, 'Conclusions' in C. Courvoisier and P. Charlot (eds), *Actualité politique et juridique de l'égalité*, Editions universitaires de Dijon, Dijon 2003, p. 245; O. Jouanjan, 'Zur Geschichte und Aktualität des Gleichheitssatzes in Frankreich' (2002) *Europäische Grundrechte Zeitschrift* 314; O. Jouanjan, 'Gleichheitssatz und Nicht-Diskriminierung in Frankreich' in R. Wolfrum (ed), *Gleichheit und Nicht-Diskriminierung im nationalen und internationalen Menschenrechtsschutz*, Springer, Cham 2003, p. 59.

apparently independent of a test of whether he or she is capable of shaping society and social structures – is in itself the decisive reason for legitimisation.[17] In the immediate successor acts, Jouanjan already sees the change towards an understanding according to which the law, and only the law, including the constitutional act, grants and confers equality rights, i.e. equality "before the law", not by nature. This was the case in the constitutions in the German *Länder* (1814–1820), and in the Paulskirche Constitution (1848), in which the contents of the principle of equality appeared, similarly "posited", as *historically* founded rights. This was followed by constitutions – of the French Third Republic, as well as of the Weimar Republic – without guarantees of fundamental rights, or with guarantees of fundamental rights that were often understood – wrongly, as we believe today – as merely programmatic exhortations. Insofar as a successive weakening can be seen – certainly in the pathos of legitimation – first in the reference to the state (constitutional) legislator, and then in the absence of even a binding obligation on the legislator, this contradicts one narrative that is often heard. This narrative wants to assume a continuously increasing legal value and power for the principle of equality in society, especially equality in status, over the centuries.

Since this development is, however, primarily related to the question of the pre-legislative nature or the binding force of the equality principle vis-à-vis the legislator, it only indirectly concerns the questions of whether and when the equality principle (or principles) developed from a more formal to a more material form, and for what reason. This question, on the other hand, is the focus of Auer's contribution, which is also historically based, but due to its conceptual orientation – legal-theoretical-ideological – can be discussed even more conclusively as a starting point for the considerations on the social theory of the equality principle (below, section 3).

3. MATERIALISATION OF EQUALITY AND SOCIAL THEORY

In a first step, we saw how a principle of equality in status emerged from an initially Christian set of values (already understood as legal principle and rule), then was seen as being anchored in the status of human being (with a rule conceived as philosophically natural law), and finally was seen as positive, 'posited' law. This first step, and its three phases, are to be compared in a second

---

17 The principle of natural equality by birth is also found in s. 1 of the Virgina Declaration of Rights, 1776: "That all men are by nature equally free and independent and have certain inherent rights, of which, when they enter into a state of society, they cannot, by any compact, deprive or divest their posterity; namely, the enjoyment of life and liberty, with the means of acquiring and possessing property, and pursuing and obtaining happiness and safety."

step with social theory and its broad array of disciplines – the latter, as it were, as an expression of a political and social *volonté générale*. A brief side glance at basic dogmatic structures may introduce categories (section 3.1 below), before concepts of materialisation are discussed (section 3.2), as well as contributions from political philosophy and constitutional theory (section 3.3) and sociology/ systems theory and economics (section 4) (some of which themselves have a background in the history of ideas).

3.1. INTRODUCTION TO MATERIALISATION – A DOCTRINAL PERSPECTIVE

This is not a contribution (or volume) of comparative private law on the principle or principles of equality.[18] Doctrinal developments in Germany and Europe (namely specific principles of equality) can, however, help clarify certain structures that are important for the broad survey in social theory as well. In German private law doctrine, most authors would seem to see the general principle of equality, and the specific principles of equality, as being grounded in a broad legal principle with uniform origin.[19] This is already supported by the terminology (epistemologically), because in legal terminology the term "specific" is regularly used to describe those norms and principles that only form (individual) manifestations of the more general norm or the more general principle. This is also supported – systematically – by the inclusion of both general and specific principle(s) as one single norm in the highest-ranking legal act (Art. 3, Grundgesetz).[20] In terms of private law doctrine, this view is also in line with the fact that the single elements that have to be scrutinised follow the same structure (only with adaptations at single points of scrutiny, albeit rather significant ones).[21] Above all, however, the same individualistic concept

---

18 See, parallel to this volume, M. Gebauer and S. Huber (eds), *Freiheit und Gleichheit im Privatrecht*, Mohr-Siebeck, Tübingen 2022.

19 For more detail, see S. Grundmann, 'Gleichheit zwischen Dogmatik und Sozialtheorie' in '*Festschrift für Singer*', above n. 8, p. 225. Important findings and passages from this publication are integrated in the present text, especially under section 3. Similarly, authors as diverse as M. Auer, in this volume, and M. Grünberger, above n. 10, esp. pp. 52–57 and 774–91; for the narrative of the common ground of all equality principles, see, for instance, A. Nußberger in M. Sachs (ed), *Grundgesetz - Kommentar*, 9th ed., C.H. Beck, Munich 2021, Art. 3, paras. 1 *et seq.*

20 The prevailing view holds that Art. 3(2) of the German Constitution (Grundgesetz), while being highly controversial in terms of legal policy at the time it was inserted, was still only seen as a special form of Art. 3(1) of German Constitution (*lex specialis* to the latter): see C. Langenfeld in T. Maunz and G Dürig (editors-founders), *Grundgesetz - Kommentar*, 93th ed., C.H. Beck, Munich 2020, Art. 3 II, para. 14.

21 For a survey on, and a brief discussion of, the most important differences, see S. Grundmann, 'Gleichheit zwischen Dogmatik und Sozialtheorie' in *Festschrift für Singer*, above n. 8, p. 225 (pp. 228–30).

of action is seen to apply: a concept in which the consequences of norms, such as sanctions, are seen as the consequences of individual wrongful action.[22]

A look around the various disciplines, then, suggests that the significant differences in the individual offence characteristics are possibly much more important in practice and theory than the uniform examination scheme suggests. Fundamental differences and decisive demarcation lines may become blurred or obscured by such an image of uniformity. A glance at the (few mentioned core moments of the) historical development already proves how much legal practice over millennia – in majority thinking, but above all in the lived (un)legal practice – fundamentally contradicted such an image of uniform concept. This also holds true for legal science, as evidenced in the *usus modernus*, for example in the leading handbook by Struve from 1670 (*Jurisprudentia Romano-Germanica Forensis*). Even in economics, as the neighbouring science that strongly influences the interpretation and further development of private law, and probably even dominates in the USA, it will probably not be possible – theoretically and with methodological honesty – to claim, even today, that the specific equality principles can be legitimised in a comparably conclusive manner as the general equality principle.

For the present discussion, in which this second consideration will be taken up in the realm of different disciplines (in section 4.2 below), the question can be put a bit differently as well. It can also be asked whether the concept of equality (and of the equality principles) at stake is a primarily formal one or, on the contrary, a more material one. It can, for instance, be asked whether it does not imply a significant increase in the actual guarantee of equality if (possibly only for the anti-discrimination rules) an individualistic concept of action is no longer assumed, but rather systemic structures are emphasised, and these are seen as the object of regulation. Such a vision of equality principles would only follow what has been taken for granted, and has been the case for many decades, in the law against restraints of competition, with its thinking in market structures and, more generally, in economic regulation. The change of perspective ensuing from such new vision becomes particularly clear in one of the best-known cases from ECJ case law on anti-discrimination law (in this case, on the grounds of foreign nationality or ethnicity), the *Feryn* case.[23] In this case, the question arose as to whether a public limited company specialising in security systems (Feryn NV)

---

22 In more detail, and with further references, see S. Grundmann, above n. 21, pp. 230–31; this is also the approach of any interpretation of the law that guides behaviour. For this comprehensively, see P. Hacker, *Verhaltensökonomik und Normativität*, Mohr Siebeck, Tübingen 2017, esp. pp. 210 *et seq.*; C. Latzel, *Verhaltenssteuerung, Recht und Privatautonomie*, C.H. Beck, Munich 2020, p. 49 *et seq.*, with stark reference to private autonomy at p. 283 *et seq.*

23 Case C-54/07, *Centrum voor gelijkheid v. Firma Feryn NV* [2008] ECR I-05187; this case is appealingly discussed by M. Renner in S. Grundmann, H-W. Micklitz and M. Renner (above n. 6), ch. 14: Non-Discrimination.

was itself already acting in a discriminatory manner when its customers refused the use of personnel of certain ethnicities for the installation of security doors. In this case, a member of Feryn's board of directors stated in an interview that this customer wish had indeed influenced the company's actions in the past, namely that it had not used ("could not employ") such personnel for the installation of security doors, not necessarily that Feryn NV had not hired personnel from such ethnicities.

3.2. MATERIALISATION – OF EQUALITY AND/OR OF FREEDOM (AUER)

The development in legal history, which was addressed via the key phrase of "equality as human beings" (see above, section 2.2) refers at the same time to a more general problem, which can be seen in the distinction between formal equality – formal enforcement of the equality principle or principles – and materialisation of the equality principle or principles. Auer takes up this question.[24] On the one hand, she assumes that only the postulate of freedom – in private law, of private autonomy – can be understood as unconditional and not contingent in time (and should therefore be seen as paramount in private law).[25] Conversely, the postulate of equality should always be thought as contingent in time, and in need of complementing value judgement. Specifically, the criterion according to which constellations are declared equal or unequal – the distinctive or incriminated criterion – must always be determined socially, politically and legally (by legislator or judge) through positive setting. On the other hand, Auer makes – and derives from the contingent nature of equality claims – a second, and in our context even more important, assumption. This is that the concept of materialisation of the fundamental right or overarching principle is coherent only for the claim to freedom, and has indeed been developed only for it, namely for private autonomy.[26] A transfer to the fundamental right or

---

24 M. Auer, in this volume.

25 The latter is not so key for the present case: for this – quite classical – view, see, path-breakingly, W. Flume, 'Rechtsgeschäft und Privatautonomie' in *Festschrift Deutscher Juristentag*, C.F. Müller, Karlsruhe 1960, p. 135 (pp. 141 *et seq.*); W. Flume, *Allgemeiner Teil des Bürgerlichen Rechts – Zweiter Band: Das Rechtsgeschäft*, 4th ed., C.H. Beck, Munich 1992, p. 1 *et seq.*; F. Bydlinski, *Privatautonomie und objektive Grundlagen des verpflichtenden Rechtsgeschäfts*, Springer, Cham 1967, p. 123 (pp. 126–31); and in this volume, M. Auer.

26 Path-breaking in this respect was C-W. Canaris (above n. 10), p. 273, as well as M. Tamm, *Verbraucherschutzrecht – Europäisierung und Materialisierung des deutschen Zivilrechts und die Herausbildung eines Verbraucherschutzprinzips*, Mohr Siebeck, Tübingen 2011; G. Wagner, 'Materialisierung des Schuldrechts unter dem Einfluss von Verfassungsrecht und Europarecht – was bleibt von der Privatautonomie?' in U. Blaurock and G. Hager (eds), *Obligationenrecht im 21. Jahrhundert*, Nomos, Baden-Baden 2010, p. 3.

overarching principle of equality – of the principle or principles of equality – is seen as being problematic. In this respect, the aforementioned essential structural differences between freedom and equality had an effect. She does not see the anti-discrimination rules – the specific equality principles – as examples of a materialisation of the general equality principle, but rather as the (first) comprehensive implementation of *formal* equality in status.[27] If Auer does not see the increasing anchoring and enforcement of discrimination bans as a case of materialisation of the principle of equality, it is hardly surprising that she also denies such a tendency in general, for the general principle of equality. In her view, guaranteeing equality in personal status ("as human beings") is nothing more than applying formal – not material – equality also to this core aspect. Formal equality has been achieved here only very recently, according to Auer. In this way, she diametrically opposes Grünberger's thesis, which not only recognises such a tendency in the advance of the specific equality principles (anti-discrimination rules), but also derives from it a true shift of paradigm for the general principle of equality (again subsequently reinforced by the stadium ban decision of the Federal Constitutional Court (Bundesverfassungsgericht)).[28] In Grünberger's view, every unequal treatment is subject to a duty to justify, and factual reasons are, furthermore, to be measured in principle – and, to an increasing extent, depending on the extent to which the public is affected – against the principle of proportionality.

Even more central to the present collection is Auer's thesis on this topic, summarised above. If it seems logical at the outset that equality in status, first of all, only formally achieves equality before the law, then if one also considers that the distinctive or incriminated criterion must always be determined socially, politically and legally through positive setting, two views seem quite conceivable. If one sees the ability of humans to shape society in a self-determined way as a distinctive characteristic for being human, and thus for the protection of equality – hence following the approach of Vitoria – then this is indeed directly related to the characteristic that distinguishes humans from a highly developed

27 M. Auer, in this volume; very differently, M. Grünberger, above n. 10, esp. pp. 52–57, 536–59 *et passim*.

28 More in detail: on the one hand, M. Auer in this volume, and, on the other hand, M. Grünberger, above n. 10, esp. pp. 52–57 (however, only "a right to ask for justification in case of unequal treatment" [translation by the author]), pp. 870–1037 *et passim*; German Constitutional Court (Bundesverfassungsgericht) (2018) *Neue Juristische Wochenschrift* 1667 (*Stadionverbot*) – discussing a direct horizontal effect (at least situational) (*unmittelbare Drittwirkung*), which has hereby become more key again; see A. Hellgardt, 'Wer hat Angst vor der unmittelbaren Drittwirkung? Die Konsequenzen der Stadionverbot-Entscheidung des BVerfG für die deutsche Grundrechtsdogmatik' (2018) *Juristen-Zeitung* 901; W. Michl, 'Situativ staatsgleiche Grundrechtsbindung privater Akteure – zugleich Besprechung von BVerfG, Beschluss vom 11.4.2018 – 1 BvR 3080/09' (2018) *Juristen-Zeitung* 910.

non-human species (for example in terms of intelligence). However, there are humans who are less intelligent than others, or even than chimpanzees. In such a case, I think it is more a question of value than of logic whether one sees in the next step, initially based on natural law, to focus solely on the descent of humans – a completion of formal equality in status ("all humanity as such") – or rather an actual strengthening of enforcement. This would then lie in granting equal treatment to all humanity even if, in a concrete case, their intelligence may not differ from that of a chimpanzee. The reason for such a step could then be, among other things, because such a test/criterion could be abused and equal treatment could always be arbitrarily denied, or because the human group is seen as a social whole and descendants are not to be excluded from it. In my opinion, when analysing whether one should speak of a materialisation of the guarantee of rights, a social view is important, because law, and especially the principle of equality, are strongly related to society. Moreover, that this discussion is not irrelevant today is shown, for example, by controversial questions (in economics) as to what normative effects it has when tests on intelligence quotients reveal differences between different ethnic groups.[29] Further materialisation – functionally, as a better chance of assertion in the contingent reality of life – then goes hand in hand with formal equal treatment. They represent nothing more than two sides of the same coin – one realising an axiom according to which all are to be thought of as human beings, or the other (functionally) focusing on the reality of life. One important circumstance in favour of the second view (at least on an equal footing with the first) may be seen in the fact that the criterion of equality or inequality is the result of a setting, whatever the basis may be. As seen, such basis can be seen in a postulate of natural law or (as would seem to be the prevalent view today) in a legal command, albeit of a constitutional nature. It may even be endowed with the eternity guarantee of Article 79(3) of the German Constitution, and with such a rank that it excludes any balancing, as is sometimes assumed in the case of the prohibition of discrimination (as part of human dignity).[30] In any case, immunisation against any counter-objection (for example, by referring to statistically higher medical costs for one sex, certainly a factual reason as such)[31] also increases the de facto enforcement of the equality postulate.

---

29 Very controversial in this respect, e.g. R. Lynn and T. Vanhanen, *IQ and the Wealth of Nations*, Praeger, Santa Barbara 2002; already cautious about the methods, R. Ram, 'IQ and economic growth: Further augmentation of Makiw-Romer-Weil model' (2007) 94 *Economics Letters* 7–11.

30 See also M. Herdegen in T. Maunz and G. Dürig, above n. 20, Art. 1 I GG, para. 49: "Thus, any discrimination on the grounds of race is a violation of dignity without regard to the severity of the consequences." [translation by the author].

31 E.g. in the case of C-236/09, *Association Belge des Consommateurs Test-Achats ASBL* [2011] ECR I-00773.

Extreme positions on both sides would seem to be debatable. When Grünberger assumes, even in the case of the general principle of equality in private law, that materialisation is always an issue, i.e. that every conclusion of a contract based on a criterion contrary to equality requires justification, should this really also apply to the choice of a preferred sex when entering into marriage? Similarly, it might be seen as debatable when Auer conceptualises any development in anti-discrimination law (in the "specific" principle of equality) as mere (residual) enforcement of a formal equality in status. For the following, conclusions may depend less on axiomatic holdings (not shared by the other side) if one sharpens the concept of "materialisation". Its core should be seen in those cases in which a state of equality is significantly facilitated and promoted via a rule that foresees that a certain differentiation criterion (for instance, gender) is immunised against the objection of factual justification. There are good examples of the latter. For example, any rule would seem to give more material protection to ("formal") equality of status, i.e. against discrimination, when justification of such discrimination is not allowed in any case, not even on such concrete terms that it is an expression of efficient risk and cost allocation (contrast, for example, the ECJ in the *Test Achats* case, mentioned in the preceding paragraph).

3.3. MATERIALISATION VIA EXTENDING ABSOLUTE EQUALITY RIGHTS

If one sees a tendency towards materialisation whenever equality as a legal position is also *de facto* more substantially guaranteed and reached, then central developments since the Second World War in the development of constitutional law, and in political philosophy, can certainly also be understood as examples of such materialisation. In accordance with the structure of this work, in which historical development and comparative social theory are in the foreground, two of the most important works of political philosophy since the Second World War – or at least those that are probably most widely discussed globally – should be taken as a starting point.

3.3.1. Theory and Idea of Justice (Rawls, Sen)

In political philosophy, the most prominent content-focused approaches to just order in the twentieth and twenty-first centuries have been *A Theory of Justice* by John Rawls[32] and *The Idea of Justice* by Amartya Sen, which responds to the

[32] See J. Rawls, *A Theory of Justice*, Harvard University Press, Cambridge, MA. 1971, esp. ch. III ('The Original Position'); contextualisation, development and introduction by S. Grundmann, in S. Grundmann, H-W. Micklitz and M. Renner, above n. 6, ch. 6: Societal Order and Private Law.

former by its very title. If one sees (as many authors do) the advance, or a central advance, in *A Theory of Justice* – beyond Kant's categorical imperative – in the fact that a mechanism is conceived that makes unbiased decision-making by all rational and benevolent decision-makers (hypothetically) possible, the reference to equality seems obvious. The famous veil of ignorance – which is not supposed to guarantee ignorance of society and its mechanisms as such, but ignorance of one's own status in society – serves the great goal of enforcing equality more reliably. Everyone is supposed to participate – in full rationality, but with self-interest securely faded out – in decisions about society; the basic decisions about the two principles of justice are even made unanimously, according to Rawls's concept. In this way, the general principle of equality is again – obviously – divorced from the "specific" ones (anti-discrimination rules). The veil of ignorance is naturally drawn primarily – or even exclusively – only for the latter.

In the present context, however, it is not only these procedural aspects, with which more actual equality is striven for by way of rational consensus, that are central. Equally important are the substantive formulations and conclusions. In terms of content, Rawls distinguishes between two principles of justice. He opts for complete equality in political participation and fundamental rights, i.e. everyone should have an equal say, the power to argue, and the power to shape the framework order in society (first principle of justice). A general principle of equality applies here for a partial section, which is resistant to deviation and further consideration and argument (no justification for exceptions for objective reasons), not only in the area of specific principles of equality, i.e. principles of equality in status. In other words, a fundamentally unbreakable principle of equality normally applies only to cases of the specific equality principles, i.e. to the central areas of status (without the possibility of deviation on objective grounds and, if necessary, reinforced by rules of evidence). However, with the first principle of justice, the same is also found to apply in (one part of) the area of the general principle of equality, for all people, not just one group (gender, ethnicity, nationality, religious affiliation, etc.). This island of an absolute principle of equality in the area of the general principle of equality naturally corresponds to the practice in today's democracies under the rule of law (and therefore does not seem revolutionary). Rawls, however, highlights the special feature (resistance to any weighing); moreover, the justification for this step becomes clear as well. In this area, we are dealing with the instruments of (participation in) constant further development of the social order, not only with individual allocations. This, then, is the key to everything else. The questions of allocation, namely the economic rights of activity, are then concerned with the second principle of justice, the so-called difference principle. Equal entitlement is not a postulate of justice in this area. Differentiation is allowed, admittedly under the (quite significant) condition that the weakest in society also benefit sufficiently from any difference in content ("maximin rule").

In his response to Rawls, Sen considerably expands the scope of absolute equality, even in the area of the general principle of equality (at least potentially). He pleads also for absolute equality in material endowment, at least up to the level at which autonomous participation in society and its opportunities is actually possible.[33] Otherwise, the possibility of political participation would be illusory, but so would meaningful human existence as such. The realm of an unconditional principle of equality – in the realm of the general principle of equality – now grows and extends, here, into the realm of allocations of material goods. This may sound revolutionary, but, after all, the Federal Constitutional Court of Germany (Bundesverfassungsgericht) recently followed it in principle.

3.3.2. Equal Human Dignity (Fabre-Magnan)

Another area of unbreakable equality exists with respect to the guarantee and inviolability of human dignity, which, as Fabre-Magnan elaborates, also implies *absolute* equality in the guarantee of human dignity for every human being.[34] According to the case law of the Federal Constitutional Court of Germany, this area is also resistant to consideration and counterarguments ('balancing');[35]

---

33 See A. Sen, *The Idea of Justice*, Penguin, London 2009 (*Die Idee der Gerechtigkeit*, C.H. Beck, Munich 2020); S. Grundmann, above n. 32; core ideas pointing in this direction already in the so-called "capabilities approach", on the basis of which Sen won the Nobel Prize in 1998: see A. Sen, *Commodities and Capabilities*, Harvard Univ. Press, Amsterdam 1985; concise summary by A. Sen, 'Development as Capability Expansion' in S. Fukuda-Parr and A-K. Shiva Kumar (eds), *Readings in Human Development*, OUP, Delhi 2003, p. 41 (best possible expansion of the actual possibilities for action and realisation of the entirety of the members of society as the core objective of "efficiency" thinking). In German constitutional practice, there is an important judgment pointing very much in this direction, namely the so-called *Hartz IV* judgment of the Federal Constitutional Court (Bundesverfassungsgericht) (BVerfGE [official reports] 152, 68), which M. Fabre-Magnan discusses in this volume.

34 See M. Fabre-Magnan, in this volume; see also, for the foundations in German constitutional law, most recently (inter alia with its anchoring in Kant's concept of man and autonomy): M. Hong, *Der Menschenwürdegehalt der Grundrechte: Grundfragen – Entstehung und Rechtsprechung*, Mohr Siebeck, Tübingen 2019, *passim*. On the German-European perspective, see S. Blömacher, *Die Menschenwürde als Prinzip des deutschen und europäischen Rechts*, Nomos, Baden-Baden 2016, *passim*.

35 From the case law, see BVerfGE [official reports] 75, 369 (380) – *Strauß-Karikatur*: "However, insofar as the general right of personality is a direct outflow of human dignity, this barrier has an absolute effect without the possibility of a balance." [translation by the author]; BVerfGE 93, 266 (293) – *Soldaten sind Mörder*: "Thus, freedom of expression must always cede where the statement affects the human dignity of another person. This principle, which applies to artistic freedom, also applies to freedom of opinion, because human dignity, as the root of all fundamental rights, cannot be weighed against any individual fundamental right." [translation by the author]; BVerfGE 107, 275 (283 *et seq.*) – *Schockwerbung II*: "Human dignity sets … an absolute limit" – "Human dignity as the foundation of all fundamental rights cannot be weighed against any individual fundamental right." [translations by the author]; in principle, as well, BVerfGE 115, 118 (153) – *Luftsicherheitsgesetz*: "Any treatment of the human being by public authority which fundamentally calls into question the quality of the human being as a subject, his status as a subject of law, by failing to respect the value

factual reasons, therefore, do not justify any deviation, for example torture to save lives, and according to Article 79(3) Grundgesetz, this area is also immune to change through amendment of the German Constitution. Fabre-Magnan indeed emphasises that the basis today – in the sense of the development in the early nineteenth century – is to be explained positivistically, from a legislative setting, but also in parallel (philosophically) with logic, because she considers a private law striving for justice without linking autonomy with respect for human dignity to be inconceivable, and as well with insights ("knowledge") from history. What will be remarkable for some private law scholars is the matter-of-factness with which she understands equal human dignity as the basis of all private law. Fabre-Magnan refers to the long tradition that the principle has had in France since the nineteenth century, namely in connection with the definite abolition and categorical outlawing of slavery (1848). In the present context, the classification under the principle of equality is particularly noteworthy, namely as an area within the general principle of equality that is resistant to consideration, i.e. not amenable to any differentiation on the basis of assumed factual grounds.

The concrete occasion of the first such determined legislative setting, in the abolition of slavery, shows, of course, as with Rawls, how islands of consideration-resistant individual areas also arise, for the general principle of equality, in connection with a factual question that is to be assigned to the area of specific principles of equality. For, of course, the history of the fundamental right to absolute respect for human dignity is closely connected in France with the abolition of slavery, and in Germany with the Holocaust (related to an ethnic group/ethnicity). However, it also extends beyond this because, for example, among the most shocking encroachments on human dignity to which Article 1 of the German Constitution responds is also, for example, the persecution and extermination of political dissidents under National Socialism – not a status, at least not in the genuine sense (and key cases decided by the German Constitutional Court on the basis of Article 1 concern such non-status-related issues as the absolute ban on torture).

---

which is due to every human being for his own sake, by virtue of his being a person, is thus absolutely prohibited" [translation by the author]; and BVerfG *Neue Juristische Wochenschrift [NJW]* 2001, 2957 (2959): "not open to a process of weighing" [translation by the author]; in the literature, for instance, H. Dreier, GG Bd. 1, 3rd ed., C.H. Beck, Munich 2013, Art. 1 I, para. 130; F. Hufen, 'Die Menschenwürde', Art. 1 GG (2010) *Juristische Schulung [JuS]* 1 (and p. 9); H-J. Papier, 'Die Würde des Menschen ist unantastbar', in *Festschrift für Starek*, Mohr Siebeck, Tübingen 2007, p. 371 (and p. 374); only a few authors plead for a certain differentiation. See, for instance, C. Bäcker, 'Begrenzte Abwägung' (2016) *Der Staat* 433 *et seq.* ("The human dignity principle is relative, the inviolability rule absolute. This assumption of the double structure of the human dignity guarantee shows why human dignity can be amenable to consideration despite the inviolability clause." [translation by the author]).

4. MATERIALISATION VIA SOCIAL IMPACT ANALYSIS

A further form of materialisation appears conceivable if we move from the perspective of the actions of individual actors as the central object of consideration, to an analysis of the effects on society as a whole. The first is traditionally the perspective in the doctrinal thinking of private law,[36] namely contract law, for which the central rules of personal equality are predominantly – and at the EU level practically exclusively – conceived.[37] The societal effects – more precisely, systemically conditioned discrimination and, correspondingly, systemically oriented responses of a regulation – suggest a disproportionately stronger, very direct and obvious look at a sociological-systems-theoretical understanding, which is then, because of the main thrust, also widely described using the term "feminist legal theory". Wielsch analyses this for the present volume and develops it further,[38] namely in the context of digitalisation. Of course, economic theory on questions of equality – unsurprisingly, in view of the core objective of maximising overall welfare[39] – also focuses on the effects of violations of the principle of equality on society as a whole. Engert, following the fundamental work of Gary Becker, justified anti-discrimination rules and

---

36 See references in n. 22.

37 The following European directives show this very clearly (insofar as employment contract law is included in this area): Council Directive 2004/113/EC of the European Parliament and of the Council of 13 December 2004 on the implementation of the principle of equal treatment between men and women in the access to and supply of goods and services; Council Directive 2000/43/EC of 29 June 2000 implementing the principle of equal treatment between persons irrespective of racial or ethnic origin; Council Directive 2000/78/EC of the European Parliament and of the Council of 27 November 2000 on establishing a general framework for equal treatment in employment and occupation; Directive 2006/54/EC of the European Parliament and of the Council of 5 July 2006 on the implementation of the principle of equal opportunities and equal treatment of men and women in matters of employment and occupation (recast). For a broader perspective, see G-K. Neuner, 'Das BVerfG im Labyrinth der Drittwirkung' (2020) *Neue Juristische Wochenschrift [NJW]* 1851 (and 1854 *et seq.*) (also discussing the criticism often found that in these cases equal treatment is not not key aim, but rather [compulsory] conclusion of a contract). This is not intended to relativise the much more far-reaching effect of the principle of equality in Art. 3 of the Constitution in private law, which in German law triggered, e.g. the fundamental reform of international family law, when the Federal Constitutional Court's verdict struck down the conflict of laws norm according to which personal statutes were subjected to the law of the nationality of the husband/father. This was seen as violating equality of women: see *BVerfGE* [official reports] 31, 58 – '*Spanierbeschluß*'.

38 See, earlier, D. Wielsch, 'Grundrechte als Rechtfertigungsgebote' (2013) 213 *Archiv für die civilistische Praxis (AcP)* 718; D. Wielsch, 'Iustitia mediatrix: Zur Methode einer soziologischen Jurisprudenz' in *Festschrift für Gunther Teubner*, De Gruyter, Berlin/New York 2009, p. 395; D. Wielsch, 'Gesellschaftliche Transformation durch subjektive Rechte', in A. Fischer-Lescano, H. Franzki and J. Horst (eds), *Gegenrechte – Recht jenseits des Subjekts*, Mohr Siebeck, Tübingen 2018, p. 141.

39 See C. Engert, 'Allied by Surprise? The Economic Case for an Anti-Discrimination Statute' (2003) 4 *German Law Journal* 685 (689 *et seq.* and 693 *et seq.*).

other mandatory standards of equality early on by arguing that the violations may be efficient according to individual utility calculations, but that they result in (higher) welfare losses for society as a whole ("total welfare").[40] In the present study, and in the studies quoted, he turns to considerations according to which these effects may also only occur indirectly (for example, mediated via information or negotiation problems).

4.1. SOCIOLOGICAL AND SYSTEMS THEORY OF EQUALITY – FROM AN ACTOR'S TO A SYSTEM'S VIEW AND THE DIGITAL AGE (MACKINNON, WIELSCH)

The most fundamental, and at the same time best-known and most visible, contribution to the discussion of the equality principles within society and its systems was made by feminist legal theory, which is based on sociology (and also, specifically, on systems theory).[41] In essence, the considerations go in the direction of not focusing solely on individual discriminatory misconduct (the so-called sex differences approach) in order to recognise and counteract the "secret design" of centuries-old discrimination of persons according to status. Just as important as a consideration of the individual logic of action was the consideration of the structures of society (the so-called sex inequality approach), and the existence of discrimination structures within it. The *Feryn* case is solved seamlessly, on the basis of this view. It may well be that Feryn NV is subject to the wishes of its customers. If, however, such wishes are no longer "given in" to across the board, but all competitors (including, of course, Feryn NV) are obliged to hire only according to individual suitability, and not to exclude according to ethnicity, three things are achieved. First, it is more likely that an educational effect will be initiated, including for the customers. Second, no signal – problematic from the point of view of human dignity – is sent to members of the ethnic group. Finally, and in any case, customer wishes can no longer be given in to without danger. Similar is the assessment of the fact that only past practices were talked about[42] – systemically, such a statement still has the

---

40 See C. Engert, 'Gleichbehandlungsgebote als Vertragshilfe' in *Festschrift für Christine Windbichler*, De Gruyter, Berlin 2020, pp. 51–67.

41 Path-breaking: C.A. MacKinnon, '*Sexual Harassment of Working Women*', above n. 12, esp. pp. 106–27; J. Butler, *Gender Trouble: Feminism and the Subversion of Identity*, Taylor & Francis, London 1990; C. Weinbach, *Systemtheorie und Gender – Das Geschlecht im Netz der Systeme*, Springer, Heidelberg 2004. Contextualisation, interdisciplinary theory review and analysis of the issues under discussion also here: A. Renner, in S. Grundmann, H-W. Micklitz and A. Renner (eds), above n. 6, ch. 14: Anti-Discrimination (discussion of the *Feryn* case).

42 Arguing in this way, for instance: V. Rieble, ('Beruf und Chance' (19/20 July 2008) *Frankfurter Allgemeine Zeitung*, Beil. C 2), who tries to prove that the ECJ has violated principles of German private law doctrine (individual perspective of action and causality requirement)

effect of promoting discrimination – up to the "self-affirmation" that it was quite comprehensible how the board of Feryn NV acted. Last but not least, thinking in such systems is much easier to bring into line with constitutional thinking in practical concordances. Human dignity, which is broadly attacked (somewhere in the system, not necessarily in the individual contractual relationship), can be directly contrasted with concerns of professional freedom, and a possible hierarchy of values comes more clearly into view.[43] Then it would be imperative to take a stand on the position of the Federal Constitutional Court of Germany that the fundamental right of human dignity is resistant to weighing.

These considerations form the background to the remarks of Wielsch, who sees the necessity of expanding the equality principle to social structures as even being exacerbated in the digital space.[44] He first states that the principle of equality has to ensure that the law not only treats individuals equally, but also takes into equal account the different social rationalities involved in a conflict ("relational reformulation of the principle of equality", demanding a legal design that is equally responsive to the concerns of all social institutions affected – guiding principle 1). Limiting equality considerations to the individual perspective of action on the part of the actor perpetrating the ban on discrimination could not do justice to this claim even at the starting point, since the crucial question is whether legal structures themselves discriminate against specific types of social action. Wielsch also refers to the logic of practical concordance between fundamental rights. In addition, there is a second guiding principle which is of special importance for the digital sphere. Here, it must be seen that only a design that allows transparency of digital regulation (irrespective of its content) can fulfil the above-mentioned desideratum that every substantial decision to be strived for must be equally responsive to the interests of all autonomies affected. Without granting such possibilities to represent the peculiar normativity of algorithmic selections, i.e. without positivisation of the

("new and absurd aggravation of sanctions", absurd in Rieble's view, is namely that a mere public confession of [past] discrimination" may as such be an act of discrimination [translation by the author]). This argument, of course, on the one hand ignores (and does not even problematise) the primacy of EU law, and on the other hand, the question of the objective of interpretation in anti-discrimination law is disregarded completely. Rieble, however, is by no means alone with this fundamental criticism, or refusal to consider different approaches. See, e.g. during the legislative process when the relevant EC directives had to be transposed: F-J. Säcker, '"Vernunft statt Freiheit!" – Die Tugendrepublik der neuen Jakobiner – Referentenententwurf eines privatrechtlichen Diskriminierungsgesetzes' (2002) *Zeitschrift für Rechtspolitik* 286; and more broadly E. Picker, 'Antidiskriminierungsprogramme im freiheitlichen Privatrecht' in E. Lorenz (ed), *Karlsruher Forum 2004: Haftung wegen Diskriminierung nach derzeitigem und zukünftigem Recht*, C.H. Beck, Munich 2005, pp. 7–115.

43 See, for instance, S. Baer, '"Ende der Privatautonomie" oder grundrechtlich fundierte Rechtsetzung? – Die deutsche Debatte um das Antidiskriminierungsrecht' (2002) *Zeitschrift für Rechtspolitik* 290.

44 D. Wielsch, in this volume.

digital normativity, any discussion about its material legality – for example, the realisation of discrimination effects – would be illusory. The second reformulation of the principle of equality therefore requires any regulator to make explicit the normative standards according to which people are to be treated. Finally, the fundamental right to be treated equally also obliges private actors to implement procedural safeguards when they deny access to digital infrastructure. Wielsch therefore understands the right to equality as a "constitutionalisation anchor" for private governance regimes in general, and for digital regulation in particular.[45]

4.2. ECONOMIC THEORY OF EQUALITY – OVERALL WELFARE LOSSES THROUGH DISCRIMINATION (BECKER, ENGERT)?

Economics has a hard time with equality, arguably apart from the special case of corporate law, where equal treatment requirements are seen as a means to avoid drawing special advantages.[46] Equality is, arguably, even seen at its core as being in conflict with the ultimate guiding goal: (overall) welfare maximisation. For at the core of every market mechanism lies a striving for free choice (normative individualism) and freedom to discriminate, also including, if necessary, error-prone (i.e. inefficient) discrimination. Early economic approaches defending anti-discrimination theorems emphasise that discriminatory choice can harm the actor itself (by reducing welfare).[47] This approach, however, incompletely depicts discrimination theorems, because, on the one hand, they prohibit (contrary to the guiding principles of normative individualism in economics) the actor from accepting this disadvantage (and possibly being punished for it

45 On the constitutionalisation of cyberspace, see also G. Teubner, 'Societal constitutionalism: alternatives to state-centred constitutional theory?' in C. Joerges, I-J. Sand and G. Teubner (eds), *Transnational Governance and Constitutionalism*, Hart Publishing, London 2004, p. 3.

46 D-A. Verse, *Der Gleichbehandlungsgrundsatz im Recht der Kapitalgesellschaften*, Mohr Siebeck, Tübingen 2006, p. 77 *et seq.*; and, in this volume, A. Engert); different in the starting point though is Case C-101/08, *Audiolux* [2009] ECR-I-09823; see comment on this judgment, for instance, in J. Basedow, 'General Principles of European Private Law and Interest Analysis – Some Reflections in the Light of *Mangold* and *Audiolux*' (2016) 24 *European Review of Private Law* 331.

47 Path-breaking for an argument in this sense (in many cases, admittedly, with the indication that the market will sufficiently "punish" inefficient discrimination anyway): G. Becker, *The Economics of Discrimination*, University of Chicago Press, Chicago 1957; on the idea that those with a "taste for discrimination" pay the price themselves, see M. Friedman, *Capitalism and Freedom*, University of Chicago Press, Chicago 1962, esp. p. 108 *et seq.*; esp. determined, R.A. Epstein, *Forbidden Grounds: The Case against Employment Discrimination Laws*, Harvard University Press, Cambridge, MA. 1992. In favour of a mandatory anti-discrimination regulation (with an economic liberal background), on the other hand, is C.R. Sunstein, 'Why Markets Don't Stop Discrimination' (1997) 8(2) *Social Philosophy and Policy* 22–37.

by being pushed out of the market), at least in many constellations. On the other hand, distinctions that may be well justified by efficiency considerations (as in the case of *Test Achats*, see above) are not even admitted for review, i.e. they are rejected *a limine*, without it being possible to check whether they may be convincing from an efficiency point of view. The general principle of equality, with the allowance of objectively justified differentiations, would perhaps also be exposed to the objection that free choice would be restricted – the efficiency goal requires unrestricted freedom of experimentation (normative individualism) – but the admissibility of objectively justified differentiations could, in most cases, be modelled with efficiency considerations. Thus, it is mainly the strict postulation of equality in personal status, i.e. the area of anti-discrimination theorems, that is problematic from the perspective of overall welfare and efficiency. For economic theory, the distinction between the general and the special equality principle is completely central and radical.

Engert, in particular, has tried to explain anti-discrimination theorems more in terms of overall welfare considerations (instead of individual utility maximisation), namely in terms of information problems, and as second-best solutions. In essence, the argument goes that, while discrimination may be individually efficient (because the discriminated-against group actually performs less well overall, for example statistically, and general exclusion can save information costs), the damage to society as a whole may be greater if the entire group no longer has an incentive to increase its own capacities.[48] This explanation may go some way to justifying anti-discrimination rules. However, the core remains irrelevant: that equality in status is centrally about human dignity, a higher value than efficiency. The theory also has to speculate very much on dynamic developments, namely that, one day, efficiency gains will actually be reaped in society as a whole if a strict anti-discrimination philosophy is enforced today. It turns out that economic theory can often also "justify" itself (sticking to its reasoning) by only dynamically and speculatively expanding the efficiency goal accordingly.[49] Especially if one adds the aspect of human dignity, and wants to see the decision-makers located behind the Rawlsian veil of ignorance, Engert's view is admittedly highly convincing. It is obvious that rational decision-makers would indeed place the possible future increase in educational capacities among a less privileged group above the current "efficiency gain" of the individual decision-maker, who wants to save information costs and, therefore, puts the aforementioned group's potential on the back-burner.

---

[48] See A. Engert, 'Allied by Surprise?', above n. 39, further developed in *Festschrift für Christine Windbichler*, above n. 40, p. 51.

[49] See F. Fukuyama, *Identity: Contemporary Identity Politics and the Struggle for Recognition*, Profile Books, London 2018, p. 13.

5. CONCLUSIONS

The lines of development are surprisingly different for a primarily substance related equality principle and an equality principle that is essentially related to status ("personal equality"). What, in the first area, was already an outstandingly important, central postulate of justice in antiquity, in the second area has only become so in modern times. It is striking that (Christian) value orientation was necessary for the implementation of "equality in being human", while thinking in categories of reason only confirmed this transition, i.e. "followed" it, as it were. However, it also turned it into a success story.

The concept of an only formal, or also material, guarantee of equality – the key question in this book – is related to the separation of the two areas (and equality principles). However, the exact delimitations are subject to disagreement. If the core issue is that, with a more material understanding of equality, above all a greater actual chance of realisation is sought, one can state three things: firstly, whether the implementation of "equality in being human" – which has been so slow and conflict-laden over centuries – already means a materialisation of the principle of equality can, and will, be seen differently. On the other hand, it should be beyond doubt that an important contribution to the materialisation of the principle of equality can be seen in all cases of a second kind. These are characterised by the circumstance that criteria that operate beyond the direct reference to status, i.e. in the area of the general, factual principle of equality, are classified as resistant to any weighing (political participation rights; equal entitlement to a subsistence minimum that allows self-realisation; and, more generally, equal human dignity). The formation of criteria as resistant to weighing is, after all, otherwise characteristic of the status-related personal equality postulate ("specific equality principles"). Thirdly, and finally, materialisation of the equality principle can also be the result of a change in thinking, namely a departure from an individual logic of action towards a logic that chooses systems and relations between persons as its focus of analysis, namely in sociologically-based conceptions of equality. This also, and even more centrally, concerns the status-related personal equality postulate ("specific equality principles"). Perhaps this view of developments and questions will also help to objectify the problem of whether Robespierre and his "Republic of Virtues" continues to have an effect in modern general equal treatment law, or whether only the social theory appropriate to the present is manifesting itself. In essence, it is a matter of weighing up positions of freedom, which are to be brought into practical concordance with interests in material equality.

THE SAME HUMAN NATURE

Some Approaches to Equality in Law

Tilman Repgen

1. DIFFERENT APPROACHES TO EQUALITY IN LAW

1.1. EQUALITY AS A QUESTION OF JUSTICE – FIRST APPROACH

When thinking about "equality", one almost inevitably falls into the footsteps of Aristotle, who distinguished between similarity – related to a quality – and equality, related to a quantity.[1] Equality, in turn, was a central concept for his

1 D. Schlüter, 'Art. Gleichheit II' in J. Ritter (ed.) *Historisches Wörterbuch der Philosophie vol. 3*, Wissenschaftliche Buchgesellschaft, Darmstadt 1979, col. 672, with reference to Aristoteles, *Metaphysik* Book V, 15, 1021a, 9 *et seq.*, here cited as Aristoteles (F.F. Schwarz, ed. and tr.), *Metaphysik. Schriften zur Ersten Philosophie*, Reclam, Stuttgart 1970, p. 139.

doctrine of justice,[2] especially for his conception of an arithmetical equality in the *iustitia commutativa*.[3]

However, I am more interested here in equality of *status*, which, following Aristotle's systematics, should rather be placed with *iustitia distributiva*, if not with justice in the general sense. However, Aristotle did not accept equality of status.

1.2. A HOPEFUL ENCOUNTER – SECOND APPROACH

The greatest conceivable legal inequality manifests itself in slavery. There, the legal personhood of individuals, or a group of people, is simply denied and the person is degraded to a mere thing: the human being is legally degenerated to the status of a thing. The problem of justice that lies therein concerns the unequal treatment of members of the human species who are actually equally qualified. In antiquity, especially in Christianity, people were already sensitive to this, without, of course, drawing any legal conclusions from it. The letter of the apostle Paul to Philemon speaks of Onesimus, a (perhaps runaway)[4] house slave. Paul sends him back to his master, the addressee of the letter. But Onesimus comes back to Philemon as a brother because of baptism, Paul writes:

> I am appealing to you for a child of mine, whose father I became while wearing these chains: I mean Onesimus. ... I am sending him back to you – that is to say, sending you my own heart. ... I suppose you have been deprived of Onesimus for a time, merely so that you could have him back for ever, no longer as a slave, but something much better than a slave, a dear brother; especially dear to me, but how much more to you, both on the natural plane and in the Lord.[5]

In civil law, Onesimus remained a slave, absolutely unequal to Philemon, but by virtue of baptism Onesimus had become a "brother" to him. Onesimus was equal in his capacity as a member of the Christian community (κοινωνία).[6]

---

2 Aristoteles, *Nikomachische Ethik*, V, p. 5 *et seq.*; here, and in the following, unless otherwise stated, the edition by G. Bien, based on the translation by E. Rolfes, 4th ed., Felix Meiner Verlag, Hamburg 1985. For an overview of Aristotle's theory of justice, see E. Schütrumpf, 'Gerechtigkeit' in C. Rapp, K. Corcilius (ed.), *Aristoteles-Handbuch. Leben – Werk – Wirkung*, Verlag J.B. Metzler, Stuttgart/Weimar 2011, pp. 226–31.

3 See Aristoteles, *Nikomachische Ethik*, above n. 2, V, 5, 1131a, and more precise in V, 7, 1132a, b.

4 In contrast to the older exegesis, it has recently been doubted that Onesimus had run away, but assumed that he had turned to Paul for mediation in a conflict situation. On this, with references, see H. Balz, 'Art. Philemonbrief' in *Theologische Realenzyklopädie vol. 26*, De Gruyter, Berlin/New York 1996, pp. 487–92, p. 489.

5 Philemon 10–16 (translation here and elsewhere according to the *New Jerusalem Bible*).

6 On this, see C. Kähler, 'Art. Sklaverei II. Neues Testament' in G. Müller (ed.), *Theologische Realenzyklopädie vol. 31*, De Gruyter, Berlin/New York 2000, pp. 373–77, p. 375.

Master and slave now faced each other in faith as equals. It is rightly emphasised that Christ was no social revolutionary; nor Spartacus, "not engaged in a fight for political liberation like Barabbas or Bar-Kochba".[7] Christ had brought a hope which referred to an "encounter with the Lord of all lords" – to "an encounter with the living God" himself – but which was not consolation for the hereafter, but meant a new, spiritual society: the Church.[8] It was Christianity that laid the roots of the idea of equality with its message – certainly, there were ideas pointing in this direction before that, but it was from Christianity that the *moral* demand for individual freedom and equality gradually took hold – not as a political programme, however, but as a consequence of a certain conception of the equal nature of man before God.[9] It was not until modern times that this also became a *legal* programme, although not only in the wake of the Enlightenment and the French Revolution, but already, as will be shown, in late scholasticism, which viewed law in its own way from a moral perspective.

1.3. THE WORLD OF THE *ANCIEN RÉGIME* – THIRD APPROACH

In a third approach, I would like to direct our attention to the legal world of the *ancien régime*. In the feudal state of the early modern era, the legal inequality is quite obvious. We are used to looking at the political inequality of the nobility, the clergy and the burghers or peasants. But private law also reflected the legal inequality. The standard textbook of the *usus modernus*, the *Jurisprudentia Romano-Germanica Forensis* by Georg Adam Struve, may serve as a source for this.[10] Regarding the title *De Jure personarum seu Statu hominum* (On the Law

---

7 Pope Benedict XVI, *Encylical letter Spe salvi 30 November 2007*, para. 4 <http://w2.vatican.va/content/benedict-xvi/de/encyclicals/documents/hf_ben-xvi_enc_20071130_spe-salvi.html> – this also contains the theological connection to the story of Onesimus.

8 Like n. 7.

9 An overview of the historical development is provided by L. Siedentop, *Inventing the Individual: The Origins of Western Liberalism*, Allan Lane, London 2014.

10 G.A. Struve, *Jurisprudentia Romano-Germanica forensis: Olim in Academia Jenensi praelecta & explanata, nunc revisa & aucta. Adiectus est index Rerum et Verborum*, Sumpt. Societas, Jena 1670. A useful bibliography of the total of 31 editions up to 1771 can be found in J. Finzel, *Georg Adam Struve (1619–1692) als Zivilrechtler*, Peter Lang, Frankfurt am Main 2003, pp. 144–53. In the following, the Jena 1701 edition is cited. Of particular interest here are the comments on lib. I, tit. 3 and 4, pp. 11–16. For further details see G.A. Struve, *Syntagma iurisprudentiae secundum ordinem pandectarum*, Nisius, Jena 1655–63, in the 4th ed., Jena 1668 (contains only the text of Struve and the registers, easily accessible also as a reprint Frankfurt am Main 2018 (Ius commune, vol. 331). The edition supplemented by Peter Müller's annotations is used here: G.A. Struve, *Syntagma Jurisprudentiæ, Secundum Ordinem Pandectarum Concinnatum, Quo Solida Juris Fundamenta Traduntur, Digestorum, Et Affines Codicis, Novellarum Ac Juris Canonici Tituli Methodice Explicantur, Controversiæ Nervose Resolvuntur, Et Quid In Foro Usum Habeat, Monetur; Cum Additionibus Petri Mülleri, editio tertia*, Vico, Frankfurt/Leipzig 1738; this last edition of the Syntagma is the best because of the rich annotation apparatus. It is available as a digital copy at the Munich Digitisation

of Persons or the Status of People), Struve explains that a distinction is made between a natural and a civil law status.

Juxta statum naturalem distinguuntur homines (1) ratione sexus ... (2) Alii sunt jam nati, alii nascituri seu in utero.[11]	According to the natural state, people are distinguished firstly according to sex. ... Secondly, some are already born, others are only about to be born or are still in the womb.

For our context of equality, however, beyond the consideration of a "natural state", the civil acceptance of inequality in the *usus modernus pandectarum* is much more important. On this, Struve wrote:

Juxta jus propter diversum statum et conditionem civilem summa et absoluta seu generalis ac prima divisio de Jure personarum haec est, quod omnes homines aut liberi sunt (1) qui habent naturalem facultatem ejus, quod cuique facere libet, nisi si quid vi aut jure prohibetur, §2 I. de jur. pers. L. 4 pr. de stat. hom.	According to the law concerning different status and civil conditions, this is the supreme, absolute, general and first division in the law of persons, that all men are either free – i.e. they have the natural possibility to act as they please, as long as they are not prevented from doing so by force or by law, as Inst. 1.3.2 and D. 1.5.4 pr.
[2] aut servi, qui dominio alieno sunt subjecti, et juribus Civilibus non fruuntur l. 4. §1. de stat. hom.[12]	Or they are slaves subject to foreign *dominium* (power) and enjoy no civil rights, like D. 1.5.4.1.

Struve paraphrased the provisions of Roman law that he had quoted. According to this, equality prevails in natural law, but not in civil law, because there a distinction is made between the free, and the unfree or slaves. Slaves "belong"

Centre at: Pars 1, [1] (Exerc. 1–8 [with pp. 1–516 of pars 1] and ca. 400 S. Indices): <https://reader.digitale-sammlungen.de/resolve/display/bsb10519853.html>; Pars 1, [2] (mit den Exerc. 9–25 [mit den Seiten 517–1767 der pars 1]): <https://reader.digitale-sammlungen.de/resolve/display/bsb10519854.html>; Pars 2 (Exerc. 26–38): <https://reader.digitale-sammlungen.de/resolve/display/bsb10519855.html>; Pars 3 (Exerc. 39–50): <https://reader.digitale-sammlungen.de/resolve/display/bsb10519856.html>. A reprint of the 1738 edition was published in Frankfurt am Main in 2016, in three volumes, whereby the indices are reprinted twice in this reprint, but not in vol. 1, but rather in vols. 2 and 3. Of particular relevance here is Exerc. 3, ad lib. 1, tit. 5, pp. 97–110, the more detailed analysis of which must be reserved for another study. On Struve now, see T. Repgen, 'Der Rechtslehrer Georg Adam Struve (1619–1692)' (2020) 28 *Zeitschrift für Europäisches Privatrecht (ZEuP)* 74–94.

11 G.A. Struve, '*Jurisprudentia*', above n. 10, lib. I, tit. III, §2, pp. 11–12.

12 Ibid., lib. I, tit. III, §4, p. 13.

to someone else, and fall under the property rights of their respective masters. But Struve also differentiates between categories of the free:

Liberi homines rursus distinguuntur in ingenuos et libertinos. Illi sunt, qui a liberis parentibus liberi nati sunt; hi vero sunt, qui ex justa servitute manumissi sunt. Tot. Tit. I de libertin.[13]	Free people are in turn divided into freeborn and freed. The former are born free of free parents. But the latter have been released from a lawful slavery, as the whole title Inst. 1.5.

The differences in status in this regard need not be of further interest here. What is important is that Struve considered slavery to be a legitimate condition, even at the end of the seventeenth century. However, he hastened to qualify this finding:

Quamvis vero hodie inter Christianos ejusmodi homines servi non habeantur, nisi quod a Turcis aliisque barbaricis gentibus capti pro servis inter Christianos censeantur, eo quod istae etiam nationes Christianos captivos pro servis habeant.	However, there are no slaves among Christians today, except that they are captured by Turks or other barbarian nations and valued as slaves among Christians, just as these nations hold captive Christians as slaves.
Sunt tamen in quibusdam locis homines proprii, own people, qui affinitatem cum servis habent, de quibus commodius cap. seq. agetur. Subjungatur text. Instit. Lib. I. Tit. III. de Jure personarum et seqq. usque ad Tit. IIX.[14]	Nevertheless, in certain regions there are *homines proprii*, proper people, who bear a resemblance to slaves, of whom the following chapter deals more fully. Added are the regulations in Inst. 1.3 to 1.8.

Struve thus conceded that real slavery based on captivity in war also existed among Christian peoples. Roman law only regarded the enslavement of foreign peoples as permissible, which the *ius commune* had adopted.[15] With good reason, Struve placed serfdom,[16] which was widespread in the system of landlordship and manorialism, close to slavery. In the *usus modernus*, there can be no question of human rights or even equal rights.

---

13 Ibid., lib. I, tit. III, §5, p. 13.

14 Ibid., lib. I, tit. III, §6, pp. 13–14.

15 T. Rüfner, 'Die Rezeption des römischen Sklavenrechts im Gelehrten Recht des Mittelalters' in T. Finkenauer (ed.), *Sklaverei und Freilassung im römischen Recht. Symposion für Hans Josef Wieling zum 70. Geburtstag*, Springer-Verlag, Berlin 2006, pp. 201–21, esp. p. 219.

16 On this further, see G.A. Struve, *'Jurisprudentia'* (n. 10), Exerc. 3, lib. 1, tit. 5, §§23, 24, pp. 108–10, with rich references from contemporary literature.

The findings on the *usus modernus*, which are only very cursory here, are important as a background for the later observations on Vitoria's discussion.

1.4. THE IDEA OF EQUALITY IN PRIVATE LAW – FOURTH APPROACH

If we look at the Bürgerliches Gesetzbuch (BGB) of the year 1900 itself, the situation is exactly the opposite of the *usus modernus*. One of the leading textbooks on the BGB from the beginning of the twentieth century was written by Ludwig Enneccerus, a member of the second BGB commission. The general and, above all, equal legal capacity of all people presupposed by the BGB was a matter of course for him, as it was for other jurisprudence at the time. He wrote in this regard:

> The legal capacity of man is taken for granted in the BG in accordance with the consciousness of the cultural nations of the present day and is therefore not particularly pronounced, since the principles are most firmly established which no longer require external certification. General freedom and legal capacity are regarded as an ethical necessity.[17]

The motives had already formulated in the same sense:

> The legal order, in recognising the legal capacity of man without regard to his individuality and without regard to his will, fulfils an imperative of reason and ethics.[18]

---

17 L. Enneccerus, *Lehrbuch des Bürgerlichen Rechts, vol. 1/1, Einleitung, Allgemeiner Teil*, 6th ed., Elwert, Marburg 1913, p. 193: "*Die Rechtsfähigkeit des Menschen ist im BG entsprechend dem Bewußtsein der Kulturnationen der Gegenwart als selbstverständlich vorausgesetzt und daher nicht besonders ausgesprochen, da die Grundsätze am festesten stehen, die einer äußeren Beglaubigung nicht mehr bedürfen. Die allgemeine Freiheit und Rechtsfähigkeit gilt [sic!] als ethische Notwendigkeit.*"

18 *Motive zu dem Entwurfe eines Bürgerlichen Gesetzbuches für das Deutsche Reich. vol. 1: Allgemeiner Theil*, Guttentag, Berlin/Leipzig 1888, p. 25 (on s. 1: 'Personen'): "*Die Rechtsordnung erfüllt, in dem sie die Rechtsfähigkeit des Menschen ohne Rücksicht auf seine Individualität und ohne Rücksicht auf seinen Willen anerkennt, ein Gebot der Vernunft und der Ethik.*" Very similarly formulated: B. Kannowski, in J. von Staudinger (founder), *Staudinger. BGB, Sellier/De Gruyter*, Berlin 2018, Vorbem zu §1 BGB, para. 15: "*Die Begriffe* 'Person' *und* 'Rechtsfähigkeit' *gehören dem positiven Recht an; Rechtsfähigkeit und Personenqualität beruhen auf der Zuerkennung durch die geltende Rechtsordnung. Dies erfüllt aber, wenn sie allen Menschen Rechtsfähigkeit zuspricht, ein sozialethisches*, naturrechtliches Postulat, *denn die Rechtsfähigkeit aller Menschen anzuerkennen, ist eine elementare Forderung des natürlichen Rechts.*" – "The terms *'person'* and *'legal capacity'* belong to positive law; legal capacity and the quality of a person are based on their recognition by the applicable legal system. However, if it grants legal capacity to all human beings, this fulfils a socio-ethical, *natural law postulate*, because recognising the legal capacity of all human beings is an elementary requirement of natural law." (emphasis in the original).

Rudolf von Jhering had said that the recognition of legal capacity was an entitlement "which every human being bears on his forehead".[19]

What was self-evident at the time of the BGB's creation was an idea that, at first glance, seems to be completely alien to the medieval systems of rule and the early modern state in Europe, whose societies were characterised by status differences. Therefore, the self-evidence with which the late nineteenth and early twentieth centuries recognised universal legal capacity, i.e. an essential expression of equality, is remarkable. The general and, thus, equal legal capacity is ultimately derived from the essence of the human being. The aim here is to show a much older approach to this idea, dating back to the sixteenth century.[20]

2. EQUALITY AS A LEGAL ARGUMENT IN LATE SCHOLASTICISM

The Spanish policy of conquest in Latin America was already subject to strong criticism in Spain in the first half of the sixteenth century. This contemporary criticism related to the question of whether the "Indios", as the indigenous people were called, were not being massively wronged by their slave-like treatment. This immediately led to very complex considerations about the legitimacy of the rule – the *dominium* – of the Spaniards in the colonies. This puts us in the middle of the legal discourse on the multilayered concept of *dominium*, which became relevant, above all, in the moral theology of the Middle Ages, but which, in terms of its subject matter, is initially assigned to private law. As will be shown, it is the claim to justice of equality in law that caused the Spaniards difficulties.

2.1. THE SERMONS OF *ANTÓN MONTESINO* IN 1511

In two sensational sermons on 21 and 28 December 1511 in Santo Domingo (on the island of Hispaniola, and now in the Dominican Republic), the Dominican priest Antón Montesino denounced the encomienda system introduced by

---

19 R. von Jhering, *Der Geist des römischen Rechts auf den verschiedenen Stufen seiner Entwicklung, vol. III/2*, Breitkopf & Härtel, Leipzig 1871, p. 322: Die Rechtsfähigkeit des Menschen ist ein Anspruch, *"den jedes menschliche Wesen auf seiner Stirn trägt."*

20 One could also think here of the famous treatise 'On Bondage' by Eike of Repgow in Sachsenspiegel Ldr. III 42, which is a particularly early testimony to the fact that slavery is not a state of law but an injustice. In detail, see T. Repgen, 'Unfreiheit ist wider die Menschenwürde – eine rechtshistorische Miniatur' in H. Thomas and J. Hattler (eds.), *Der Appell des Humanen. Zum Streit um Naturrecht*, Ontos Verlag, Heusenstamm 2010, pp. 125–52. Additionaly: T. Repgen, 'Eike von Repgow and the Christian Character of his Sachsenspiegel' in M. Schmoeckel (ed.), *Great Christian Jurists in German History*, Mohr Siebeck, Tübingen 2020, pp. 13–25, esp. pp. 21–23.

the Spaniards in the new Spanish possessions as a sinful injustice before the assembled *encomenderos* and *conquistadores*.[21] These sermons were preceded by a joint consultation of the Dominicans, in the convent in Santo Domingo, on the practices of the Spaniards in the fledgling colonies. Montesino, as the one who knew best how to preach, was chosen to deliver the sermon. The first of the two sermons was written at the time, and signed by all the members of the convent to express that it was not an individual opinion of one monk but the conviction of all in the monastery.[22] In his sermon on 21 December 1511, Montesino condemned the behaviour of the Spaniards as sinful. For our context, it is significant that behind this theological assessment was a legal evaluation. His sermon stated:

> You are all in mortal sin and live and die in it because of the cruelty and tyranny you use against those innocent peoples. Tell me, by what right and by what justice do you hold those Indians in such cruel and terrible servitude? With what authority have you waged such despicable wars against these people who calmly and peacefully inhabited their land, countless of whom you have exterminated with death and unheard-of devastation? How can you thus oppress and afflict them without giving them food, nor nursing them in their diseases, which they contract by the excess of labour you inflict upon them, and let them die, or more plainly, whom you kill to

21 Described in detail, and with verbatim quotations from Montesino's sermon, in B. de las Casas, 'Geschichte Westindiens' (translation of 'Historia de las Indias') in M. Delgado (ed.), *Werkauswahl, vol. 2: Historische und ethnographische Schriften*, Schöningh, Paderborn 1995, pp. 161–324, esp. ch. III, 3–5, pp. 219–31; H. Pietschmann, 'Die iberische Expansion im Atlantik und die kastilisch-spanische Entdeckung und Eroberung Amerikas' in W. Bernecker, R. Th. Buve, J. R. Fisher, H. Pietschmann, H. W. Tobler (eds.), *Handbuch der Geschichte Lateinamerikas. Bd. 1: Mittel-, Südamerika und die Karibik bis 1760*, Klett-Cotta, Stuttgart 1994, pp. 207–74, esp. pp. 224 *et seq.*, recalled that Henry the Navigator applied a model reminiscent of medieval feudal law to the Portuguese colonisation of unsettled islands in the 15th century, while Portugal established trading colonies in the settled countries. Castile, on the other hand, tried out a feudal system on the inhabited Canary Islands (l.c., p. 227 *et seq.*).

22 M. Sievernich, 'Anfänge prophetischer Theologie. Antonio de Montesinos Predigt (1511) und ihre Folgen' in M. Sievernich (ed.), *Conquista und Evangelisation*, Matthias-Grünewald-Verlag, Mainz 1992, pp. 77–98, p. 86. Doubts about the written version, and thus the report of de las Casas: A. García y García, 'La ética de la Conquista en el pensamiento español anterior a 1534' in A. García y García (ed.), *Iglesia, Sociedad y Derecho*, Universidad Pontificia de Salamanca, Salamanca 1985, pp. 341–71 (Reprint of this edition in *V Centenario del Descubriminento de América. Actas del I Simposio sobre la ética en la conquista de América [1492–1573]*, Salamanca 1984, pp. 77–104), pp. 343–45. But García y García also believes that Montesino denounced the abuses of slavery in the Caribbean (p. 345). García y García has not put forward any compelling arguments against the correctness of de las Casas's report. That Montesino preached an inspiring sermon is indisputable. An important reason for doubt, for García y García, is that normally sermons are not written down, and that Montesino was chosen precisely because of his rhetorical skills. De las Casas, however, did not claim that writing was the normal procedure, but described the written version and signing as an exception made because of the explosive content, and plausibly motivated this exception with the danger for the preacher.

dig and gain gold daily? And what care do you take to teach them to know God their Creator, to be baptised, to hear mass, and to keep Sundays and feast days?

Are these not human beings? Have they not rational souls (*ánimas racionales*)? Are you not obliged to love them as yourselves? Do you not understand this? Do you not feel this? What deep sleep, what lethargy holds you? Be sure that in the state you are in you will no more attain salvation than Moors or Turks who do not believe in Jesus Christ and do not want to.[23]

Of course, the questions are purely rhetorical. However, two points should already be noted:

(1) The link between sinfulness and unlawfulness. Whoever does wrong, at the same time commits a sin, in this case even a grave sin that leads to the loss of salvation. This is an unusual perspective for today's legal thinking, since law appears first and foremost as a state system of social order, strictly separated from morality. But the fact that legal norms are also binding on the conscience, and thus have a moral dimension, is not really alien to our thinking.
(2) The second important point of view in the quoted passage of the sermon directly concerns our framework theme: equality. Montesino's central argument to justify the injustice of the Spaniards' behaviour is that the Indios are just as human as the Spaniards, i.e. equal and, therefore, bearers of their own rights and duties. If one wants to curtail these rights of the natives, one needs – as with all subjective rights – a justification, a *iustus titulus*; and it was precisely at this point of justifying unequal treatment of the Indios that the discussion began.

Among Montesino's listeners was Bartolomé de Las Casas, then still an *encomendero* himself. Moved by Montesino's sermons, and due to the impression left on him by a massacre of Indios in Caonao in 1512 on Kuba, Las Casas, however, moved away from the encomienda system.[24]

Queen Isabella I of Castile had, by a law of 1503, divided the Spanish colonies in America into territorial structures for the purpose of administration. These encomiendas were "entrusted" (*encomendar*) to so-called *conquistadores* to rule

23 Cited according to the German translation by M. Sievernich, 'Anfänge prophetischer Theologie', above n. 22, p. 87; see also T. Engl, 'Die Adventspredigt des Antón Montesinos' in E. Schmitt (ed.), *Der Aufbau der Kolonialreiche. Dokumente zur Geschichte der europäischen Expansion, vol. 3*, C.H. Beck, Munich 1986, pp. 489–97, p. 494; also, with slight deviation in the formulations, by B. de las Casas, 'Geschichte Westindiens', above n. 21, p. 226.

24 See N. Brieskorn, 'Die Kritik von Bartolomé de Las Casas an der *Relectio de Indis*' in N. Brieskorn and G. Stiening (eds.), *Francisco de Vitorias 'De Indis in interdisziplinärer Perspektive'*, Frommann-Holzboog Verlag, Stuttgart/Bad Cannstatt 2011, pp. 219–49, p. 219.

there on behalf of the Spanish Crown. Following the papal bulls Inter caetera of 3 and 4 May 1493 and Piis fidelium of 25 June 1493 by Pope Alexander VI, the mandate referred to the mission and protection of the indigenous population;[25] in practice, however, it meant rigorous exploitation of the Indios through forced labour and taxes[26] – in short, slavery. The encomienda system has been appropriately described as an "adapted form of European landlordism".[27] However, the Spanish Crown had reminded the people very early on that "the Indians were not slaves but free men".[28] In 1508, the Crown also received the right of patronage over the Church in its colonies, i.e. organisational sovereignty, including the appointment of bishops.[29] Michael Sievernich has rightly remarked that the Church lost its independence here, and became dependent on the Crown.[30]

The economic connection between political and ecclesiastical interests explains the reaction of Montesino's audience after the first sermon in 1511:[31] after the mass on 21 December 1511, the audience, led by the royal governor,

---

25 On Inter cetera, see J. Höffner, *Kolonialismus und Evangelium*, 3rd ed., Paulinus-Verlag, Trier 1972, pp. 212–16.

26 A fact-rich overview of the history of European expansion to America is H. Pietschmann, 'Die iberische Expansion im Atlantik', above n. 21, pp. 207–74, with extensive bibliography at pp. 889–910; pp. 207–11 also a historiographical classification; for a shorter account, see H. Pietschmann, 'Das spanische Kolonialsystem' in H. Thomas (ed.), *Amerika, eine Hoffnung, zwei Visionen*, Busse Seewald, Herford/Stuttgart/Hamburg 1991, pp. 59–75; also useful is the overview (in the section 'Immigration and composition of the population', although [too] much influenced by the Zeitgeist of the 1930s and 1940s) is R. Konetzke, 'Das spanische Weltreich' in F. Valjavec (ed.), *Historia Mundi, vol. 8*, Francke, Bern 1959, pp. 319–73, esp. pp. 365–70; on the intellectual-historical questions and discussions, a fundamental text is J. Höffner, *'Kolonialismus'*, above n. 25, esp. pp. 173–88 on the history of the conquests; on the spiritual-moral classification from a historical perspective, see also A. Milhou, 'Die neue Welt als geistiges und moralisches Problem (1492–1609)' in *Handbuch der Geschichte Lateinamerikas. vol. 1* (above n. 21), pp. 274–96, with bibliography pp. 910–12.

27 J. Höffner, *'Kolonialismus'*, above n. 25, p. 181. For an overview of the encomienda system, with further literature references, see T. Eggensperger, 'Die encomienda – Dreh- und Angelpunkt der Kritik des Las Casas an der Kolonisierung Westindiens' in M Delgado (ed.), *Bartolomé de Las Casas, Werkauswahl, vol. 3/2: Sozialethische und staatsrechtliche Schriften*, Schöningh, Paderborn 1997, pp. 67–81; see also S. E. Ramírez, 'Encomienda' in B. A. Tenenbaum (ed.), *Encyclopedia of Latin America History and Culture, vol. 2*, Charles Scribner's Sons, New York 1996, pp. 492–93.

28 J. Höffner, *'Kolonialismus'*, above n. 25, p. 182. With reference to Queen Isabella's decree: *Real Cédula para que los vecinos de la Española sirvan á los cristianos en la labranza é granxeria é les ayuden á sacar oro, pagandoles sus xornales*; Medina del Campo, '20/12/1503' in *Col. de Doc. Inéd., vol. 31*, Madrid 1879, pp. 209 *et seq*. Already in reaction to Christopher Columbus's attempt to sell captured Indios as slaves in Seville in 1495, Queen Isabella had sought advice and ordered the release and repatriation of the prisoners: see A. Pagden, *The Fall of Natural Man: The American Indian and the Origins of Comparative Ethnology*, CUP, Cambridge 1982, p. 31.

29 M. Sievernich, 'Anfänge prophetischer Theologie', above n. 22, p. 78.

30 Ibid., p. 79.

31 The following after the report by B. de las Casas, *Historia de las Indias*, lib. III, ch. III–V (Bibliotheca de Autores españoles, vol. 96), Editorial Atlas, Madrid 1957, pp. 174–79; German translation by T. Engl in *'Der Aufbau der Kolonialreiche'*, above n. 23, pp. 494–97; also in B. de las Casas, 'Geschichte Westindiens', above n. 21, pp. 222–31.

Don Diego Colón, angrily demanded that the preacher publicly recant his teachings. He had "incited" against the king and his rule, and had thus done a disservice to the Crown. Montesino replied that he had only preached the truth, that this was what he was called to do, and that there was in no way any harm in this for the king and the kingdom. It was finally agreed that on the following Sunday, 28 December 1511, Montesino would "say what seems appropriate to him about what was preached and, if possible, try to satisfy them and explain what was said".[32] Based on a sentence from Job, *"[r]epetam scientiam meam a prinicipio et sermones sine mendatio esse probabo"*,[33] Montesino spoke to the faithful. On this occasion, however, Montesino did not recant his exhortations, but – according to Las Casas's report – deepened the arguments of the previous week, and increased the conclusions, by announcing to the *encomenderos* that they would have to die in their mortal sins if they did not make restitution to the Indians, because only then could they hope for absolution of their sins. Otherwise, the monks would no longer hear their confessions.[34]

The question raised by Montesino about the legitimacy of the Spanish practice of rule found – hardly surprisingly – a lively echo in Spain. At least the short-term economic goals seemed to have been thwarted if the Indians had been given back their freedom and their domicile. The *encomenderos*, through the Franciscan superior Alfonso de Espinal,[35] indignantly appealed to the Spanish King Ferdinand, who replied to Diego Colón as early as 15 March 1512, saying that the "scandalous sermon" had "no good foundation in theology as well as in canon and civil law", since forced labour was permitted by divine and human law, and was based here on a royal command.[36] Even though the provincial of the Dominicans in Spain, Alonso Loaysa, agreed with this view, and forbade further preaching on the matter, the debate could no longer be stopped.[37] Both sides sent their representatives to Spain. The disputes led to new legislative efforts, first of all the Leyes de Burgos of 1512, which at least aimed at a basic protection

---

32 B. de las Casas, *'Historia de las Indias'*, above n. 31.

33 "I repeat my original insight and prove that my words need no improvement": that is how B. de las Casas *'Historia de las Indias'*, above n. 31, reproduces Job 36:3 in a slight modification of the wording in the Vulgate, where it says *"repetam scientiam meam a principio et operatorem meum probabo iustum"*: "I shall range far afield for my arguments to prove my Maker just".

34 B. de las Casas, *'Historia de la Indias'*, above n. 31, lib. III, ch. III–V, pp. 174–79: German translation in *'Der Aufbau der Kolonialreiche'*, above n. 23, p. 497 and in B. de las Casas, 'Geschichte Westindiens', above n. 21, pp. 229–30.

35 J. Höffner, *'Kolonialismus'*, above n. 25, p. 193.

36 Cited after M. Sievernich, 'Anfänge prophetischer Theologie', above n. 22, p. 90. As early as 1504, King Ferdinand had secured, through a junta, that the Indios were subject to the Spaniards, according to human and divine law: see: A. Pagden, above n. 28, pp. 28 *et seq.*

37 M. Sievernich, 'Anfänge prophetischer Theologie', above n. 22, pp. 90 *et seq.*; S. Zavala, 'Introducción' in *De las Islas del mar Oceano por Juán López de Palacios Rubios, Del dominio de los Reyes de España sobre los indios por Matías de Paz*, Fondo de Cultura Económica, Mexico 1954, pp. VII–CXXX, XI–XII.

of the Indios.[38] This need not be described here. Sievernich summarised the development thus:

> The thesis of the juridical justification of the *repartimientos* is contrasted with the theological qualification of this very institution as gravely sinful; the one legitimises the existing order, while the other insists on the necessity of a new order and inculcates the duty of restitution *in solidum*.[39]

Even if the impetus behind the criticism of colonial practice was religiously motivated – Montesino and his confreres were primarily concerned with the salvation of the Spaniards and the Indios – the criticism ultimately rested on a *legal* consideration. Montesino had already asked the rhetorical question after stating that the colonists were living in a state of mortal sin:

¿Con qué derecho y con qué justicia teneís en tan cruel y horrible servidumbre aquestos indios?[40]	By what *right* and by what justice do you keep those Indios in such cruel and terrible bondage?[41]

The decisive criterion for the evaluation as a sin was, therefore, a legal one. Brieskorn aptly said, "[w]hoever wanted to take action against sin had to attack the 'right'",[42] namely the supposed right of the Spaniards vis-à-vis the Indios. Seen in the light of day, it was not a theological argument against a legal one, but rather the legal question of whether the Spaniards were legitimately exercising their rule. If this question was answered in the negative, as Montesino and the other Dominican friars in Santo Domingo judged the matter, then the Spaniards were obliged to restitute. With this, however, we find ourselves in the midst of a discourse that had begun with Augustine, and had already found an intensive deepening in the High Middle Ages.[43]

---

38 See the description of the individual steps in M. Sievernich, 'Anfänge prophetischer, above n. 22, pp. 93–96; J. Höffner, *'Kolonialismus'*, above n. 25, pp. 194 *et seq.*

39 M. Sievernich, 'Anfänge prophetischer Theologie', above n. 22, p. 92: *"Der These von der juridischen Rechtfertigung der Repartimientos steht die These von der theologischen Qualifizierung eben dieser Institution als schwer sündhaft gegenüber; die eine legitimiert die bestehende Ordnung, während die andere auf die Notwendigkeit einer neuen Ordnung besteht und die Pflicht zur Restitution in solidum einschärft."*

40 B. de las Casas, '*Historia de las Indias*', above n. 31, p. 176.

41 Translation according to T. Engl in '*Der Aufbau der Kolonialreiche*', above n. 23, p. 494.

42 N. Brieskorn SJ, 'Las Casas und das römische Recht' in M. Delgado (ed.), *Bartolomé de Las Casas, Werkauswahl, vol. 3/1: Sozialethische und staatsrechtliche Schriften*, Schöningh, Paderborn 1996, pp. 13–32, p. 14.

43 On the doctrine of restitution, see, above all, N. Jansen, *Theologie, Philosophie und Jurisprudenz in der spätscholastischen Lehre von der Restitution. Außervertragliche Ausgleichsansprüche im frühneuzeitlichen Naturrechtsdiskurs*, Mohr Siebeck, Tübingen 2013; T. Repgen, 'De restitutione – eine kommentierende Einführung' in J. Stüben (ed, tr),

At this point, a few references to the background must suffice.[44] It was Anselm of Canterbury who interpreted the Christian doctrine of redemption to the effect that redemption requires the participation of the individual. In this view, a sentence of Augustine's took on new relevance. In his letter to Macedonius, Augustine had said:

Si enim res aliena, propter quam peccatum est, cum reddi possit, non redditur, non agitur poenitentia, sed fingitur: si autem veraciter agitur, non remittetur peccatum, nisi restituatur ablatum; sed, ut dixi, cum restitui potest.[45]	For if a foreign thing, on account of which someone has sinned, can be returned and is not returned, no repentance is made, but a hypocrisy. Even if he has truly repented, the sin is not remitted if you do not restitute what you have taken. But, as I said, if restitution is possible.

Almost identical in wording, this consideration had found its way into the *Decretum Gratiani*.[46] And in the *Liber Sextus* it stated succinctly:

Peccatum non dimittitur, nisi restituatur ablatum.[47]	A sin is not remitted if you do not restitute what you have taken.

To a certain extent, this is where the debate has its legal starting point: were the Spaniards liable to restitution or not? This is not the place to unfold the restitution doctrine of the Middle Ages. The idea of equality, which is already echoed in Montesino's question, "*¿[e]stos, no son hombres? ¿No tienen ánimas racionales?*"[48] – whether the Indios were not also human beings – together with the restitution of property and the freedom of the Indios that he demanded, unleashed an explosive force that required legal analysis, but was also accessible.

Francisco de Vitoria, De Iustitia – Über die Gerechtigkeit, Teil 2, Frommann-Holzboog Verlag, Stuttgart-Bad Cannstatt 2017, pp. XVII–LVII; T. Repgen, 'De restitutione – Fortsetzung der kommentierenden Einführung' in J. Stüben (ed, tr), *Francisco de Vitoria, De Iustitia – Über die Gerechtigkeit, Teil 3*, Frommann-Holzboog Verlag, Stuttgart-Bad Cannstatt 2020, pp. XVII–LVI.

44 For more detail, see T. Repgen, 'De restitutione – eine kommentierende Einführung', above n. 43, pp. XXII–XXXIV.

45 Augustinus, 'Epistola CLIII (ad Macedonium)', ch. 6, para. 20 in *Opera omnia Augustini Hipponensis, Patrologia Latina, vol. 33*, Migne, Paris 1865, Sp. 662.

46 *Decretum Gratiani*, C. 14 q. 6 c. 1: *"Si res aliena, propter quam peccatum est, cum reddi possit, non redditur"*.

47 VI 5.12, reg. iur. 4.

48 B. de las Casas, '*Historia de las Indias*', above n. 31, p. 176.

2.2. *DE INDIS*

Francisco de Vitoria, a Dominican monk and professor of theology in Salamanca, presented such an analysis in his *Relectio De Indis*[49] at the turn of the year 1538/39. Although one would have thought that more than 40 years after the beginning of the Spanish conquests in Latin America, and more than 25 years after Montesino's famous Advent sermons, the arguments had all been exchanged, Vitoria took up the question raised by Montesino – *"¿con qué derecho?"*[50] – of what right the Spanish had based their actions on, and whether restitution was not owed.

The *Relectio De Indis* is divided into three parts. The first part deals with the question of whether Spanish rule over the Indios itself is justified,[51] the second with the powers of the Spanish rulers that follow from this legal situation, and the third with the powers of the Church vis-à-vis the Indios. In the first part in particular, as we shall see, the legal equality of the people plays a decisive role.

As always in the texts of the late scholastics, the initial question is that of the salvation of human beings. Those who live in mortal sin miss their eternal goal. Montesino had told the colonists this consequence in no uncertain terms. However, there were also dissenting voices – not least those of the Spanish kings – that justified the actions of the colonial lords. Thus, there was a real "case of doubt".

---

49 F. de Vitoria, '[Relectio] De Indis' in J. Stüben (Latin–German text, intro., trs. and annotations), *Vorlesungen II (Relectiones). Völkerrecht, Politik, Kirche*, Kohlhammer, Stuttgart 1997, pp. 370–541. The Latin text follows the edition of L. Pereña and J. M. Perez Prendes, *Corpus Hispanorum de Pace, vol. 5*, Consejo Superior de Investigaciones Científicas, Madrid 1967. On the text's history, see J. Stüben, *Vorbemerkungen zum zweiten Band der Lateinisch-deutschen Gesamtausgabe*, in J. Stüben (ed.), Vorlesungen II (Relectiones) (as before), pp. 13–35, pp. 18–25; on the transmission of the complete works of Vitoria, see H-G. Justenhoven, *Francisco de Vitoria zu Krieg und Frieden*, Bachem, Cologne 1991, pp. 10–12. Justenhoven has made the De Indis lecture the focus of his dissertation. He is concerned with a reconstruction of Vitoria's doctrine of just war. Also useful is D. Deckers, *Gerechtigkeit und Recht. Eine historisch-kritische Untersuchung der Gerechtigkeitslehre des Francisco de Vitoria (1483–1546)*, Universitäts-Verlag, Freiburg (Switzerland) 1991, pp. 229–41.
On the classification of the Relectio De Indis esp., see U. Horst, 'Leben und Werke Francisco de Vitorias' in *Vorlesungen I (Relectiones). Völkerrecht, Politik, Kirche*, Kohlhammer, Stuttgart 1995, pp. 13–99, pp. 84–98; a great contect overview is N. Brieskorn, 'Die Kritik von Bartolomé de Las Casas', above n. 24, pp. 228–44.
The term *"relectio"* means the systematic revisiting of questions that have arisen in the course of the academic year in the regular lectures: H-G. Justenhoven, *'Francisco de Vitoria'* (ibid.), p. 10.

50 B. de las Casas, *'Historia de las Indias'*, above n. 31, p. 176.

51 The *pars prima* is again divided into an introduction (*praeludium*) and three *sectiones* (divisions, namely: (1) Were the barbarians real lords before the arrival of the Spaniards?; (2) On the (seven) illegitimate titles of dominion; (3) On the (seven)legitimate titles of dominion). Introduction and sections are divided into numbered paragraphs.

In this situation, Vitoria taught, in accordance with the "probabilism" prevalent in moral theology at the time,[52] that even he who does not inform and consult himself sins.[53] Conscience must be guided by what is at least probably right and true.[54] In the questions of how to deal with the "barbarians", there is not, after all, an *"evidenter iniustum ... nec rursus ita evidenter iustum"*:[55] no obvious wrong, or its converse, an obvious right. Vitoria wants to contribute to clarifying the question of doubt, whether they were actually slaves.

Presuppositionally, Vitoria asks the basic question, were the barbarians true masters (*domini*) or were they slaves from the beginning? If they were slaves, they had nothing of their own (arg. Inst. 2.9.3. and Ulpian D. 29.2.79) and the Spaniards, therefore, did not take anything from them that would now require restitution.[56] But it seemed twofold.

In scholastic fashion, Vitoria begins with the antithesis, namely slavery by nature, as described by Aristotle in his *Politics*.[57] There are, Aristotle taught,

---

52 On this, see T. Repgen, 'Naturrecht in action. Rechtliche Argumentation *in foro conscientiae* anhand von Beispielen aus Vitorias Summenkommentar' in S. Lepsius, F. Vollhardt, O. Bach (eds.), *Von der Allegorie zur Empirie. Natur im Rechtsdenken des Spätmittelalters und der Frühen Neuzeit*, Erich Schmidt Verlag, Berlin 2018, pp. 63–84, p. 82 with reference to R. Schüßler, *Moral im Zweifel. vol. 1: Die scholastische Theorie des Entscheidens unter moralischer Unsicherheit*, Mentis, Paderborn 2003 and *vol. 2: Die Herausforderung des Probabilismus*, Mentis, Paderborn 2006; R. Schüßler, 'Probability in Medieval and Renaissance Philosophy' in *The Stanford Encyclopedia of Philosophy (Spring 2015 Edition)* <http://plato.stanford.edu/archives/spr2015/entries/probability-medieval-renaissance/>; a good overview was already offered by G. Otte, 'Der Probabilismus. Eine Theorie auf der Grenze zwischen Theologie und Jurisprudenz' in P. Grossi (ed.), *La Seconda Scolastica nella Formazione del Diritto Privato Moderno. Incontro di studio*, Giuffrè, Milan 1973, pp. 283–302.

53 F. de Vitoria, 'De Indis', above n. 49, I prael., 2: *"si iste non consuluit sapientes in re dubia, excusari non potest."* – "If someone does not consult with the wise in a case of doubt, he cannot be excused."

54 Ibid., I prael., 3

55 Ibid., I prael., 7.

56 Ibid., I 1, 1; de Vitoria had already addressed this question in his *Relectio de potestate ecclesiae I*, in 'De potestate ecclesiae I/Erste Vorlesung über die Gewalt der Kirche', in F. de Vitoria, 'Vorlesungen (Relectiones)' in J. Stüben (ed., tr.), *Völkerrecht, Politik, Kirche*, vol. 1, Kohlhammer, Stuttgart 1995, pp. 162–277, qu. 1, para. 8, p. 178, with the argument that Christians in antiquity had been subject to their pagan authorities. This was true as long as these rulers did not commit injustice. On this, and on the parallel argumentation of Las Casas, see N. Brieskorn, 'Die Kritik des Bartolomé de Las Casas', above n. 24, p. 229.

57 Aristoteles, *Politik*, ed. and translated by E. Rolfes, Felix Meiner: Hamburg 1958, I, 4 and 5 (1254a–1255a). A still useful, source-based overview of Aristotle's position is provided by F. Schaub, *Studien zur Geschichte der Sklaverei im früheren Mittelalter*, Rothschild, Berlin 1913, pp. 5–8; also A. Pagden, above n. 28, pp. 41–48. For a brief classification, see also H. Flashar, *Aristoteles. Lehrer des Abendlandes*, 2nd ed., C.H. Beck, Munich 2013, pp. 110–13; Aristotle sees people as inherently unequal. He understands "nature" in a biological sense, not normatively. Flashar rightly points out a certain inconsistency in Aristotle, when Aristotle does not see a way to assigning the legally free, who are not gifted with sovereignty, to the slave state.

people who are rational to such a small extent that they hardly differ from animals. For Aristotle, the physique is an indication of this.

With reference to the Indios, Vitoria counters Aristotle's teaching with an observation that has the effect of reversing the burden of proof:

Illi erant in pacifica possessione rerum et publice et privatim.	But those people were in undisturbed possession of their goods in the public as well as in the private sphere.
Ergo omnino, nisi contrarium constet, habendi sunt pro dominis.[58]	So, unless the contrary is established, they must necessarily be regarded as dominions.[59]

Until the arrival of the Spaniards, the Indians did not live as slaves, but as their own masters, and in this respect they were equal to the Spaniards. If the Spaniards now wanted to treat them as slaves, they needed a justifying reason.

Aristotle had provided such a reason in the eyes of some, such as Juán Gines Sepúlveda.[60] The background to Aristotle's differentiation is that the good life for which man should strive is not found through the application of abstract rules, but through experience and wise counsel.[61] But then the wiser men should guide the rest. For Aristotle, this is the inner reason for "natural slavery". If one's intellectual abilities are not sufficient to lead such a good life, it is better, according to Aristotle, to entrust oneself to another. The latter, however, should also strive for the best for his slave.[62]

Aristotle's view of natural slavery was shared by many until the sixteenth century. John Mair (1467–1550) had applied it without hesitation to the inhabitants of the Antilles.[63] It was, therefore, no small leap for Vitoria[64] to reject

58 F. de Vitoria, 'De Indis', above n. 49, I 1, 1.

59 Translation in according to J. Stüben, '*Vorlesungen II*', above n. 49, p. 387.

60 On Sepúlveda, see C. Schäfer, 'Einleitung' in C. Schäfer (ed., tr.), *Juan Ginés Sepúlveda, Democrates Secundus – Zweiter Demokrates*, Frommann-Holzboog Verlag, Stuttgart-Bad Cannstatt 2018, pp. XIII–LXXIV; H. Pietschmann, 'Aristotelischer Humanismus und Inhumanität? Sepúlveda und die amerikanischen Ureinwohner' in W. Reinhard (ed.), *Humanismus und Neue Welt*, Wiley-VCH Verlag, Weinheim 1987, pp. 143–66; A. Pagden, above n. 28, pp. 109–18.

61 Aristoteles, '*Nikomachische Ethik*', above n. 2, VI, 9, 1142a, 14.

62 On this see: C. Dierksmeier, 'Globalization Ethics in the Sixteenth Century? Why We Should Re-Read Francisco de Vitoria' in D. Th. Orique O.P., Rad Roldán-Figueroa (eds.), *History, Philosophy, and Theology in the Age of European Expansion*, Brill, Leiden/Boston 2019, pp. 197–217, esp. pp. 198–201.

63 J. Major, *In secundum librum sententiarum*, Paris 1519, fol. clxxxvij v.

64 A. Pagden, above n. 28, pp. 15–24, rightly referred to Aristotle's view of the world, promimently represented in the Middle Ages, according to which the "barbarians" live outside the polis, i.e. ultimately outside "civilised" legal systems, but it is first and foremost

the Aristotelian concept of natural slavery, and to replace it with the legal concept of the *equal human nature* of all.

Vitoria immediately eliminated a possible theological counterargument: according to the teaching of John Wicliff (1330–1384),[65] every *dominium* was based on the grace of God. According to this doctrine, anyone who did not live in the state of grace could not have *dominium*. Applied to the situation of the unbaptised Indios, this would mean that they lacked the state of grace and, therefore, could not be *domini*.[66] The Council of Constance (1415) had already rejected these teachings of Wicliff long before the discovery of the New World by Columbus,[67] which Vitoria also emphasised.[68] It was true, Vitoria continued, that every *dominium* was derived from God.

Apparet, quod dominium fundetur in imagine Dei.[69]	It is obvious that the *dominium* is based on the image of God.

What is decisive, then, is to whom the image of God belongs, of which Genesis speaks, as Vitoria reminded us.[70] Genesis says:

> God said, "Let us make man in our own image, in the likeness of ourselves, and let them be masters of the fish of the sea, the birds of heaven, the cattle, all the wild

the political community in which a humane relationship between man and man is realised. For Aristotle, there was no difference between "barbarians" and natural slaves, cf. Aristoteles, *Politik*, (above n. 57) I, 2 (1252 b). With this preconceived expectation, the Europeans came to America (which they initially thought was India). It was not surprising, then, that the Spaniards identified the Indios as "barbarians" who were characterised by passions but not by reason; Bernardo de Mesa and Gil Gregorio, for example, argued at the junta of Burgos in 1512 (in reaction to Montesino's sermons): A. Pagden, above n. 28, p. 48 with verbatim quotation from the handwritten copy of Gregorio's statement in *Real Academia de la Historia* (Madrid) 9-17-93688, 33, with annotations 90 et seq. and pp. 49 et seq. with quotations from Las Casas's report on the position of Bernardo de Mesa; see also T. de Mercado, *Summa de tratos y contratos*, Sevilla 1571, lib. II, ch. XXI, fol. 108r.

65 On this in more detail, see A. Conti, 'Art. John Wyclif' in *Stanford Encyclopedia of Philosophy 2017*, online <https://plato.stanford.edu/archives/spr2017/entries/wyclif/>.

66 See also ibid., para. 5.2, with reference to J. Wicliff, *De civili dominio*, ed. by R. L. Poole, J. Loserth and F. D. Matthew, Trübner, London 1885, vol. 1, p. 1 – Vitoria had already stated in his 1528 *Relectio de potestate civili* that the rights of political organisation were not dependent on the state of grace and also not on the cultural level; see N. Brieskorn, 'Die Kritik von Bartolomé de Las Casas', above n. 24, p. 220, pointing out that Vitoria had not considered the conquest of Peru to be justified in any way.

67 A. Conti, above, n. 65, n. 1.1.

68 F. de Vitoria, 'De Indis', above n. 49, I 1, 2.

69 Ibid., I 1, 2.

70 Ibid. On the argumentation with the image of God, see A. Masferrer, 'Human dignity in the early sixteenth century Spanish scholasticism. Francisco de Vitoria and Fray Bartolomé de las Casas' in H. Dondorp, M. J. Schermaier, B. Sirks (eds.), *De rebus divinis et humanis: Essays in honour of Jan Hallebeek*, V&R unipress, Göttingen 2019, pp. 203–13, 208–11.

animals and all the creatures that creep along the ground." God created man in the image of himself, in the image of God he created him, male and female he created them.[71]

Even a mortal sin, Vitoria argued, does not change the God image of man and the *dominium* associated with it:

Quia non perdit dominium super pro-prios actus et super propria membra.[72]	For [the sinner] does not lose dominion over his actions and himself.

Since Thomas Aquinas, the ability to control one's own actions was the essential characteristic of the *dominium*.[73] Aquinas saw man's rational and volitionally controlled self-rule as the essential distinguishing feature from the animal:

Ad secundum dicendum quod ex hoc contingit quod homo est dominus sui actus, quod habet deliberationem de suis actibus, ex hoc enim quod ratio deliberans se habet ad opposita, volun-tas in utrumque potest.	Secondly, as far as this is concerned, it must be said that man is master of his action because he can reflect on his actions. For since reason is reflective (also) of the opposite, the will can be directed to both.
Sed secundum hoc voluntarium non est in brutis animalibus, ut dictum est.[74]	But this willing does not exist in animals, as is said above.

The excerpt is, first of all, interesting with regard to the theory of action. Aquinas combines voluntaristic and rationalistic elements in such a way that a strict assignment to one of the two camps is not advisable.[75] For our question, however,

71 Genesis 1: 26 *et seq.*

72 F. de Vitoria, 'De Indis', above n. 49, I 1, 3.

73 Going into the development of the *dominium* especially: M. J. Schermaier, 'Dominus actuum suorum. Die willenstheoretische Begründung des Eigentums und das römische Recht' in (2017) 134 *Zeitschrift der Savigny-Stiftung für Rechtsgeschichte, Romanistische Abteilung*, 49–105, esp. 57 *et seq.*

74 Thomas Aquinas, *Summa Theologiae (STh) I-II*, q. 6, art. 2, ad 2; here and in the following, quotations from the *STh* are taken from the Editio Leonina, Rome 1891, easily accessible at <www.corpusthomisticum.org>.

75 In this sense also, convincingly, with detailed argumentation, see S. Schweighöfer, *Die Begründung der normativen Kraft von Gesetzen bei Francisco Suárez*, Aschendorff Verlag, Münster 2018, pp. 55–57, 85–101.

this is not important. What is decisive here is that both the image of God and the *dominium suorum actuum* are linked to the characteristic of belonging to the species "man", and to this characteristic alone. Vitoria consistently emphasised that:

Dominium fundatur in imagine Dei.	*Dominium* is founded in the image of God.
Sed homo est imago Dei per naturam, scilicet per potentias naturales.	But man is the image of God by virtue of [his] nature, namely by virtue of his natural endowments.
Ergo non perditur per peccatum mora-le.[76]	So one does not lose *dominium* through mortal sin.

To reaffirm this, Vitoria recalled that the Old Testament kings Saul and David were clearly sinners, but nevertheless also exercised dominion according to law.[77] Temporal goods were given by God to all men without regard to their state of grace.[78] Infidelity did not change the *dominium*,[79] and in the Book of Tobit the restitution of stolen goods to pagans was ordered.[80] This also seems consistent because the *dominium* is based on natural law. According to Vitoria, no one was allowed to take a thing from a "Saracen" or a Jew because they were unbelievers:

Sed est furtum vel rapina non minus quam a Christianis.[81]	Rather, it is then theft and robbery, no less than taking something away from Christians.

It becomes clear that religion is not, for Vitoria, a legally relevant distinguishing criterion in relation to the *dominium*. This addresses a central aspect of legal equality. This equality, which is, ultimately, founded religiously in the image of

76 F. de Vitoria, 'De Indis', above n. 49, I 1, 3.
77 Ibid.
78 Ibid.
79 Ibid., I 1, 4, with reference to *STh* II-II, q. 10, a. 12 resp., where Thomas states that the children of the pagans must not be baptised against the will of their parents.
80 Ibid., with reference to Tob 2:13.
81 Ibid., I 1, 4.

God, rather abstracts from faith and thus also from faith's claim to truth. As an interim result, Vitoria then stated:

Ex ominbus his sequitur conclusio, quod barbari nec propter peccata alia mortalia nec propter peccatum infideli-tatis non impediuntur, quin sint veri domini tam publice quam privatim nec hoc titulo possunt a Christianis occu-pari bona terrae illorum.[82]	From all this it is concluded that the barbarians are not prevented from being true dominions in the public as well as in the private sphere, either because of other mortal sins or because of the sin of unbelief, and the goods of their country cannot be taken possession of by Christians on this legal basis.

Another possible objection to a genuine *dominium* of the "*barbaren*" was discussed as the endowment of reason, since unreasonable creatures could not be rights-bearers,[83] which corresponded to the aforementioned Aristotelian position.[84] Thomas Aquinas had declared:

Sola creatura rationalis habet dominium sui actus.[85]	Only a rational creature is master of its actions.

82 Ibid., I 1, 10, with reference to THOMAS DE VIO (CAJETAN), ComSTh II-II, q. 66, a. 8 in *Sancti Thomae Aquinatis Opera omnia, iussu impensaque Leonis XIII*, vol. IX, Roma 1897, pp. 94 (online at <http://archive.org/stream/operaomniaiussui09thom#page/ii/mode/2up>). On Cajetan's commentary on Thomas Aquinas, which was of paramount importance for the discussion of legal titles in 16th century Spain, see M. DELGADO, 'Glaubenstradition im Kontext. Voraussetzungen, Verdienste und Versäumnisse lascasianischer Missionstheologie' in M. Delgado (ed.), *Bartolomé de Las Casas, Werkauswahl, vol. 1: Missionstheologische Schriften*, Schöningh, Paderborn 1994, pp. 35–58, pp. 41 *et seq.*; D. DECKERS, 'Restitution – Das Beichthandbuch und die Schultheologie im 16. Jahrhundert' in M. DELGADO (ed.), *Bartolomé de Las Casas, Werkauswahl, vol. 3/1: Sozialethische und staatsrechtliche Schriften*, Schöningh, Paderborn 1996, pp. 128–36, pp. 134 *et seq.* On the text of Vitoria, see also D. DECKERS, *'Gerechtigkeit'*, above n. 49, p. 231, pp. 220 and 234 also on the Thomas Aquinas comment by Cajetan.

83 See *STh* I-II, q. 1, a. 1 resp.: *"Est autem homo dominus suorum actuum per rationem et voluntatem, unde et liberum arbitrium esse dicitur facultas voluntatis et rationis."* ("Man is master of his actions by virtue of his reason and will, and therefore freedom of choice is called a faculty of the will and reason."); *STh* I-II, q. 1, a. 2 resp.: *"Illa ergo quae rationem habent, seipsa movent ad finem, quia habent dominium suorum actuum per liberum arbitrium, quod est facultas voluntatis et rationis."* ("But those who have reason move towards [their] goal because they are masters of their actions by virtue of freedom of choice, which is a faculty of the will and of reason.")

84 See, above n. 57. Sepúlveda had wanted to justify the masterlessness of the Indios with a lack of reason: see N. BRIESKORN, 'Die Kritik des Bartolomé de Las Casas', above n. 24, p. 230.

85 THOMAS AQUINAS, *Summa contra gentiles*, lib. III, c. 111 <www.corpusthomisticum.org>.

And Vitoria adds:

Per hoc aliquis est dominus suorum actuum, quia potest hoc vel illud eligere.[86]	For he who can choose this or that is master of his own hands.

The *potestas eligendi* is only granted to rational beings. Vitoria only very briefly emphasised that even children can have their own rights, which have to be exercised by a guardian.[87] Nor can one deny that children are created in the image of God.[88] With this statement, Vitoria rejected the view that the Indians were "barbarians" without reason, and should, therefore, be treated like children. Private law already gave the appropriate answer to this idea, with the institute of paternal authority or guardianship,[89] since the child itself is legally capable of acting through parents or guardians.

After all, Vitoria continued, one could not deny the barbarians reasonableness per se, as is shown by the existence of a political order, a legal system and a religious cult.[90] However, the fact that there are also less rational people everywhere was a fact that was also known in Spain.[91]

In a somewhat daring manoeuvre, Vitoria, at the end of this chapter of his lecture, tried to find a common ground with Aristotle, whose teaching is opposed to the idea of equality. Aristotle, Vitoria explained, did not know slavery by nature, but only considered the weakly gifted to be in need of leadership, analogous to the situation of guardianship.[92] Certainly, an unbiased reading of

86 F. de Vitoria, 'De Indis', above n. 49, I 1, 12 with reference to *STh* I, q. 82, a. 1, ad 3: "*Ad tertium dicendum quod sumus domini nostrorum actuum secundum quod possumus hoc vel illud eligere.*" ("Thirdly, it must be said that we are masters of our actions because we can choose this or that ourselves").

87 Ibid., I 1, 13. Vitoria leaves the problem of how to deal with *amentes* – madmen – to the legal scholars.

88 Ibid., I 1, 13.

89 On this, see T. Repgen, '§§1773–1895 – Vormundschaft über Minderjährige' in M. Schmoeckel, J. Rückert and R. Zimmermann (eds), *Historisch-kritischer Kommentar zum BGB, vol. IV: Familienrecht*, Mohr Siebeck, Tübingen 2018, pp. 1346–1505.

90 F. de Vitoria, 'De Indis', above n. 49, I 1, 15. In another context, Vitoria emphasises that what is decisive is the fundamental talent for reason, i.e. potentiality, which is of the same kind in all human beings: see: F. de Vitoria, 'De eo, ad quod tenetur homo, cum primum venit ad usum rationis, n. 8' in U. Horst, H-G. Justenhoven, J. Stüben (eds.), *Vorlesungen II (Relectiones). Völkerrecht, Politik, Kirche*, Kohlhammer, Stuttgart 1997, pp. 112 *et seq.* On *Vorlesungen II (Relectiones). Völkerrecht, Politik, Kirche*, Kohlhammer, Stuttgart u.a. 1997, pp. 112 *et seq.* On this, also see K. Bunge, *Gleichheit und Gleichmaß. Zur Rechtsphilosophie Francisco de Vitorias*, Frommann-Holzboog Verlag, Stuttgart-Bad Cannstatt 2018, pp. 61–63.

91 F. de Vitoria, 'De Indis', above n. 49, I, 15.

92 Ibid., I 1, 16. The same idea is echoed later by Vitoria in I 3, 17, when he considers whether the barbarians would have to tolerate foreign rule in the sense of guardianship, Vitoria is not determined, but tends to answer the question in the affirmative, which has led Las Casas to accuse him of contradiction, because Vitoria in the *sectio prima* [namely in the passage

Aristotle will allow us to understand him differently, but for our context it is not this that is significant, but Vitoria's effort to uphold the idea of equality based on the image of God.

Restat ergo conclusio certa, quod antequam Hispani ad illos venissent, illi erant veri domini et publice et privatim.[93]	So we are left with the safe conclusion that before the arrival of the Spaniards, those [barbarians] were real dominions, both in the public and private spheres.

This concludes the first section; the *prima pars* of the *Relectio De Indis.*

For Vitoria, it was clear – against the medieval ideas of papal universalism[94] – that the Indios had *dominium* over their goods like all other people, and that the Spaniards were, therefore, not allowed to appropriate the goods or enslave the Indios. One could say that the Indios were equally free and sovereign because of their innate likeness to God, and thus their dignity.[95]

Vitoria's comments on the Aristotelian doctrine of slavery already indicated that he had considered justifications other than natural slavery, which he rejected on the grounds of equal human nature. Among such potential reasons was the assertion of a kind of humanitarian intervention, since cannibalism and incest were practised among the Indios.[96] If this were to legitimise a war

quoted here] has described the Indios as *veri domini*; see: N. Brieskorn, 'Die Kritik des Bartolomé de Las Casas', above n. 24, p. 242. On F. de Vitoria, 'De Indis', above n. 49, I, 1, 16, also K. Bunge, above n. 90, p. 151.

93 F. de Vitoria, 'De Indis', above n. 49, I 1, 16. In this sense, Vitoria also made himself unmistakably clear in his regular lecture on the *Summa Theologiae*: see F. de Vitoria, *De iustitia II*, above n. 43, ComSTh II-II q. 62, a. 1 para. 28, p. 42 *et seq.*; on this, see also D. Deckers, '*Gerechtigkeit*', above n. 49, pp. 228 *et seq.*, who rightfully notices that 'De Indis' is basically an elaboration of the line of thought presented in ComSTh II-II q. 62, a. 1 para. 28.

94 On this, e.g. J. Höffner, '*Kolonialismus*', above n. 25, pp. 9–41, 209–32, 264–303.

95 Even if the natural law thinkers have sought other lines of reasoning, the results are not far apart, e.g. when I. Kant, *Die Metaphysik der Sitten (The Metaphysics of Morals)*, 1797, Akademie Ausgabe, Bd. VI, 2nd ed., Berlin 1914, pp. 237 *et seq.* (<https://korpora.zim.uni-duisburg-essen.de/kant/aa06/237.html>) writes, "*Die angeborene Gleichheit, d.i. die Unabhängigkeit, nicht zu mehreren von anderen verbunden zu werden, als wozu man sie wechselseitig auch verbinden kann; mithin die Qualität des Menschen, sein eigener Herr (sui iuris) zu sein … alle dieses Befugnisse liegen schon im Prinzip der angebornen Freiheit, und sind wirklich von ihr nicht … unterschieden.*" ("The innate equality, i.e. the independence, of not being joined to several by others, as to which they can also be mutually joined; consequently the quality of man to be his own master (*sui iuris*) … all these powers already lie in the principle of innate freedom, and are really not … distinguished from it."); on I. Kant, see G. Luf, *Freiheit und Gleichheit*, Springer, Vienna 1978, p. 60.

96 F. de Vitoria, 'De Indis', above n. 49, I 2, 21. On the background of the argument of barbarism and lack of culture as a reason for slavery, see J. Höffner, '*Kolonialismus*', above n. 25, pp. 233–42; and Pagden's position as presented above n. 64. On the discussion of Vitoria's position, see G. Cavallar, *The Rights of Strangers: Theories of International Hospitality, the Global Community, and Political Justice since Vitoria*, Ashgate, Aldershot 2002, pp. 98–107.

against the Indios, one would also arrive at a justification for enslavement, in Vitoria's view, because in accordance with the legal tradition of the Middle Ages, Vitoria considered it permissible under *ius gentium* to enslave prisoners of war.[97] However, Vitoria rejected such a justification, in the specific case of the Indians. He recalled that Christians were not called to be judges.[98] There was also no criterion of distinction, since sins were committed all the time in Christian kingdoms as well, and no one would think of swapping kingdoms.[99] In this respect, the argumentation here also boils down to an equality argument.

An equality argument is also encountered in the case of those legal titles which, in Vitoria's view, could justify the Spaniards' stay in the territories of the Indians, but not the way in which they actually exercised their rule.[100] Thus, according to Vitoria, there is a *ius communicationis* on the basis of a "natural society and community" of people. From this follows a right of travel and residence,[101] as long as one never harms anyone, because:

Omnem hominem proximum esse.[102]	Every human being is a neighbour.

And so there is also a right to trade:

Non enim "homini homo lupus est".[103]	For "man is not a wolf to man".

[97] See F. de Vitoria, ComSTh II-II q. 57, art. para, n. 5, in J. Stüben (ed.), *De iustitia - Über die Gerechtigkeit, Teil 1*, Frommann-Holzboog Verlag, Stuttgart - Bad Cannstatt 2013, pp. 40 *et seq*. What remains unresolved, moreover, is the tension between this statement by Vitoria and a remark made by him in the margins of the discussion of the admissibility of private property in ComSTh II-II q. 62, art. 1, n. 20, where he says, unchallenged, *"ut libertas dicitur esse de iure naturali, quia stando in solo iure naturali nulla est libertas, quae admittat secum ser-vitutem"* – "Freedom comes from natural law, because from the point of view of mere natural law there is no freedom that simultaneously admits slavery": F. de Vitoria in J. Stüben (ed.), *De iustitia - Über die Gerechtigkeit, Teil 2*, Frommann-Holzboog Verlag, Stuttgart - Bad Cannstatt 2017, p. 32 *et seq*. If one takes into account the view, also shared by Vitoria, that the *ius gentium* must not contradict natural law, Vitoria would have to reject the position reported in ComSTh II-II q. 57, art. 3, para. 5 of the *ius gentium*.

[98] This consideration is an important argument for Las Casas in his dispute with Juan Gínes de Sepúlveda: see J. Höffner, *'Kolonialismus'*, above n. 25, p. 239 with annotations.

[99] F. de Vitoria, 'De Indis', above n. 49, I 2, 22.

[100] On this part of the *relectio*, which is also viewed very critically, see N. Brieskorn, 'Die Kritik des Bartolomé de Las Casas', above n. 24, pp. 232–44, with reference to R. Hernández, *Derechos humanos en Francisco de Vitoria*, Editorial San Esteban, Salamanca 1984, pp. 345–81.

[101] On this, see also H-G. Justenhoven, *'Francisco de Vitoria'*, above n. 49, pp. 96–108; G. Cavallar, '*The Rights of Strangers*', above n. 96), pp. 107–12.

[102] F. de Vitoria, 'De Indis', above n. 49, I 3, 1.

[103] Ibid., I, 3, 2.

Instead, man is an equal human being. However, measures are never permitted that would not also be permitted in a war against Christians:

Non licet ultra progredi, quam si bellum susciperetur contra Christianos.[104]	It is not permissible to go beyond what would be acceptable in war against Christians.

It is undeniable – and Vitoria was already criticised for this by Las Casas, for example – that in his *Relectio De Indis* he cited various reasons that *could* legitimise the warfare of the Spanish against the Indios.[105] This included the right to install a Christian ruler if a large number of Indios had adopted the Christian faith, since otherwise there was a danger of their turning away from the faith.[106] A detailed critique of the legitimations of war presented by Vitoria in the *sectio tertia* of the *prima pars* of his *Relectio* is not necessary here, since it is the justification of the idea of equality, and not the history of the Spanish colonies, that is at issue.[107]

Vitoria's consideration is problematic in two ways: on the one hand, he also held that conversions to the faith always had to be voluntary, about which there was often reasonable doubt. In this respect, however, it must also be said that Vitoria treats this reason for war as merely hypothetical.[108] More weighty, on the other hand, is the fact that Vitoria also saw no reason to favour Christian rule over other rulers, which is why the legal title for conquest derived from

104 Ibid., II, 11.

105 K. Bunge, n. 93, p. 254, fn. 274, is incomplete in that it only mentions the potentially unsuitable reasons for war for Vitoria, but passes over the potentially suitable ones. H-G. Justenhoven, *'Francisco de Vitoria'*, above n. 49, p. 98, rightly emphasises that Vitoria was not concerned with making an apology on behalf of the Spaniards, but with clarifying the legal situation, so that he also discussed possible legitimate reasons for war.

106 F. de Vitoria, 'De Indis', above n. 49, I, 3, 13.

107 On this, see N. Brieskorn, 'Die Kritik des Bartolomé de Las Casas', above n. 24, pp. 232–44 with reference to R. Hernández, *Derechos humanos en Francisco de Vitoria*, Editorial San Esteban, Salamanca 1984, pp. 345–81; R. Marcus, 'Las Casas admirateur critique de Vitoria' in (1987) 184 *Revue d'éthique et de théologie morale*, pp. 67–72, who recalls that Vitoria had already replied clearly by letter to a question in 1534 that he saw no just reason for the war of the Spaniards in the New World (ibid., p. 68). Las Casas, too, Marcus emphasises, had seen that Vitoria had spoken in *conditionalis* (ibid., p. 71). The medieval *ius commune* – building on the ancient texts of Roman law – certainly knew slavery and considered it legitimate, especially as a consequence of captivity in war. On this (with an outlook on Jean Bodin), see T. Rüfner, above n. 15, pp. 201–21. Since there was to be no legitimate state of war within the – broadly defined – *populus Romanus*, whose lord was the emperor, enslavement of Christians on the basis of captivity in war seemed legally impossible (T. Rüfner, ibid., p. 218).

108 F. de Vitoria, 'De Indis', above n. 49, I 3, 13: "*Alius titulus* potest *esse* ..." ("Another legal ground *may* be ...") (emphasis added).

a violation of the right to mission seems contradictory.[109] This attempted justification of Spanish conquest, however, does not change the fact that Vitoria clearly articulated and justified the equality argument.

One can sum up as follows: from Vitoria's point of view, the decisive injustice of the Spaniards towards the Indios lay in the unequal treatment, which was reflected in the disregard for the rights (*dominium*) of the Indios.[110]

2.3. *SUBLIMIS DEUS*, 2 JUNE 1537

The Spanish debates about the legality of the conquests in America and the treatment of the Indios did not leave no trace in the legislature. The ecclesiastical legislator was the most outspoken: in the papal bull Sublimis Deus of 2 June 1537, Pope Paul III[111] declared on the question of dealing with the Indios that neither the Indios nor any other peoples "discovered" by Christians should be deprived of their freedom and property, regardless of whether they accepted faith in Christ or not. Under no circumstances should they be enslaved.[112] The papal document is particularly noteworthy, in our context, because it could claim (ecclesiastical) legal binding force for itself. With the Breve Pastorale officium of 29 May 1537, the pope had authorised the Archbishop of Toledo to excommunicate those who treated Indios like slaves.[113]

---

109 See the text to n. 104; on the right to mission as a reason for war, see also H-G. Justenhoven, *'Francisco de Vitoria'*, above n. 49, pp. 103–08; D. Deckers, *'Gerechtigkeit'*, above n. 49, pp. 238–40.

110 Thus also rightly, H-G. Justenhoven, *'Francisco de Vitoria'*, above n. 49, pp. 101 *et seq.* with reference to F. de Vitoria, ComSTh II-II q. 66, a. 1 para. 2., in V. Beltrán de Heredia (ed.), *Comentarios a la Secunda secundae des Santo Tomás*, tom. III, Apartado 17, Salamanca 1934, p. 323. There, Vitoria emphasises that the mineral resources belong to the one who first discovered and took possession of them. The Spanish kings, therefore, could not appropriate these treasures *"sine causa rationabili"* – without a reasonable, i.e. legitimate, reason.

111 On this, see K. Ganzer, 'Art. Paul III' in G. Müller (ed.), *Theologische Realenzyklopädie*, vol. 26, de Gruyter, Berlin 1996, pp. 118–21 (elected Pope on 13.10.1534). The opening of the Council of Trent on 13.12.1545 took place during his pontificate.

112 Pope Paul III, 'Bulle "Sublimis Deus" 2 June 1537' in M. Sievernich, *Conquista und Evangelisation*, Matthias-Grünewald-Verlag, Mainz 1992, pp. 475–76 (German translation); on all, see H. Gründer, 'Conquista und Mission' in *Christliche Heilsbotschaft und weltliche Macht. Studien zum Verhältnis von Mission und Kolonialismus. Gesammelte Aufsätze*, LIT Verlag, Münster 2004, pp. 23–46, initially in W. Hofmeister, 'Dezentralisierung in Lateinamerika' (1992) 42 *Aus Politik und Zeitgeschichte* Nr. 37 3–15.

113 Pope Paul III, 'Breve "Pastorale officium" an den Erzbischof von Toledo vom 29. Mai 1537' in *Heinrich Denzinger, Enchiridion Symbolorum et Definitionum. Kompendium der Glaubensbekenntnisse und kirchlichen Lehrentscheidungen*, 44th ed., Herder, Freiburg i. Br. 2014, Nr. 1495, p. 459, with reference to the fact that the penal provision was repealed again by a breve of 19 June 1538 (Non indecens videtur). See also N. Brieskorn, 'Die Kritik von Bartolomé de Las Casas', above, n. 24, p. 221. It cannot be overlooked that the insight gained in Sublimis Deus 1537 has not been consistently applied: see, as an overview, J. Andrés-Gallego and J.M.G. Añoveros, *La iglesia y la esclavitud de los negros*, Ediciones Universidad de Navarra, Pamplona 2002; H. Gründer, *Welteroberung und Christentum.*

2.4. *NOVAS LEYES* OF 20 NOVEMBER 1542

In the "New Laws" of 20 November 1542, Emperor Charles V (Carlos I of Spain) drew legal consequences from the criticism of *Las Casas*, but also of *Vitoria* and others:

> We order and decree that from now on no Indio may be enslaved under any pretext, whether under martial law or for any other reason ... that an Indio may be enslaved.[114]

The fact that a legal regulation does not necessarily change reality was, unfortunately, confirmed here as well. The king complied with the rejection of these "New Laws" and repealed them in 1545.[115]

2.5. THE SAME HUMAN NATURE

In the reflections of Francisco de Vitoria presented here, one notices the clear confession that the Indios are *veri domini*; that is, they have their own masters, true *dominium*, and are therefore no one's slaves. Even more important than this statement seems the justification, namely the derivation of this insight from the same human nature – the essential characteristic of which lies in the image of God. Of course, Vitoria did not use the concept of equality or *aequalitas* in this context, but in fact this is exactly where the train of thought led, since a problem of regulation was addressed here, which was later addressed with the concept of legal equality.

Even though we have seen that Montesino already had this idea in mind when he preached his sermons in Santo Domingo in the Advent of 1511, we can also see that his contemporaries had difficulty with this argument. Matías de Paz, for example, then a professor in Valladolid, and also a Dominican priest, had attended the Junta of Burgos[116] in 1512 to discuss the injustice of the *conquista* deplored by Montesino. He wrote down his ideas in a treatise called *De dominio regum*

Ein Handbuch zur Geschichte der Neuzeit, Gütersloher Verlagshaus Mohn, Gütersloh 1992, Kap. XV, pp. 503–18, 679–82; here, p. 505 reminds us that in the 17th and 18th centuries in Latin America many slaves were "owned" by the Church. This is not to be pursued further here, because the epistemological interest of this article does not aim at the history of slavery, but at the justification of the idea of equality in law.

114 Cited in J. Höffner, '*Kolonialismus*', above n. 25, p. 204.

115 See A. Pagden, above n. 28, p. 108.

116 Critical of the real political significance of such commissions is A. Pagden, above n. 28, pp. 27–28, who assigned them more of a legitimising role than a decision-making role. With regard to the ad hoc significance, one may agree, but one must not overlook the fact that questions of legitimacy were of the greatest importance for the lasting viability of political decisions in the eyes of almost all actors of the time *sub specie aeternitatis*. It was a matter of one's own salvation. From this perspective, the question of legitimacy gained the highest relevance. This is where the discussion took on its seriousness.

Hispaniae super Indos, which has survived as a manuscript.[117] De Paz borrowed a theological argument from Jesus Sirach 10:8 and Matthew 21:43 for the transfer of dominion to the Spaniards,[118] and argued that the Spanish king had been justified in waging war.[119] On the other hand, the rule of the Indios was illegitimate. But the king was not allowed to rule tyrannically and turn the natives into slaves.

Unlike most of his contemporaries, Vitoria's assessment of the *conquista* did not depend on whether the Indios accepted the Christian faith. De Paz had a different opinion:

Unde sic victi non statim efficiuntur sclavi ipso jure, donec pertinaciter nolint supradicto principi obedire, aut se jugo suavissimo Salvatoris subjicere.[120]	And therefore the conquered do not automatically become slaves as long as they do not stubbornly refuse obedience to the superior ruler and reject the sweetest yoke of the Saviour.

According to de Paz, baptised persons were not allowed to be enslaved at all,[121] in accordance with the medieval understanding of Roman law.[122] Here, an important difference from Vitoria's text became apparent. Vitoria clearly rejected a differentiation according to faith with regard to the *dominium*, and focused on the same human nature, which rested in the image of God and the associated ability of man to control his actions wilfully and rationally.[123] This also differed

117 M. de Paz, 'De dominio regum Hispaniae super Indos', in excerpts, in V. Beltrán de Heredia, 'El padre Matias de Paz OP, y su tradado "De dominio regum Hispaniae super Indos"' (1929) 40 *La Ciencia Tomista* 173–90. Beltrán de Heredia comments on the origin of the treatise, and gives a description of its contents; on this, see J. Höffner, '*Kolonialismus*', above n. 25, pp. 216–18.

118 V. Beltrán de Heredia, above n. 117, 183.

119 Ibid., 187.

120 Ibid., Secunda conclusio, Primum corollarium, p. 182, cited by J. Höffner, '*Kolonialismus*', above n. 25, p. 218.

121 See above n. 15.

122 V. Beltrán de Heredia, above n. 117, 188. De Paz based his position on the universalist teachings of Henry of Segusia (Hostiensis) on the *orbis christianus*, see: V. Beltrán de Heredia, above n. 117, 183, 186; J. Höffner, '*Kolonialismus*', above n. 25, p. 216, annotation 34; further, on de Paz, S. Zavala, above n. 37, pp. XXVII–LXXXVII, XCVI–CXXX; A. García y García, 'La ética', above n. 22, pp. 346–53.

123 Similarly, see also B. de Las Casas, 'Traktat über die königliche Gewalt (De imperatoria vel de regia potestate)' in M. Delgado (ed.), *Werkauswahl, vol. 3/2: Sozialethische und staatsrechtliche Schriften*, Schöningh, Paderborn 1997, pp. 191–248, p. 197 (§1 n. 1): "As for men, it is proved that by reason of their rational nature they were originally born free, says Digesta (De iustitia et iure: l. manumissiones [D. 1.1.4]). Because of this nature, God did not make the one the servant of the other, but gave free will to all. The reason for this, according to Thomas Aquinas (In II Sententiarum d. 44, q. 1., a. 3), is that rational nature is not in itself ordered towards anything else as an end, so neither is one man towards another man. For freedom is a right necessarily and per se inherent in man from the beginning of rational nature" (according to the German translation of Thomas Eggensperger OP). But even Las Casas considered an accidental slavery of man to be compatible with the right to freedom, see ibid., §1 n. 2.

clearly from the theocratic ideas of Juan López de Palacios Rubio,[124] and pointed in the direction of general equality. For Vitoria, it is rooted in an image of man that is ultimately determined by Christian eschatology, as Thomas Aquinas developed with particular clarity in his *Summa Theologiae*.[125] This image of man virtually shapes the structure of the leading text of the late scholastics (*exitus-reditus* scheme). According to this, every human being, regardless of his or her status, takes his or her origin from God, and is called to return to God. Although man is also part of a human community, and a member of a public community – the State – he is not part of it; he does not "belong" to the State, as can be seen in the following excerpt from the *Summa Theologiae*:

> *Ad tertium dicendum quod homo non ordinatur ad communitatem politicam secundum se totum, et secundum omnia sua, et ideo non oportet quod quilibet actus eius sit meritorius vel demeritorius per ordinem ad communitatem politicam. Sed totum quod homo est, et quod potest et habet, ordinandum est ad Deum, et ideo omnis actus hominis bonus vel malus habet rationem meriti vel demeriti apud Deum, quantum est ex ipsa ratione actus.*[126]

> On the third point, it must be said that man is not altogether subordinate to the political community and to all that he possesses. And therefore one is not allowed to judge his actions as more meritorious or less valuable according to the order of the political community. Rather, everything that constitutes man, what he can do and what he possesses, must be ordered towards God. And therefore every action of man is good or bad in the sense of meritorious or worthless before God, as it results from its very nature.

124 On this, see C. Birr, 'Dominium in the Indies. Juan López de Palacios Rubios' Libellus de insulis oceanis quas vulgus indias appelat (1512–1516)' in (2018) 26 *Rechtsgeschichte. Legal History (RG)* 264–83. Birr offers a clear summary of the history of the transmission and content of the Libellus, which amounted to a legal justification of Spanish rule in the New World, and sought to derive it from tradition; see also S. Zavala, above n. 37, pp. XIII–XXVII, XXXII–LXXXVII; J. Höffner, *'Kolonialismus'*, above n. 25, p. 219, which at p. 225 argues that most of the Spanish court lawyers of the time considered the Spanish conquests to be justified. The Spanish dispute was primarily about the justification of political rule. Admittedly, this is a somewhat different perspective than the one I am pursuing here. However, it should also be emphasised that Juan López de Palacios Rubios, *De las Islas del Mar Océano* (Libellus de Insulis Oceanis) (written between 1512 and 1516), Introducción, texto crítico y traducción de Paulino Castañeda, EUNSA, Pamplona 2013, ch. 3, pp. 126, 130, considered the unbelievers as well as the believers as rational creatures for their own masters, from whom one should not take away property without just cause. In this context, he also referred (ch. 3, p. 122 fn. g) to Genesis 1:26, without explaining the idea of the image of God, as Vitoria did later. J. L. de Palacios Rubios (ibid., ch. 4, p. 280) also advocated duties of solidarity and assistance towards the Indios: *"ratione humanitatis, cum sint nostrae naturae participes"* ("by virtue of their being human, because they participate in our nature"). See also A. García y García, 'La ética', above n. 22, pp. 353–57, esp. 355; A. Pagden, above n. 28, pp. 50–55; C. Birr (ibid.), 270–72.

125 See, further, T. Repgen, 'De restitutione', above n. 43, 2017, pp. XXI–XXXII.

126 Thomas Aquinas, *STh* I-II, q. 21, a. 4, ad. 3. On this, see also J. Höffner, *'Kolonialismus'*, above n. 25, pp. 265 *et seq.*

Therefore, the human being is not to be evaluated with regard to the community, but rather as an end in him- or herself. This is how Thomas Aquinas expressed it in his *Summa contra Gentiles*:

Primum igitur, ipsa conditio intellectualis naturae, secundum quam est domina sui actus, providentiae curam requirit qua sibi propter se provideatur: aliorum vero conditio, quae non habent dominium sui actus, hoc indicat, quod eis non propter ipsa cura impendatur, sed velut ad alia ordinatis. … Disponuntur igitur a Deo intellectuales creaturae quasi propter se procuratae, creaturae vero aliae quasi ad rationales creaturas ordinatae.[127]	First, the situation of the rational being, according to which it is the master of its action, requires the care of providence, with which it provides for its own sake. The situation of others (creatures), which do not have dominion over their actions, means that the care for them is not for their own sake, but in relation to others. … The rational creatures (i.e. man) are created for their own sake (*propter se*), but all other creatures are ordered towards them.

Thus, there was already an argumentation in scholastic theology that was a solid basis for the idea of equality in law. Vitoria effectively applied this idea to the questions of the legal legitimacy of the rule of the Spaniards in America.

3. YIELDS

Georg Friedrich Hegel opined in 1817, in his *Encyclopaedia of the Philosophical Sciences*:

> The common proposition that all men are equal by nature [contains] the misconception of confusing the natural with the concept; it must be said that by nature men are rather only unequal … That citizens are equal before the law contains … expressed in this way, a tautology; for only the legal state in general, that the laws prevail, is thereby pronounced. … The laws … presuppose the unequal conditions and determine the unequal legal competences and duties arising from them.[128]

127 Thomas Aquinas, *Summa contra gentiles*, lib. 3, ch. 112 para. 1 <www.corpusthomisticum.org>. Translation based on Thomas Aquinas, *Summa contra gentiles, Dritter Band, Teil 2, Buch III, Kapitel 84–163*, edited and translated [in German] by K. Allgaier, 4th edn., Lambert Schneider Verlag, Darmstadt 2013, p. 155. The excerpt quoted is also found in J. Höffner, *'Kolonialismus'*, above n. 25, p. 266.

128 G.F.W. Hegel, *Enzyklopädie der philosophischen Wissenschaften im Grundrisse*, with the collaboration of U. Rameil, edited by W. Bonsiepen and H-C. Lucas, Felix Meiner Verlag, Hamburg 1992 (Gesammelte Werke, vol. 20), §539, p. 510: *"der geläufige Satz, daß alle Menschen von Natur aus gleich sind, [enthält] den Mißverstand, das Natürliche mit dem Begriffe zu verwechseln;*

For Hegel, as for his time in general, equality is first and foremost a question of equal rights: equality before the law. For Hegel, this equality does not follow from the concept of nature, but from that of civil law. The equality of man before the legal acts or, more precisely, before the law, is of course a millennia-old topos, mentioned over and over again in discussions about justice, and the basis of the demand that judges should judge without regard to the person.[129]

In our sources from late scholasticism, on the other hand, we see a justification for equality that is linked to the nature of human beings; admittedly not to the empirical nature, but to the spiritual nature that finds expression in the relationship of human beings to God. In this relationship, human beings are equal. They are all created in the image of God and, *therefore*, also *true domini*: masters of themselves, subject to no one by nature, as Vitoria emphatically taught.[130]

The assumption of an equal human nature was not new as such. Already Aristotle had reported in his *Politics* the view held by some pre-Socratics that the distinction between freemen and slaves was violence and unjust coercion, since the two did not differ by nature.[131] Alcidamas (436–338 BC), in his speech on the release of the Messenian prisoners, also mentioned by Aristotle, is said to have said: "The God has created all free, and none has nature destined to be a slave".[132]

The same pre-Socratics, however, relativised their point of view through a radical subjectivity that makes normative content dependent on the will of the person acting, but rejects metaphysical ties.[133] We should also remember the Stoa,[134] who emphasised the commonality of humanity and whose ideal

es muß gesagt werden, daß von Natur die Menschen vielmehr nur ungleich sind ... Daß die Bürger vor dem Gesetz gleich sind, enthält ... so ausgedrückt eine Tautologie; denn es ist damit nur der gesetzliche Zustand überhaupt, daß die Gesetze herrschen, ausgesprochen ... Die Gesetze ... setzen die ungleichen Zustände voraus und bestimmen die daraus hervorgehenden ungleichen rechtlichen Zuständigkeiten und Pflichten; similarly, *Grundlinien der Philosophie des Rechts*, edited by K. Grotsch, Felix Meiner Verlag, Hamburg 2017, §200, pp. 199–200.

129 Here a reference to Deuteronomy 1:16–17 and Leviticus 19:15 will suffice.

130 See, in particular, the quotation in the text by n. 76.

131 Aristoteles, *Politik* (above n. 57), I, 3 (1253b); on this, see also E. Zeller, *Die Philosophie der Griechen in ihrer geschichtlichen Entwicklung: Erster Teil, Zweite Abteilung: Allgemeine Einleitung. Vorsokratische Philosophie, zweite Hälfte*, Reisland, Leipzig 1920 [Reprint Hildesheim 1963], p. 1400.

132 Cited after O.A. Baumhauer, 'Art. Alkidamas' in H. Cancik, H. Schneider (eds.), *Der Neue Pauly. Enzyklopädie der Antike*, Metzler, vol. 1, Stuttgart – Weimar 1996, Sp. 503; see also W. Waldstein, 'Zum Menschsein von Sklaven' in H. Bellen, H. Heinen (eds.), *Fünfzig Jahre Forschungen zur antiken Sklaverei an der Mainzer Akademie*, Franz Steiner Verlag, Stuttgart 2001, pp. 31–49, p. 34 with references in text.

133 See: E. Zeller, above n. 131, pp. 1403, 1410.

134 I.e. L. A. Seneca, 'De beneficiis lib. III', ch. 28, §1 in *Philosophische Schriften, Lateinisch und Deutsch, vol. 5*, translated, introduced and with annotations by M. Rosenbach, Wissenschaftliche Buchgesellschaft, 2nd ed., Darmstadt 1995, pp. 260–63: "*Eadem omnibus principia eademque origo; nemo altero nobilior, nisi cui rectius ingenium et artibus bonis aptibus.*" ("All men have the same beginnings, the same origin; no one is more distinguished than another, unless he has a straighter and better disposition through good character traits.")

denied differences, but at the same time came to terms with the Roman reality of slavery.[135] In Roman law, which was influenced by the Stoa, the equality of all human beings was, accordingly, asserted, but not legally implemented. Ulpian taught:

Quod attinet ad ius civile, servi pro nullis habentur; non tamen et iure naturali, quia, quod ad ius naturale attinet, omnes homines aequales sunt.[136]	As far as the *ius civile* is concerned, slaves are considered nothing [i.e. have no legal capacity]. But not according to natural law, because, as far as natural law is concerned, all men are equal.

As a matter of course, slavery remained a fixed institution, either due to descent from a slave, as a consequence of a war captivity, or as a punishment.[137]

With the Church Fathers, the idea of equality now received a Christian grounding. Basil the Great (330–379 AD) declared that slavery did not exist naturally among human beings.[138] His brother Gregory of Nyssa (335–394 AD) was even more explicit. For him, slavery was a violation of divine law. Alluding to the Genesis account of creation, Gregory reminded us that only animals should be subject to humans.[139] Finally, Gregory of Nazianzus (329–390 AD) emphasised that humans had all been free in the beginning, and explained slavery as a consequence of the fall from grace.[140]

On Seneca, in detail, see W. Waldstein, above n. 132, pp. 36–49. Further references to other writings of the Stoa can be found in F. Schaub, above n. 57, pp. 9–14, specifically, on Seneca, pp. 12–13.

135 Cf. the description close to the source in F. Schaub, above n. 57, pp. 9–17. Remarkable, for example, is the thesis that slaves are spiritually *sui iuris*, i.e. legally free and independent: L.A. Seneca, above n. 134, ch. 20, §1, pp. 248–51: *"Errat, si quis existimat servitutem in totum hominem descendere. Pars melior eius excepta est: corpora obnoxia sunt et adscripta dominis, mens quidem sui iuris"* ("It is mistaken if one thinks that slavery transforms man completely. His better part is excluded from it: the body is subjected and attributed to the masters, the spirit, however, is of its own right"). See W. Waldstein, above n. 132, pp. 41, 48.

136 Ulp. D. 50.17.32.

137 Details in M. Kaser, R. Knütel and S. Lohsse, *Römisches Privatrecht*, 21st ed. C.H. Beck, Munich 2017, §15 n. 15 *et seq.*

138 Basilius, 'Liber de Spiritu sancto', ch. 20, para. 51 in J. P. Migne (ed.), *Patrologia Graeca, tom. 32*, Paris 1886, col. 160 D; see F. Schaub, above n. 57, p. 33. On Basil and the two following Church Fathers, see R. Klein, *Die Haltung der kappadokischen Bischöfe Basilius von Caesarea, Gregor von Nazianz und Gregor von Nyssa zur Sklaverei*, Franz Steiner Verlag, Stuttgart 2000; on this, a detailed review can be found in V.H. Drecoll, (2002) 45 *Jahrbuch für Antike und Christentum* 220–22.

139 G. von Nyssa, 'In Ecclesiasten, homilia IV' in J. P. Migne (ed.), *Patrologia Graeca, tom. 44*, above n. 138, col. 664 s. C-A; see: F. Schaub, above n. 57, p. 34 fn. 1.

140 G. von Nazianz, 'Oratio XIV, De pauperum amore, ch. 25' in J. P. Migne (ed.), *Patrologia Graeca, tom. 35*, Paris 1886, col. 892 A; see F. Schaub, above n. 57, p. 36. In this sense, also, see C. von Alexandrien, 'De adoratione in spiritu et veritate, lib. VIII' in J. P. Migne (ed.), *Patrologia Graeca, tom. 68*, Paris 1864, col. 552 B; see F. Schaub, above n. 57, p. 43.

But even the Church Fathers did not reject slavery as a state of injustice.[141] The clear recommendation of the Apostle Paul in 1 Corinthians 7:21[142] had an effect here. Christianity did not directly address the social environment, but man's individual relationship with God. Slaves, however, had the opportunity to belong to the Church from the very beginning.[143] Free persons and slaves were treated equally there. This also corresponded to the ideas of justice of Lucius Caecilius Firmianus (Lactanz) (c. 250 to c. 320), who regarded the equality of all men as a requirement of justice.[144] Fittingly, Friedrich Schaub summarised the attitude of late antique Christian authors up to Augustine thus:

> In general, the principle prevails that God created man free, that all men are equal by nature .... The sentence of Ulpian: "Quod ad ius naturale attinet, omnes homines aequales sunt", corresponds to: "omnes namque homines natura aequales sumus" of Gregory the Great.[145]

If I see it correctly, Pope Leo the Great, in the fifth century, was the first to establish the idea of equality, with the idea of the likeness of God. He declared that believers had the same nature as those who had not yet accepted the Gospel.

> *Simul enim et cum istis habemus, quod ad imaginem Dei conditi sumus, nec carnali origine a nobis, nec spirituali nativitate divisi sunt.*[146]

> For we have the same [nature] with these [unbelievers], because we are created in the image of God. And we are not separated either by fleshly origin or by spiritual birth.

However, this remained irrelevant in social reality, if one disregards monasticism, which practically implemented the equality of people, even within the orders.[147]

141 See F. Schaub, above n. 57, pp. 37–40, with detailed evidence from the work of John Chrysostom.

142 1 Corinthians 7:21: "So, if when you were called, you were a slave, do not think it matters – even if you have a chance of freedom, you should prefer to make full use of your condition as a slave."

143 F. Schaub, above n. 57, pp. 49–51; Pope Benedict XVI, above n. 7, para. 4.

144 L. Lactanz, *Institutiones Divinae*, lib. V, 14: *"Ubi enim non sunt universi pares, aequitas non est, et excludit inaequalitas ipsa iustitiam"* ("For where all are not equal, there is no *aequitas*, and this inequality itself excludes justice."). For the whole, with references from the sources, see F. Schaub, above n. 57, pp. 52–56, p. 54.

145 F. Schaub, above n. 57, p. 67.

146 Pope Leo the Great, 'Sermo XLI (De Quadragesima III)' in J. P. Migne (ed.), *Patrologia Latina*, vol. 54, Paris 1846, ch. III, col. 274A-B <http://gateway.proquest.com/openurl?url_ver=Z39.88-2004&res_dat=xri:pld&rft_dat=xri:pld:ft:all:Z500042152>; see F. Schaub, above n. 57, p. 67 fn. 2.

147 F. Schaub, above n. 57, pp. 112–14, with references esp. from the *Regula S. Benedicti.*

Otto Dann saw the development of legal equality essentially as a product of the rational-legal theories of the Enlightenment period.[148] Indeed, one finds many things there that represent this idea. Nevertheless, it seems to me that late scholasticism already conceived of human equality as a legal position, not just as a moral demand. Vitoria's *Relectio De Indis* is only one piece of evidence for this, albeit a remarkable one, because Vitoria not only made a legal demand, but backed it up with a justification for the equality of human nature. The key concept here is the dominium: that subjective legal position that follows from each person's sovereignty over his or her own actions. For Vitoria, this sovereignty is based on the image of God.[149] The latter characterises the nature of every human being, and is, therefore, the reason for equality in law. Even before the rational-legal theoretical approaches of the seventeenth and eighteenth centuries, a justification for the "equal human nature" that has legal quality is, thus, found.

148 O. Dann, 'Art. Gleichheit' in O. Brunner, W. Conze, R. Koselleck (eds.), *Geschichtliche Grundbegriffe*, vol. 2, Klett-Cotta, Stuttgart 1975, pp. 997–1046, esp. pp. 1008–10.

149 See above the text by n. 76.

TWO CENTURIES OF PRIVATE LAW THEORY ON FORMAL AND MATERIAL EQUALITY

Marietta AUER

Two centuries of private law theory concerning formal and material equality: such a title suggests a rather optimistic perspective regarding the development of the concepts of equality in modern private law thinking. Drawing upon the work of Franz Wieacker, this narrative suggests a historical development in which formal equality continuously progresses towards an ever-greater level of material equality, a development that continues along this path until a legal state of actual equality and freedom from discrimination is achieved in private law.[1]

The following analysis will put the viability of this narrative to the test. On the one hand, it seems to find ample support in the development of the principle of equality in private law during the past two centuries. On the other hand, the newest developments show that we might have reached a turning point, and possibly even a dividing line. In recent times, the trend towards constitutionally

[1] F. WIEACKER, *Das Sozialmodell der klassischen Privatrechtsgesetzbücher und die Entwicklung der modernen Gesellschaft*, C.F. Müller, Karlsruhe 1953, p. 18; F. WIEACKER, *Privatrechtsgeschichte der Neuzeit*, 2nd ed, Vandenhoeck & Ruprecht, Göttingen 1967, p. 543 *et seq.*; F. WIEACKER, *Industriegesellschaft und Privatrechtsordnung*, Athenäum-Fischer, Frankfurt 1974, p. 24.

anchored equality in private law has run into serious conflict with fundamental structures of private law.

In section one of this chapter, I will define and explain the concepts of formal and material freedom, as well as formal and material equality and justice. On this basis, I will reconstruct the relationship between freedom and equality in private law, stemming from Enlightenment thinking (section 2). The next section identifies the historical and theoretical establishment of general formal equality as the first level of equality in private law (section 3). The following part distinguishes general formal equality from a second level of special principles of equal treatment and the more recent anti-discrimination law that has emerged within private law (section 4). Finally, this analysis concludes by asking whether a general principle of equal treatment under private law can be derived from these developments; one which no longer represents an exception requiring justification, but has instead become the rule, even in private law relationships guided by private autonomy.

1. CONCEPTUAL FOUNDATIONS: FORMAL AND MATERIAL FREEDOM AND EQUALITY

In order to approach the question whether there is now a general principle of equal treatment under private law, it is first necessary to clarify the conceptual foundations of private law thinking about equality. In this context, it is quite useful to apply the distinction between a formal and material perspective, commonly used in the debate on freedom of contract, to the variants of meaning of equality in private law. Whereas the *formal* paradigm of freedom of contract denotes a purely legal freedom without regard to the person, a *material* understanding takes into account the actual chances of realising freedom under private law, i.e. it understands freedom of the person in terms of actual freedom of choice, with its corresponding legal consequences. For instance, in cases of seriously unequal bargaining power, there would be a demand for an equalisation via the creation of "contractual parity".[2] This means that a distinction can also be made between a formal paradigm of equality under private law, in the sense of formal legal equality in private law relationships, and a material understanding of equality as a condition for the possibility of actual equality.[3]

---

2 For this terminology, see C-W. Canaris, 'Wandlungen des Schuldvertragsrechts – Tendenzen zu seiner "Materialisierung"' (2000) 200 *Archiv für die civilistische Praxis (AcP)* 273, 277 *et seq.*; see also M. Auer, *Materialisierung, Flexibilisierung, Richterfreiheit*, Mohr Siebeck, Tübingen 2005, p. 23 *et seq.*; for a critical treatment, see G. Wagner, 'Materialisierung des Schuldrechts unter dem Einfluss von Verfassungsrecht und Europarecht – Was bleibt von der Privatautonomie?' in U. Blaurock and G. Hager (eds), *Obligationenrecht im 21. Jahrhundert*, Nomos, Baden-Baden 2010, pp. 13, 18 *et seq.*

3 M. Grünberger, *Personale Gleichheit*, Nomos, Baden-Baden 2013, pp. 34 *et seq.*, pp. 57 *et seq.*

Following Michael Grünberger, it is possible to speak of a first, and a second, problem of freedom and equality in private law. The first problem of freedom and equality marks the beginning of the egalitarian understanding of law in modernity, which is primarily concerned with the abolition of feudal status law and the creation of a general legal capacity that applies to every person qua personhood. The second problem of freedom and equality, on the other hand, only comes to light when this first stage has been mastered, and it becomes apparent that formal equal freedom in no way results in like chances of realising individual claims to freedom and equality. Instead, a considerable amount of effort is necessary to effect change and bring about real freedom and real equality.[4]

Yet this distinction already bears an insight that needs to be taken into account in the following analysis: freedom and equality are not, in and of themselves, desirable; instead, their value is derived with their respective inherent degrees of justice. In the end, all considerations of formal or material freedom and equality in private law aim at a specific conception of justice understood in terms of private law. In particular, this pertains to contractual justice, which can also be interpreted either formally, materially or procedurally.[5] Once again, *formal* justice is understood to mean justice in the sense of strict equal treatment without consideration of the person, while *material* justice strives toward actual equality of outcome with regard to the person. The in-between *procedural* concept of justice means that a chance for material contractual justice or, as Walter Schmidt-Rimpler put it, a sufficient "guarantee of correctness of the contractual mechanism" can already be procedurally justified through the mere mechanism of contracting without material intervention in the nature of the contract. Procedural justice thus minimises the impact on contractual freedom. This, however, presupposes that one ensures appropriate chances to realise a mechanism of contractual bargaining on the prior level of contractual freedom, by means of suitable material interventions which ensure a sufficient level of contractual parity.[6] To put it succinctly: procedural justice follows from material freedom, thus overcoming the formal/material dichotomy.[7]

Is this conceptual framework still viable when extended to equality? Here, two questions need to be raised. On the one hand, the distinction between a formal and a material reading already faces serious conceptual problems in the context of contractual freedom, where it was initially developed.

4 Ibid., pp. 110 *et seq.*

5 C-W. Canaris, 'Wandlungen des Schuldvertragsrechts', above n. 2, 282 *et seq.*

6 W. Schmidt-Rimpler, 'Grundfragen einer Erneuerung des Vertragsrechts' (1941) 147 *Archiv für die civilistische Praxis (AcP)* 130, 152 *et seq.*; W. Schmidt-Rimpler, 'Zum Vertragsproblem' in F. Baur, J. Esser, F. Kübler and E. Steindorff (eds), *Funktionswandel der Privatrechtsinstitutionen. Festschrift für Ludwig Raiser*, Mohr Siebeck, Tübingen 1974, pp. 3 *et seq.*; see also C-W. Canaris, 'Wandlungen des Schuldvertragsrechts', above n. 2, 284 *et seq.*; G. Wagner, above n. 2, p. 19 *et seq.*

7 For a similar argument, see BVerfGE 89, 214, 231 *et seq.*

From what has just been said about the material preconditions of procedural justice, it follows that, contrary to the seemingly clear dichotomous differentiation sketched above, there can be no purely formal conception of freedom in private law that does not always presuppose an inalienable core of structural parity, or substantial capacity for the same use of freedom.[8] Thus, the distinction between such seemingly "neutral", "necessary" or "apolitical" modifications of freedom of contract serving to establish parity, as opposed to deliberately distributive or paternalist restrictions of contractual freedom, falls apart and becomes conceptually impossible.[9]

On the other hand – and this represents an even more substantial objection – semantic parallelisms such as those between formal and material freedom as well as equality, just as between the first and second problems of freedom and equality, conceal the fact that freedom and equality, as legal and ethical conditions of justice, do not exhibit parallel structures. In accordance with its structure, freedom can be understood as a self-legitimising principle of justice, precisely when it is understood formally and devoid of content. Herein lies the core of all conceptions of justice that prioritise freedom over equality. Equality, on the other hand, exhibits a different structure. Unlike freedom, it always requires a qualitative, material fulfilment in accordance with a given standard of equal treatment. This, characteristically, results in a situation where possible claims to equal treatment – bar those aiming at a complete and actually unachievable equality, which paradoxically are not (and cannot be) the point of the law – are limitless and, ultimately, can never be attained. It is no secret that this represents the Achilles heel of modern equal treatment and anti-discrimination law, especially in societies in which egalitarian principles have already been extensively put into practice.[10]

2. ENLIGHTENMENT FOUNDATIONS OF PRIVATE LAW: INNATE EQUAL FREEDOM AND THE PRIMACY OF PRIVATE AUTONOMY

The asymmetrical relationship between freedom and equality becomes all the more apparent when considering the foundations of the idea of universal equality

8 For a critique, see also G. Wagner, above n. 2, pp. 18 *et seq.*

9 See also M. Auer, '*Materialisierung, Flexibilisierung, Richterfreiheit*', above n. 2, pp. 28 *et seq.*

10 Paradoxically, egalitarian societies exhibit stronger gender differences when it comes to the course of studies and professions. For this "paradox of equality", see G. Stoet and D. C. Geary, 'The Gender-Equality Paradox in Science, Technology, Engineering, and Mathematics Education' (2018) 29(4) *Psychological Science* 581 <https://doi.org/10.1177/0956797617741719>; G. Stoet and D. C. Geary, 'Corrigendum: The Gender-Equality Paradox in Science, Technology, Engineering, and Mathematics Education' (2019) 31(1) *Psychological Science* 110 <https://doi.org/10.1177/0956797619892892>.

in Enlightenment philosophy. These foundations can be referenced quickly, and are easy to grasp.[11] Modern law, and particularly private law, is essentially based on the Enlightenment concept of the social contract. According to this concept, the only legitimate way to establish legitimate State institutions possessing normatively valid law making and law-enforcement power is a contract concluded between all members of the society as free and equal parties.[12] This basic idea also holds true on a smaller scale: the freely concluded contract has a self-legitimating effect not only as a social contract, but also as a consensus of wills between private individuals, regardless of its content, *if* and *because* it was concluded between equals acting in a free and self-responsible fashion.[13] Both on the macro level of constitutional law and on the micro level of private law, the contract principle might, thus, be described, without exaggeration, as the most powerful legitimising principle of modern law. Even when taking into account the recent global shift to constitutionalism, which has dominated the international scene since the second half of the twentieth century, and is increasingly superseding private law as the historical core of legal doctrine, the current discourse on private law, in principle, still relies on the classic Enlightenment principle of self-legitimising freedom. Despite its increasingly constitutional framing, this discourse is still based on the model of the free contract guided by private autonomy. The future viability of this basic doctrinal structure, when it comes to equal treatment claims under private law, remains to be seen.[14]

The basis of the universal legitimising power of the contract principle, as already found in Immanuel Kant, is the maxim *"volenti non fit iniuria"*. This means that *because* and *insofar* as the person consents, no injury can come to a willing person, irrespective of the content of the contract.[15] The form of consent itself thus replaces the evaluation of the content of consent, by means of the mechanism of freely responsible consent. This is expressed in the maxim *"stat pro ratione voluntas"*, according to which the pure form of the will takes the place

11 See M. Grünberger, above n. 3, pp. 71 *et seq.*

12 W. Kersting, 'Zur Logik des kontraktualistischen Arguments' in V. Gerhardt (ed), *Der Begriff der Politik: Bedingungen und Gründe politischen Handelns*, Metzler, Stuttgart 1990, pp. 216 *et seq.*

13 W. Flume, 'Rechtsgeschäft und Privatautonomie' in E. von Caemmerer, E. Friesenhahn and R. Lange (eds), *Hundert Jahre deutsches Rechtsleben. Festschrift zum hundertjährigen Bestehen des Deutschen Juristentages*, C.F. Müller, Karlsruhe 1960, vol. 1, pp. 135, 141 *et seq.*; W. Flume, *Allgemeiner Teil des Bürgerlichen Rechts, Bd. 2: Das Rechtsgeschäft*, 4th ed., Springer, Berlin 1992, pp. 1 *et seq.*

14 See also M. Auer, 'Selbstreflexion der Privatrechtswissenschaft: Formation, Herausforderungen, Perspektiven' in E. Hilgendorf and H. Schulze-Fielitz (eds), *Selbstreflexion der Rechtswissenschaft*, 2nd ed., Mohr Siebeck, Tübingen 2020, pp. 301 *et seq.*

15 I. Kant, 'Die Metaphysik der Sitten: Rechtslehre' in Königlich Preußische Akademie der Wissenschaften (ed), *Kants Werke. Akademie-Textausgabe, Bd. 6*, De Gruyter, Berlin 1968, §46, pp. 203, 313.

of the rationality of the intended content.[16] This mechanism of legitimation is structurally necessary such that freedom is fundamentally understood in terms of formal freedom, i.e. the presence of a materially unrestricted freedom to consent, equally available to all rational subjects. The basis of this principle of will is the Enlightenment idea that only human reason can be considered the source of interpersonally valid norms; for only reason – the presupposed metaphysical universal, within the Western worldview – is equally available to all rational beings. Therefore, equality in the sense of Enlightenment rationalism is not just any kind of equality. It should be understood as specific equality in the *ability to use reason and freedom*; that is, what equally belongs to all rational human beings. To differentiate here instead, and to limit freedom from the very outset, simply because some individuals are incapable of fully utilising their freedom to act in a freely responsible manner, despite the basic assumption of the universally equal capacity for reason, stands in fundamental contradiction to the legitimising basic principle underlying the enlightened worldview. This conception of reason loses its legitimising power due to inner contradiction if its universality is inherently understood to be limited by its antithesis, or if it is relativised in more than just marginal cases such as legal incapacity. In Kantian terms, freedom – the only thing capable of serving as a justifying principle equally accessible to all rational beings – can then no longer serve as a condition for the possibility of private law.

As a principle of legitimation, reason, thus, always pushes for the most abstract, formal universalisation possible. It is at this point that equality, as defined above, comes into play as the necessary condition for this universalisation, which in turn requires an a priori formal understanding of equality. This has to do with the fact that the aforementioned idea of general innate equality is only relevant with regard to the sole human characteristic pertinent to the rational mechanism of legitimation, namely the universal capacity of reason. At the same time, in the Kantian world view, this unique capacity establishes the dignity of human beings as moral persons, and their universally equal legal capacity as bearers of rights.[17] That human beings differ in their accidental individual characteristics and capacities, and even in group characteristics with a susceptibility to discrimination, such as gender, descent, etc., is of no consequence from the perspective of rational law. Much like the empirical differences in individual abilities to make use of freedom, these differentiating characteristics are, by definition, irrelevant, because all that matters for participation in the rational mechanism of legitimation is the equality of all people – as equals in their

16 W. Flume, 'Rechtsgeschäft und Privatautonomie', above n. 13, p. 141; W. Flume, *Allgemeiner Teil des Bürgerlichen Rechts*, above n. 13, p. 6.

17 See M. Auer, 'Die Substanz der Freiheit: Pufendorfs Begriff der moralischen Person' in R. Gröschner, S. Kirste and O.W. Lembcke (eds), *Person und Rechtsperson*, Mohr Siebeck, Tübingen 2015, pp. 81 *et seq.*

personhood – under the law. And by all people, we really mean *all* people, even if 300 years ago it would never have occurred to the architects of these ideas to grant women or slaves the same civil legal capacity as white men of European descent. The revolutionary power of the Enlightenment mechanism of legitimation lies precisely in the fact that it has developed its own unstoppable historical-normative momentum ever since its initial formulation; a directional dynamic towards the ever-increasing realisation of the claim to universalisation inscribed within it. As a result, more and more groups have been staking a claim to equal legal capacity by virtue of their equal claim to human dignity. This was done (in this historical order) first by men of non-European descent, then by women, and might in the future also be claimed by non-human entities capable of bearing rights.[18]

On this basis, it is certainly correct to speak of a "preponderance of freedom over equality" in a strictly qualified sense.[19] Even though it is true that the Enlightenment mechanism of legitimation always presupposes equality in the sense of an equal innate capacity for reason, contracts are valid not simply because they have been agreed upon between equals, but only if and when these contracts have genuinely been concluded in a free, self-determined manner by these equals. In that case, the legitimising mechanism *always* lies in freedom, and not in equality. No allocative or distributive decision can be considered legitimate merely because everyone is treated equally. Decisive here is the normative Enlightenment claim to submit all heteronomous systems of justice to a critique of reason, and to replace them with the only unquestionable principle of legitimacy in modern society: the principle of individual autonomy. Although Enlightenment thinking always presupposes equality, the true driver of all its conceptions of justice remains – and I am again repeating myself – freedom. The same applies to an understanding of private law that reconstructs the Enlightenment principle of autonomy in terms of private autonomy. Thus, private autonomy also has to be understood in a fundamentally formal sense, because its legitimising structure shares all the characteristics of Enlightenment contractualism just discussed. This is, for instance, expressed by the assumption of the equal legal capacity of all legal subjects in section 1 of the German Civil Code (Bürgerliches Gesetzbuch or BGB).[20]

---

18 This subcategory covers contemporary debates on animal rights and legally capable artificial intelligences. See A. Peters, 'Rights of Human and Nonhuman Animals: Complementing the Universal Declaration of Human Rights' (2018) 112 *American Journal of International Law Unbound (AJIL Unbound)* 355 *et seq.*; G. Teubner, 'Digitale Rechtssubjekte? Zum privatrechtlichen Status autonomer Softwareagenten' (2018) 128 *Archiv für die civilistische Praxis (AcP)* 155 *et seq.*

19 Original quote: "*Präponderanz der Freiheit vor der Gleichheit*" (author's translation); see M. Grünberger, above n. 3, pp. 35, 312, 749, 810 *et seq.*

20 See, e.g., L. Raiser, 'Der Gleichheitsgrundsatz im Privatrecht' (1948) 111 *Zeitschrift für das gesamte Handelsrecht und Wirtschaftsrecht (ZHR)* 75, 78; cf. M. Grünberger, above n. 3, pp. 32, 82 *et seq.* and p. 224 *et seq.*

3. FORMAL EQUALITY AS THE FIRST LEVEL OF THE PRIVATE LAW PROBLEM OF EQUALITY

The actual history of the past two centuries of private law thinking about equality, however, has not actually been touched upon, let alone exhaustively dealt with. Without a doubt, there is a considerable difference between the theoretical preconditions of the Enlightenment concepts of freedom and equality described above and their actual historical implementation in private law since the turn to modernity. As mentioned above, however, the history to be told here deviates from Wieacker's narrative of a development from formal to ever-greater concern about material equality in private law. I will avoid this reconstruction, because Wieacker's transformation story from the allegedly formal ethics of freedom of the nineteenth century to the material ethics of social responsibility of the twentieth century already misrepresents the development of freedom. After all, such a purely formal concept of freedom did not even exist in the nineteenth century.[21] The same holds – if not more so – for private law thinking about equality. Moreover, as seen above, freedom and equality do not work in the same way as justifying principles, so that a parallelisation through the same linear transformation narrative would not only be an oversimplification, but indeed misleading and wrong.

Here, it is again worth reminding ourselves of the structural differences between the histories of ideas behind the normative ideal of freedom, as opposed to that of equality. As a constructive principle of private law relationships, freedom was realised from the outset in various amalgamations, both in its formal and material dimensions, so that its development since the nineteenth century can be described as mere variations on the theme of how the formal and material aspects can be integrated into one coherent system of law. The situation regarding equality, however, is very different. The struggle for equality in the law was, first and foremost, concerned with the realisation of formal equality, i.e. the inclusion of previously excluded groups such as non-white men and women, before the issue of material equality could be addressed at all. Thus, Michael Grünberger's description of a first and second problem of equality in private law, in analogy to a first and second problem of freedom, where both sides denote the same difference between a formal and a material realisation of equality or freedom, misses at least part of the point.[22] Even if one advocates the primacy of formal over material freedom, the question of just how formal freedom can fulfil its ultimately procedural claim to justice always arises equiprimordially. Formal equality, on the other hand, had to be fought

---

[21] See, e.g., M. Auer, *Der privatrechtliche Diskurs der Moderne*, Mohr Siebeck, Tübingen 2014, p. 1 *et seq.* and p. 135 *et seq.*

[22] See above n. 4.

for centuries before the plateau of legal egalitarianism could even be set foot on. In contrast, everything that has been achieved since then, in terms of claims towards material equality for marginalised groups, i.e. non-discrimination law, pertains to a completely different normative level of inquiry. Here, the question at stake is not the inclusion of groups previously excluded from any legal right, but rather a reconfiguration of social groups along new lines of unequal treatment, which cover even those who were never excluded from formal legal equality in the first place.[23] An example of this point is discrimination based on sexual orientation.[24]

Against this background, two centuries of equal treatment discourse in private law can be summarised as follows; starting from the first problem of establishing formal legal equality, the milestones of the past two hundred years involve, on the one hand, the extension of formal equal treatment to women, and, on the other, the arduous dismantling of disenfranchisement resulting from discrimination according to origin, religion, descent or "race".[25] When examining such serious cases of formal disenfranchisement of entire segments of the population, however, the main problems usually lie outside the sphere of private law, and concern issues of status involving public law, such as citizenship, freedom of mobility, voting rights, social insurance, freedom of opinion and access to profession and education.[26] It is no coincidence that serious curtailments of the general equality of rights in private law became relevant precisely in those areas where private law relationships most closely correspond to the status relationships governed by public law, namely in family and personal status law, and for this reason are sometimes referred to as the "nucleus of the State". Thus, it is widely known that when the BGB came into force, family law was riddled with a number of privileges afforded to the husband over the wife, the dismantling of which was only completed very recently, and was only made possible by the pressure exerted by the German Federal Constitutional Court (Bundesverfassungsgericht or BVerfG) in its numerous interventions.[27] It is also no coincidence that the fundamental disenfranchisement of the Jewish population during the National Socialist dictatorship also found parallels in the discrimination against other groups during the same period, thus pointing to a totalitarian pattern of unequal treatment. In particular, this included a social rollback that aimed to drive women away from an increasingly egalitarian understanding of their roles that was already emerging at the time – a development that, ultimately, could not be

23 On the structural distinction between general equal treatment law and specific non-discrimination law, see M. Grünberger, above n. 3, p. 527 *et seq.*, pp. 550 *et seq.*

24 For example, equal treatment of homosexual and heterosexual men as *men*, as opposed to women, was never a subject of debate. For an argument along these lines, see BVerfGE 105, 313, 351 on the German Civil Partnership Act (LPartG) from 2002.

25 On the conceptual discussion, see M. Grünberger, above n. 3, p. 561 *et seq.*

26 For historical detail, see ibid., p. 116 *et seq.*

27 See ibid., p. 88 *et seq.*

stopped. The first lesson we can take from this is: never again! The second lesson is that the Enlightenment philosophy of right, with its insistence on universal formal equality and legitimising freedom, actually captures the core of what one can, and should, meaningfully understand by justice under the rule of law.

This reading is confirmed by the well-known "Radbruch formula", first formulated by Gustav Radbruch in 1946, against the backdrop of Nazi injustice, and widely used as a model for ethical assessment of unjust law ever since. The formula consists of two parts. The second part, pertinent here, goes beyond the more widely known first part, in that it not only postulates the loss of validity of intolerably unjust law, but in fact confidently assumes the loss of the legal quality, as such, in cases where law fundamentally runs counter to equality:

> Where justice is not even striven for, where equality, which comprises the core of justice, has been consciously denied in the establishment of positive law, the law is not only 'unjust' law, but rather it altogether lacks a legal nature. For one cannot define law, even positive law, in any other way than as an order and statute the purpose of which is to serve justice.[28]

Justice essentially means equality.[29]

4. SPECIAL NORMS OF EQUALITY AND ANTI-DISCRIMINATION LAW AS THE SECOND LEVEL OF THE PRIVATE LAW EQUALITY PROBLEM

According to the Radbruch formula, law that fundamentally denies the value of equality as the core of justice is no law at all. It is precisely this strict consequence, however, that shows that the second level of the equality problem in private law follows – indeed, must follow – other rules. This is yet another way of criticising the picture that the first and second equality problems in private law can, or should be, described in terms of a continuum of steadily increasing guarantees of justice, all pointing towards the transition from formal equality to an increasing state of actual, material equality.

---

28 Original quote: "*[W]o Gerechtigkeit nicht einmal erstrebt wird, wo die Gleichheit, die den Kern der Gerechtigkeit ausmacht, bei der Setzung positiven Rechts bewußt verleugnet wurde, da ist das Gesetz nicht etwa nur 'unrichtiges' Recht, vielmehr entbehrt es überhaupt der Rechtsnatur. Denn man kann Recht, auch positives Recht, gar nicht anders definieren als eine Ordnung und Satzung, die ihrem Sinne nach bestimmt ist, der Gerechtigkeit zu dienen*" (author's translation); G. Radbruch, 'Gesetzliches Unrecht und übergesetzliches Recht' (1946) *Süddeutsche Juristen-Zeitung (SJZ)* 105, 107.

29 But equality of what? For this question, see also A. Sen, *Inequality Reexamined*, Harvard University Press, Cambridge, MA 1995, p. 11; cf. M. Grünberger, above n. 3, p. 871, p. 902 *et seq.*

That full material equality cannot be the aim of the modern society and its legal set-up, especially through the ground rules of private law, should be clear when one looks at what could be called the "aporia of bourgeois law". While guaranteeing formal equality and equal participation through civil liberties on the constitutional level, the bourgeois society, at the same time, uses the same civil liberties to justify the factual inequality found within the society governed by private law, and thus petrifies factual inequality in the guise of equal constitutional rights.[30] Recently, the argument that the ground rules of private law help to create and perpetuate an unequal distribution of wealth on a global scale last seen in feudalism has actually gained new momentum.[31] There is no easy way out of this aporia of the bourgeois society. The equal constitutional rights afforded to all citizens, in the shadow of which inequality looms large, cannot be dismissed as mere ideology. In fact, their exercise is regarded as socially desirable. The freedoms to develop different abilities, to realise different life plans, and to engage in any form of competitive development of individual and social goals in general, are the signature of social productivity of the modern individualistic-pluralistic society.[32] Thus, no matter the form of individualistic ethics one follows – whether utilitarian, Kantian or Rawlsian – one becomes entangled in contradictions if one wishes to enjoy the advantages of individualisation and pluralisation, but is unwilling to pay the price they exact, i.e. the acceptance and dynamic self-reinforcement of individual and group-specific differences. The question thus shifts to asking about *which* inequalities are so normatively undesirable in a pluralistic, yet still egalitarian, society (according to its own self-understanding) that they are considered to be in need of correction. This question is especially pertinent for inequalities generated by the ground rules of private law, or, even more suggestively, through the "private law society" (*Privatrechtsgesellschaft*).[33]

We are dealing with a dual structural problem here. The already tense relationship between equality and individualistic freedom within modern society collides, above all in the area of private law, with the heightened significance of

---

30 See, classically, K. Marx, 'Zur Judenfrage' in K. Marx and F. Engels, *Werke (MEW), Bd. 1*, Dietz, Berlin 1981, pp. 347, 368 *et seq.*; cf. F. Böhm, 'Privatrechtsgesellschaft und Marktwirtschaft' (1966) 17 *ORDO: Jahrbuch für die Ordnung von Wirtschaft und Gesellschaft* 75, 121 *et seq.*; M. Grünberger, above n. 3, pp. 51 *et seq.*, 111 *et seq.*

31 See K. Pistor, *The Code of Capital*, Princeton University Press, Princeton, NJ and Oxford 2019.

32 F. Böhm, above n. 30, 89 *et seq.*; cf. C-W. Canaris, 'Verfassungs- und europarechtliche Aspekte der Vertragsfreiheit in der Privatrechtsgesellschaft' in P. Badura and R. Scholz (eds), *Wege und Verfahren des Verfassungslebens: Festschrift für Peter Lerche*, C.H. Beck, Munich 1993, pp. 873, 875 *et seq.*

33 The concept was coined by F. Böhm, above n. 30, 75 *et seq.*; for a more recent treatment, see K. Riesenhuber (ed), *Privatrechtsgesellschaft: Entwicklung, Stand und Verfassung des Privatrechts*, Mohr Siebeck, Tübingen 2007; cf. M. Grünberger, above n. 3, pp. 32, 254 *et seq.*, 899 *et seq.*, 975 *et seq.*

freedom as the constructive basis of private law relationships. The problem of equality as a principle of private law ultimately results from the interference of two equally socially effective normative structures of individualistic society: the desired egalitarianism, on the one hand, and the individualistic self-initiative as a specific private law aim, on the other. This impasse cannot be conclusively resolved in one direction or the other. Against this background, not only does the normative emptiness of the general principle of equality come into view, but it should also become intelligible why the doctrinal handling of principles of equal treatment in German private law, until recently, was always characterised by a conspicuous normative restraint. Until the Federal Constitutional Court's "stadium ban" decision in 2018,[34] it was widely recognised that a liberal understanding of private law based on private autonomy would be incompatible with the recognition of a general principle of equality amongst private parties, especially on a direct constitutional basis.[35] However, this did not impede the development of numerous sector-specific principles of equal treatment in subfields of private law such as labour law, corporate and capital market law, and competition and cartel law, and, moreover, in the law of debtor and creditor majorities, as well as in the area of the general obligation to contract.[36] The recognition of such sector-specific principles of equal treatment, however, has always required a sector-specific legitimation emanating from genuine private law considerations, and thus not derived from a direct or indirect application of Article 3 of the German Constitution (Grundgesetz or GG). With regard to the general principle of equal treatment under labour law, such considerations have, since the 1930s, drawn upon, for example, the employer's duty of loyalty and care, the company-community relationship, the implementation of self-imposed company norms, the employer's structural authority or unilateral structuring power, and the equitability requirement of §315 BGB,[37] whereas Article 3 of the GG – according to Götz Hueck's skillful dialectical treatment in 1958 – establishes "the general principle on which the principle of equal treatment in private law is based", but is not able to serve as "the actual legal basis for equal treatment in private law".[38]

It should be added that, for a long period of time (reaching back to the 1950s), at least outside of family law, there was no actual push in the direction of

---

34 Decision of 11.04.2018, 1 BvR 3080/09; BVerfGE 148, 267.

35 See M. Grünberger, above n. 3, pp. 267 *et seq.*, 311 *et seq.*

36 Ibid., pp. 315 *et seq.*

37 Ibid., pp. 320 *et seq.*

38 Original quote: *"Mit der Feststellung, daß das privatrechtliche Gleichbehandlungsprinzip auf den in Art. 3 GG verkörperten allgemeinen Rechtsgrundsatz zurückgeführt werden kann, sind somit zwar wichtige Zusammenhänge aufgedeckt worden; die eigentliche Rechtsgrundlage der Gleichbehandlung im Privatrecht, die besonderen Elemente, die im einzelnen für ihre Geltung maßgebend sind, ergeben sich daraus jedoch noch nicht"* (author's translation); G. Hueck, *Der Grundsatz der gleichmäßigen Behandlung im Privatrecht*, C.H. Beck, Munich 1958, p. 97 *et seq.*; cf. M. Grünberger, above n. 3, pp. 247 *et seq.*, 325 *et seq.*

ever-greater realisation of equal treatment under private law. Instead, the sector-specific equal treatment provisions in commercial law remained discrete and closely tied to specific purposes in their various contexts. Consequently, it is misleading to situate them in the same narrative of continual development as modern anti-discrimination law. Yet, this is precisely what Grünberger does when he proclaims that a "paradigm shift" has occurred towards the recognition of a general principle of non-discrimination under private law in the General Act on Equal Treatment (Allgemeines Gleichbehandlungsgesetz or AGG), which came into force in 2007, and the underlying European non-discrimination law.[39] He does not see, here, a conflict between equal treatment and private autonomy resulting in a loss of freedom. Instead, he describes the restriction of the free choice of the contractual partner by means of principles of non-discrimination as a configuration of private autonomy, through access rules resulting in a mere redistribution and extension of the freedom to choose contractual partners to other actors, namely to previously excluded groups, and thus resulting in an overall expansion of freedom.[40] The latter line of argumentation can be extended specifically to family law, with reference to both the Civil Partnership Act that came into force in 2001, and the dynamic towards "marriage for all", which became the law in Germany in 2017.

5. FROM SPECIFIC NORMS OF EQUALITY TO GENERAL CLAIMS FOR EQUAL TREATMENT UNDER PRIVATE LAW?

What is the main takeaway from this analysis? In his truly monumental study on the principle of equal treatment in private law, Michael Grünberger argued in 2013 that the classical view of the primacy of freedom over equality, when seen against the backdrop of the current state of the private-law right to equal treatment, was no longer a convincing description of the existing state of law. In contrast, Grünberger argues that the tension between freedom and equality in private law should be resolved in favour of equality and not freedom.[41] He sees the traditional view in which freedom is the principle, and equal treatment the exception in need of justification, as normatively anachronistic when held up against the background of contemporary understandings of society and law. And when seen in the context of current debates about sexism, racism and the

---

39 M. Grünberger, above n. 3, p. 54.

40 Ibid., pp. 894 *et seq.*, 962 *et seq.*, with reference to D. Wielsch, *Zugangsregeln*, Mohr Siebeck, Tübingen 2008. For a related approach, see A. Hellgardt, *Regulierung und Privatrecht*, Mohr Siebeck, Tübingen 2016, p. 280; A. Hellgardt, 'Wer hat Angst vor der unmittelbaren Drittwirkung?' (2018) *Juristenzeitung (JZ)* 901, 906 *et seq.*

41 M. Grünberger, above n. 3, pp. 54 *et seq.*, 749 *et seq.*

colonial legacies of Western thought, Grünberger has certainly exposed a weak spot in the classical doctrine, which, in part, explicitly emphasises the "freedom to discriminate" as the core value of private autonomy.[42] Against this, one could, indeed, argue that a society governed by a private law which emphatically professes the value of discrimination is neither likely to have a promising future, nor be worth living in – not to mention the relevance of a private law scholarship that affirms this in a tone reminiscent of the imperial era.

Yet the question arises whether this normative disaffection, itself bound to the zeitgeist of the time, is sufficient to justify the purported adoption of a *general* principle of equal treatment under private law. Grünberger contends that this principle constitutes a reversal of the rule–exception relationship between freedom and equality at the level of the burden of justification.[43] The conceptual consequence following from this is that future instances of unequal treatment, even between private individuals, will, generally speaking, require justification, while the exercise of rights of freedom will constitute the "theoretically and practically most important justification ground" for unequal treatment of private individuals by private individuals, but no more than that.[44] Therefore, it comes as no surprise that Grünberger also transfers the doctrinal justification for such a legal-ethical landslide from the very bottom to the very top, and finds its basis not only in the constitution – instead of in autonomous considerations of private law – but also in a direct horizontal effect of Article 3(1) of the GG.[45] If one assumes that this is true, the libertarian contract law maxim *stat pro ratione voluntas* no longer holds, for it explicitly states that the core of private autonomy lies precisely in the absence of need for justification, both against potential contractual partners, and against society as a whole. According to Werner Flume, "as far as the law recognises it, the design of legal relationships through private autonomy requires no other justification than that the individual wants it".[46] In contrast, a general principle of equal treatment under private law

---

42 See, e.g., K. Riesenhuber, 'Privatautonomie – Rechtsprinzip oder mystifizierendes Leuchtfeuer?' (2018) *Zeitschrift für die gesamte Privatrechtswissenschaft (ZfPW)* 352, 366; K. Riesenhuber, 'Privatautonomie und Diskriminierungsverbote – Grundlagen im deutschen Recht und europäische Regulierung' in K. Riesenhuber and Y. Nishitani (eds), *Wandlungen oder Erosion der Privatautonomie?*, De Gruyter, Berlin 2007, pp. 20, 25; cf. also M. Grünberger, above n. 3, p. 39.

43 M. Grünberger, above n. 3, pp. 61, 809, 823 *et seq.*, 864 *et seq.*

44 Original quote: *"theoretisch und praktisch wichtigsten Rechtfertigungsgrund"* (author's translation); M. Grünberger, above n. 3, p. 804.

45 Ibid., pp. 1004 *et seq.*, 1018 *et seq.*; cf. also A. Hellgardt, *'Regulierung'*, above n. 40, pp. 265 *et seq.*; A. Hellgardt, 'Wer hat Angst vor der unmittelbaren Drittwirkung?', above n. 40, 901 *et seq.*; F. Rödl, *Gerechtigkeit unter freien Gleichen*, Nomos, Baden-Baden 2015, pp. 363 *et seq.*

46 Original quote: *"Die privatautonome Gestaltung von Rechtsverhältnissen bedarf, soweit sie vom Recht anerkannt wird, keiner anderen Rechtfertigung, als daß der einzelne sie will"* (author's translation); W. Flume, 'Rechtsgeschäft und Privatautonomie', above n. 13, p. 141; cf. W. Flume, *'Allgemeiner Teil des Bürgerlichen Rechts'*, above n. 13, p. 6. For a critique, see M. Grünberger, above n. 3, p. 931 *et seq.*

would amount to a universal, discourse ethics-tinged "right to justification" in private legal transactions.[47] Amidst all of this, Grünberger is by no means blind to the fact that such a general, publicly effective obligation to justify acts and behaviour will always be accompanied by restrictions on the freedom of the person obligated to provide this justification.[48]

The fact that this new conception of equality under private law has, apparently, struck a chord at this point in time is demonstrated by the debate surrounding the above-mentioned stadium ban decision issued by the Federal Constitutional Court.[49] In this decision, the Court assumed that Article 3(1) GG takes precedence over the organiser's contractual freedom under private law when individuals are excluded from private events organised "for large audiences to the effect that admission is granted without distinguishing between individual persons". In this specific case, it was a nationwide stadium ban at football matches. The decision to exclude potential participants in such cases on the basis of "house rules" (*Hausrecht*) under private law is, therefore, unconstitutional and voidable when "such exclusion has a considerable impact on the ability of the persons concerned to participate in social life".[50] In procedural law, the principle of equal treatment in private law can be made operational through requirements such as duties of those who wield such "house rules" to respond to the individuals excluded, and to offer justifications aimed at ensuring that their decisions to exclude someone are not arbitrary, which in turn can be challenged in a civil court.[51] In the language of the Federal Constitutional Court, all of this is ostentatiously dressed in the doctrine of the indirect horizontal effect

---

47 M. Grünberger, above n. 3, pp. 55, 550, 768, 918 *et seq.*

48 Ibid., p. 934.

49 BVerfGE 148, 267; cf. also BVerfGE 81, 242; 89, 241; 128, 226; 138, 377; BVerfG NJW 2015, 2485. For the debate, see, e.g. A. Hellgardt *'Regulierung'*, above n. 40, 901 *et seq.*; S. Jobst, 'Konsequenzen einer unmittelbaren Grundrechtsbindung Privater' (2020) *Neue Juristische Wochenschrift (NJW)* 11 *et seq.*; F. Michl, 'Situativ staatsgleiche Grundrechtsbindung privater Akteure' (2018) *Juristenzeitung (JZ)* 910 *et seq.*; C. Smets, 'Die Stadionverbotsentscheidung des BVerfG und die Umwälzung der Grundrechtssicherung auf Private' (2019) *Neue Zeitschrift für Verwaltungsrecht (NVwZ)* 34 *et seq.*; M. Ruffert, 'Privatrechtswirkung der Grundrechte: Von Lüth zum Stadionverbot – und darüber hinaus?' (2020) *Juristische Schulung (JuS)* 1 *et seq.*; J. Neuner, 'Das BVerfG im Labyrinth der Drittwirkung' (2020) *Neue Juristische Wochenschrift (NJW)* 1851 *et seq.*; A-B. Kaiser, 'Privatautonomie: Von der unmittelbaren zur mittelbaren Drittwirkung und zurück?' in M. Jestaedt and H. Suzuki (eds), *Verfassungsentwicklung III*, Mohr Siebeck, Tübingen 2021, p. 3 *et seq.*; M. Auer, 'Selbstreflexion der Privatrechtswissenschaft', above n. 14, p. 319 *et seq.*

50 Original quote: "*Mittelbare Drittwirkung entfaltet Art. 3 Abs. 1 GG etwa dann, wenn einzelne Personen mittels des privatrechtlichen Hausrechts von Veranstaltungen ausgeschlossen werden, die von Privaten aufgrund eigener Entscheidung einem großen Publikum ohne Ansehen der Person geöffnet werden, und wenn der Ausschluss für die Betroffenen in erheblichem Umfang über die Teilhabe am gesellschaftlichen Leben entscheidet*" (author's translation); BVerfGE 148, 267 (headnote 2, cf. also p. 284 at fn. 41).

51 BVerfGE 148, 267, 285 f. (fn. 45 *et seq.*).

of fundamental rights, as laid out in the *Lüth* decision, and therefore initially comes across as a mere harmless repetition of this venerable doctrinal figure.[52] Upon closer inspection, however, the decision realises precisely the model envisaged by Grünberger of a comprehensive, constitutionally based procedural claim to equal treatment under private law, and thus has the potential to trigger a doctrinal landslide towards the universal direct applicability of fundamental rights within private-law legal relationships.[53]

We must forego a discussion of the constitutional doctrinal problems connected with the horizontal effect of fundamental rights between private actors, which are thrust into the spotlight by this decision. For the purposes of the present analysis, it must suffice to direct our attention once again to the broader coherence of the overarching conception of the relationship between freedom and equality under private law developed by Grünberger, and portrayed in terms of a paradigm shift. Grünberger's concrete explanations of how freedom and equality interact in private law begin with the presentation of three alternative solution models. The first of these is the "priority model" (*Vorrangmodell*), which corresponds to the classical priority of freedom over equality.[54] From this, he distinguishes the "applicability model" (*Tatbestandsmodell*). This model already partially reverses the rule-exception relationship by placing equal weight on freedom and equality, while the exercise of freedom rights exerts an exceptional exclusionary effect in relation to equality, according to a rule scheme operating on a yes/no basis.[55] The approach favoured by Grünberger, however, is the "justification model" (*Rechtfertigungsmodell*). According to this model, the exercise of freedom rights only comes into play on a secondary level, as an exception from the prioritised general claim to equal treatment under private law. When balanced against equality, individual freedom rights open up a spectrum of different degrees of justifying power (*Rechtfertigungskontinuum*), ranging from an exclusion of the principle of equal treatment by mere reference to the exercise of freedom rights to the opposite strict exclusion of any freedom to differentiate.[56] The decisive factor for the intensity of control, according to Grünberger, is always the context of the specific question of equal treatment.

---

52 F. Michl, above n. 49, 911.

53 This is structurally based on the balancing of conflicting constitutional rights, which no longer allows for a differentiation of the theoretically lower burden of justification in cases of horizontal constitutional effect. See M. Kumm, 'Who is Afraid of the Total Constitution? Constitutional Rights as Principles and the Constitutionalization of Private Law' 7 *German Law Journal* 341, 352 *et seq.*; cf. also M. Grünberger, above n. 3, p. 1019 *et seq.* For a critique, see G. Wagner, above n. 2, p. 64 *et seq.*; M. Auer, 'Selbstreflexion der Privatrechtswissenschaft', above n. 14, p. 319 *et seq.*

54 M. Grünberger, above n. 3, p. 810 *et seq.*

55 Ibid., p. 816 *et seq.*, with reference to G. Bachmann, 'Der Grundsatz der Gleichbehandlung im Kapitalmarktrecht' (2006) 170 *Zeitschrift für das gesamte Handelsrecht und Wirtschaftsrecht (ZHR)* 159 *et seq.*

56 M. Grünberger, above n. 3, p. 823 *et seq.*

For Grünberger, the burden of justification for private actors – contrary to what is implied in the stadium ban decision – is generally set lower than for public authorities. In accordance with the stadium ban decision, however, he also argues that the burden of justification intensifies with the increasing public relevance of a given private legal act.[57]

Consequently, following Grünberger, it would be logical – and this can also be seen as in line with the stadium ban decision – to interpret the entire doctrinal interplay of freedom and equality in private law as a balanced coexistence of two principles, with the principle of equality based on direct constitutional effect possessing general priority over freedom. And yet, Grünberger does not draw this conclusion. He instead emphasises the variety of regulatory approaches in the applicable law, which does not correspond to any of his three models in their pure form, but rather combines as a rule at least two of them.[58] With regard to the goal of a general principle of equal treatment under private law, this flight into regulatory pluralism is quite surprising, if not self-defeating: was the whole point not to reconstruct all cases as henceforth justified exceptional cases within a new model of private law based on a general maxim of *in dubio pro aequalitate*? Is this not precisely the point at which the justification model should prove its doctrinal and theoretical superiority? The justification model begs for an interpretation as the pre-eminent doctrinal model of the relationship between private law freedom and equality. However, if one looks at the burden of proof required to justify potentially discriminatory uses of private freedom, the same picture emerges: a general rule is not discernible. Instead, one is again confronted with a plurality of individual cases in which the burden of justification is sometimes set higher, and is sometimes dropped completely. In the end, this burden of justification does not follow any rule other than the "context of equality", as Grünberger rightly emphasises.[59] Thus, one searches for generalities but finds only particularities.

Finally, the question arises whether there is a conceptual flaw in the basic assumption that something like the claimed general principle of equal treatment must follow from the individual cases at all.[60] This leads back to the point, stated above, that the normative relevance of equal treatment problems can only unfold in a given context with regard to specific features measured against a specific comparison group. That Grünberger comes to exactly this conclusion therefore comes as no real surprise; rather, it befits the normative structure of equality. Against this, it cannot be maintained that the normative structure of freedom is empty too, unless its content is concretised through individual cases concerning

57 Ibid., p. 824 *et seq*. The postulate of a lower burden of justification for private actors, however, remains doubtful for the reason of structural non-differentiability explained above in n. 53.

58 Ibid., p. 808 *et seq*.

59 Ibid., p. 828.

60 Grünberger himself asks this question; see ibid., p. 809.

the actual use of freedom.[61] The main insight here is that the law does not only protect context-dependent individual freedoms, but also, and primarily, the abstract, indeterminate principle of freedom, as the source of future innovations of freedom.

Therein lies a crucial difference to equality. The constitutional principle of equal treatment and the specific prohibitions of anti-discrimination law do not protect any and all future innovations of equality. It is true that the constitutional principle of equal treatment makes it possible to identify and address new problems of equality. However, it is anything but a foregone conclusion that all new and yet to be discussed future claims for equal treatment always automatically possess a presumptive added value in terms of social justice or expedience.[62] And it is insufficient to simply respond that the same holds for the scope of future freedoms. To return to the beginning of this analysis, and in this insight ultimately lies the entire background of two hundred years of the history of ideas on freedom and equality: freedom, in contrast to equality, carries a principle of legitimacy within it. The pathos of freedom – and *only* of freedom – consists in conferring persons who are formally equal in their ability to reason with the power to take decisions about their own normative goals, and freeing them from having God, nature or the well-intentioned State decide how they are to live their lives. The empty space of freedom is a principle of legitimacy. The empty space of equality, on the other hand, is just empty.

61 Ibid., p. 812.
62 See above n. 29.

EQUAL DIGNITY OF HUMAN BEINGS

The Philosophical and Methodological Foundations of Private Law

Muriel FABRE-MAGNAN

All the words in this title may seem, if not provocative, at least highly questionable:

- To say that private law has a foundation.
- To affirm that it is the equal dignity of human beings that is at its foundation.

I will not dwell here on the first point, which is actually obvious: that private law has a foundation (in the sense of a *Grundnorm*). This is not a jusnaturalist position, and even less a theological conviction, but a structural and logical necessity. All the greatest philosophers have said so, at least since Aristotle. In law, Kelsen memorably explained it: although the jurist, in a pure theory of law, does not have to concern himself with the *Grundnorm*, a legal system necessarily presupposes such a logico-transcendental hypothesis. If each norm derives its validity from a norm that is superior to it, things must, at some point, come to a halt with a dogmatic statement of a different nature from the norms laid down. It is futile to try to go beyond this and to try to found the foundation, because the foundation is without foundation. The search for reasons necessarily stumbles upon an ultimate "why" that cannot, in turn, be founded.[1]

I will focus here on the second question, or rather the second assertion, namely that it is the equal dignity of human beings that is the basis of private law. The examination of this question implies the recognition that, contrary to Kelsen's view, the jurist must be concerned with the question of the foundation.

[1] For more developments, see: M. FABRE-MAGNAN, *L'institution de la liberté*, PUF, 2018.

It also means recognising that this foundation is not merely a structural place about which there is nothing to say, but that it must be given substance. The foundation cannot be a simple empty space, a purely formal logico-transcendental condition, or, as those interested in the dignity of the human person[2] sometimes put it, a simple "placeholder".[3] In other words, something must be said about the substantive content of the *Grundnorm*.

This is, in fact, what the legal texts do by expressly giving a name to the foundation of human rights – that is to say, to the heart or hard core of private law – and calling it the dignity of the human person. In this sense, far from being inspired by a jusnaturalist or even theological ideology, the assertion that the dignity of the human person is the foundation of human rights is, therefore, in the first place a purely positivist statement.

The 1948 Universal Declaration of Human Rights states that "recognition of the inherent dignity of all members of the human family … is the foundation of freedom, justice and peace in the world", "*die Grundlage von Freiheit, Gerechtigkeit und Frieden in der Welt bildet*". The Charter of Fundamental Rights of the European Union, proclaimed at Nice on 7 December 2000, devotes its entire first chapter to dignity, and states, in Article 1 (entitled "Human Dignity") that "[h]uman dignity is inviolable. It must be respected and protected". Here, dignity seems, at first sight, to simply be the first of the fundamental rights, i.e. also a fundamental right (*primus inter pares*). The explanations appended to the Charter specify, however, that "the dignity of the human person is not only a fundamental right in itself, but constitutes the very basis of fundamental rights", "*bildet das eigentliche Fundament der Grundrechte*", thus re-establishing the special status of dignity, the first of the human rights, but having the particularity of founding all the others.

Finally, Article 1 of the German Basic Law, which, after having affirmed that the dignity of the human being is intangible, deduces from it, in paragraph 2, that it is "as a consequence" ("*darum*") that "the German people recognise inviolable and inalienable rights for the human being". However, one can go further and argue that the principle of dignity does not only have a value by a decree of positive law. It responds to other, deeper, requirements, and even to a necessity.[4]

---

2 In particular, see C. McCrudden, 'Human Dignity and Judicial Interpretation of Human Rights' (2008) 19 *European Journal of International Law* 722: "if these arguments are accepted, then from a substantive point of view, dignity is a placeholder".

3 A linguistic term for a word, sign or other mark that stands in for unknown or unidentified content.

4 See, in this sense, V. Descombes, *Le complément de sujet: Enquête sur le fait d'agir de soi-même*, Gallimard, NRF essais, Paris 2004, who explains (p. 464) that the question of foundation must ultimately respond to a necessity: "The answer [to the question of the authority of norms] must appeal to a practical necessity (the necessity that attaches to such and such a thing to be done) that is no longer deontic. One can justify a particular norm by another norm, the existence of a right by the existence of another right, but one cannot base all norms on a fundamental norm (which would necessarily be empty since it would say in sum: there is a rule that there are rules)."

The dignity of the human person responds to a requirement of the meaning of words (see section 1 below); it is a logical condition (section 2) and, finally, it can even be said to be a matter of knowledge (section 3).

1. A REQUIREMENT FOR THE MEANING OF WORDS

Concepts naturally refer to something substantial, in the basic sense of content, and even more simply, a definition. Law, like all concepts, and even like all words, automatically has a definition, and thus an antonym, whether this is called arbitrary, brute force, or, as Olivier Jouanjan says very well in his magnificent latest book to describe the Nazi system, "domination without form".[5] Law must thus have a minimum of form in order to be qualified as such, it being understood that, as he rightly points out, "the problem of legal form is not one of pure form".[6]

Some of Kelsen's formulations could be interpreted in this sense. In a 1953 article clarifying his thinking, the great legal theorist states,

> as regards the interpretation of concrete norms by legal science, the pure theory of law highlights the almost always present and more or less important ambiguity of the 'material' to be interpreted. It assigns to scientific interpretation the sole task of revealing the possible meanings of a concrete norm and of leaving to the body responsible for applying the law the choice, determinable only in terms of political considerations, between the various theoretically possible interpretations.

And he adds, "[t]hat only one of these is 'right' cannot be sustained from the point of view of legal science".[7] The choice between the different theoretically possible interpretations or, a fortiori, of the "just" norm, is indeed a political choice, but the pure theory of law allows us to exclude certain meanings: the impossible meanings of a norm. It can, therefore, be said that it is through scientific interpretation that the impossible meanings of norms can be excluded. To do this, one must necessarily look at the content of the norms. Words must have the minimum meaning required by the normativity of language, if not by that of law. Wittgenstein explained this, in a famous passage, in relation to chess. The game of chess, like all games, has no meaning without constitutive rules, i.e. without some basic rules that give it meaning.[8] As the philosopher Vincent

---

5 O. Jouanjan, *Justifier l'injustifiable. L'ordre du discours juridique nazi*, PUF, Léviathan, Paris 2017, p. 290.

6 Ibid., p. 286.

7 H. Kelsen, 'Qu'est-ce que la théorie pure du droit?' (1992) 22 *Droit & Société* 559. This is a translation of the article called 'Was ist die Reine Rechtslehre', first published in *Demokratie und Rechstaat: Festschrift für Zaccharia Giacometti*, Zürick 1953, pp. 143–61.

8 L. Wittgenstein, *Recherches philosophiques*, original ed. (published posthumously) 1953, Gallimard, 2004, ss. 66 *et seq.*, or s. 567: "the game must be determined by the rules!"

Descombes summarises, "the constitutive rules do not exclude possibilities, but only nonsense, that is to say, in reality, logical impossibilities".[9]

Now, by definition, the law must say what has value, since it must say not what is, but what must be. It must, therefore, necessarily define the axiology giving the horizon of this must-be. Castoriadis shows that the idea was already present in Aristotle. In the *Nicomachean Ethics*, Aristotle defines distributive justice as an equality of relations that must be done "according to value (*ek tou kat' axian*)". Every society, thus, always posits an axia; that is, Castoriadis says, a "proto-value" (a primary value) – serving as a basis for establishing this proportionality. Whether one translates axia as value, dignity or merit, one is thus obliged, Castoriadis continues, "to posit a value as the value, an attribute of men as the attribute that will define the 'weight' of each individual for sharing". Thus,

> the just distribution is relative to what each individual is/has already in terms of a 'value' which is not 'relative' to anything, is not in terms of …, but posited absolutely, the point of origin of justice, the basis of reference which cannot be referred to anything other than itself.[10]

In this sense, moreover, even a totalitarian or fascist legal system expresses what is valid in relation to its objectives.[11]

In short, by definition, law must indicate the minimum substance necessary to give it meaning, and define what must be; in particular, what must be the distribution key proclaimed as just.

If we were to leave it at that, however, this would imply a relativism of values. We would be left with a kind of nominalism, putting dignity at the centre but with variable definitions, or even imposing any other value chosen by the regime in place. We need to go further.

2. A LOGICAL CONDITION

The principle of dignity signifies both the infinite value of the human being and the resulting fundamental duty to respect the other, and in particular the place reserved for the other.

---

9 V. Descombes, 'L'institution au sens large' in *Les équivoques de l'institution: normes, individu et pouvoir*, ed. by E. Djordjevic, S. Tortorella, M. Unger, Classiques Garnier, Paris 2021, which describes these logical impossibilities as "combinations of gestures (chess) or signs (speech) that do not make sense in the system created by the institution".

10 C. Castoriadis, *Les carrefours du labyrinthe 1*, Points Essais, Paris 1978, pp. 372–74.

11 It is also interesting to note that, as Olivier Jouanjan shows very well in his book cited above in n. 5, contrary to popular belief, Nazi jurists, far from being pure positivists, were on the contrary keen to introduce substance into the law (see, in particular, p. 126). This cannot, of course, be sufficient to guarantee the rule of law.

This duty is a logical, almost tautological, condition of possibility of private law. There is no private right if there are no autonomous subjects of law recognised as such.

Of course, the relationship between dignity and autonomy varies according to culture. In the United States and Germany, the two terms are often equated, since the dignity of the human person lies in his or her freedom and autonomy. It is, thus, on the basis of the right to dignity protected by Article 1 of the German Basic Law that a general right to self-determination ("*Selbstbestimmung*") is recognised, invoked in particular in questions of end of life, or surrogate motherhood. In France, on the other hand, the two terms are often perceived as antagonistic, with dignity being invoked to limit the freedom of individuals to do things perceived as unworthy (for example, limiting freedom of expression). In reality, the dialectic between these two concepts does not fit into either of these two opposing approaches.

Dignity is a precondition for freedom and autonomy of persons. More precisely, it is a condition of possibility. Human beings cannot act freely, as autonomous persons, if they are treated by others as things or animals. The Schœlcher decree of 27 April 1848 abolishing slavery in France explained that, if "slavery is an attack on human dignity", it is because "by destroying man's free will, it suppresses the natural principle of right and duty". Nor is a human being free if his basic needs are not being met. As Lord Chancellor Robert Henley said in the 1762 US Supreme Court decision *Vernon v. Bethell* (the phrase was taken up by Roosevelt at the time of the New Deal), "necessitous men are not, truly speaking, free men".[12]

In line with the work of Levinas, philosophers generally understand better than jurists that the absolute and unconditional recognition of the other is a prerequisite for his or her freedom. Today, on the contrary, inspired by the American notion of privacy, the European Court of Human Rights deduces from Article 8 of the European Convention of Human Rights (right to respect for private and family life) a right to personal autonomy interpreted as the right to make all choices for oneself, including those that ultimately lead to the loss of one's freedom and autonomy. It thus recognises a "right to make choices about one's own body" which may lead the person to validly consent to others infringing on their bodily integrity. In other words, the right to personal autonomy could lead to the recognition of a right to consent to the renunciation of one's fundamental rights and freedoms, for example, the right to bodily integrity. The result is a reversal of freedom, which is no longer an impassable space protected from the encroachment of others, but the right to consent to this encroachment. However, the law cannot be asked to guarantee the autonomy of individuals while, at the same time, validating the possibility for these same individuals to lose their autonomy.[13]

---

12 *Vernon v. Bethell* (1762) 28 ER 838.

13 On this thesis, and on this reversal of freedom, see M. Fabre-Magnan, above n. 2.

Since dignity signifies the infinite value of the human being, it necessarily implies the equal dignity of all human beings, and of each one of them. It is not possible to identify, for example, a legal concept of humanity that would have a higher value than individuals, since the value of each individual is infinite. Nor is it possible to consider that some individuals could be sacrificed to save the lives of others. As the Bundesverfassungsgericht rightly ruled in its decision of 15 February 2006 on the Air Safety Act passed in 2004, following the attacks in New York on 11 September 2001, it is contrary to the principle of dignity to authorise the German Minister of Defence, even as a last resort, to order the air force to shoot down a hijacked aircraft that is threatening to crash into an urban area or a nuclear power plant. It is the same calculation of utility that we want to inculcate today with the famous "trolley cases" that we would like to make a moral guide for action, when these little perverse tales actually lead to accustoming minds to break with the equal dignity of human beings, since we would have to learn (moreover by means of little games) which human beings to sacrifice to save which others.[14]

3. A QUESTION OF KNOWLEDGE

We are familiar with the famous distinction made by Kelsen, in his pure theory of law, between causality (scientific) and imputation (legal). In causation, if A is, then B is: if water is heated above a certain temperature, it turns into steam. In imputation, if A is, then B must be. The consequence is imputed to the premise by the legal system; it does not follow naturally from it, that is, without human intervention.

In a way, then, one could say that the dignity of the human person is a matter of scientific causation or, to use another Kelsenian distinction, it is a matter of knowledge. Experience has indeed shown what happens if a human being is treated in an undignified way. This scientific causality can be demonstrated by the absurd, or more precisely by horror and barbarism.

The 1948 Universal Declaration of Human Rights recalls that "disregard and contempt for human rights have resulted in barbarous acts". The French Declaration of the Rights of Man and of the Citizen of 1789 already stated,

> the Representatives of the French People, constituted as a National Assembly, considering that ignorance, forgetfulness or contempt for Human rights are the sole causes of public misfortune and of the corruption of Governments, have resolved to

---

[14] See my chapter, 'La perversion des petits contes moraux: des tramways aux véhicules autonomes' in *Concerter les civilisations: Mélanges en l'honneur d'Alain Supiot*, Le Seuil, Paris 2020, pp. 153–67.

> set forth, in a solemn Declaration, the natural, inalienable and sacred rights of Man, so that this Declaration, which will be kept constantly before all the Members of the social body, will constantly remind them of their rights and duties.

The word "dignity" was also invoked in the Schœlcher decree of 27 April 1848, which abolished slavery in France; the text states, in its opening words, "that slavery is an attack on human dignity".

Treating human beings with dignity is not just one possible political choice among others, but a "scientific" condition – in the sense of a necessary condition – of their humanity. In the famous words of Erasmus, "men are not born such, they become such" ("*finguntur*": they are made, or fashioned such).[15] In this sense, the principle of dignity has to do with truth, in the sense of a truth of law and justice, as opposed to brute force:[16] there is a form of knowability of values, and a form of predictability of law.

One author has spoken of an "apophatic"[17] theory of law[18] in relation to dignity, in the sense that dignity is seen, above all, when it is violated. It is, undoubtedly, a trait of human beings to understand the value of what they had only when they are deprived of it.

It is only now – far too late – that we are beginning to understand that maintaining a healthy environment is also a natural condition of human existence. The preamble to the Charter of the Environment adopted in France in 2004, which now has constitutional status, states – or, more accurately, describes in "scientific" terms –

> that natural resources and balances have conditioned the emergence of humanity; That the future and very existence of humanity are inseparable from its natural environment; That the environment is the common heritage of human beings; That man exerts an increasing influence on the conditions of life and on his own evolution; That biological diversity, the fulfilment of the individual and the progress of human societies are affected by certain modes of consumption or production and by the excessive exploitation of natural resources.

---

15 *"At homines, mihi crede, non nascuntur, sed finguntur"* (*Traité de l'éducation des enfants*, 1529).

16 See A. Montaut in P. Legendre (ed), *Tour du monde des concepts*, Fayard, Paris, coll. 'Weights and measures of the world', pref. J. N. Robert, postface S. Sharma (p. 282) on the word "truth" in Hindi. She refers to *"satyāgraha"* – literally "seizing the truth" – which was Gandhi's motto for substituting the force of truth for that of arms. She reminds us that "clutching the truth and not your club or gun was the most effective counter-power to colonial rule in the second quarter of the 20th century". India's motto then was, "truth alone triumphs" (*"satyam eva jayate"*).

17 According to the Larousse dictionary, "apophatic" (from the Greek *apophatikos*, meaning "negative"), "is said of a theology that approaches knowledge of God from what he is not rather than from what he is".

18 M. Terestchenko, 'Le principe de dignité. Petite contribution à une théorie apophatique du droit' in *L'institué*, Bruylant, 2015, p. 67.

This is a description of causal consequences, not just one that is imputed by the legal system to certain premises. To put it another way, there is an act of knowledge, or a knowability of the value of the environment.

It is not, however, a matter of directly deducing norms from the nature of things, as the jusnaturalists maintain. This problem is one of the most classical in legal theory, and refers in particular to Hume's famous law that what ought to be cannot be deduced from what is.

It is possible, however, to conceive of a (just) middle ground between the confusion of the two notions of "is" and "ought", and their total disjunction. The philosopher Jean-Louis Gardies has, thus, proposed a middle way to respond to what he considered to be Hume's "error".[19] There is certainly a gap and a rupture between facts and institutions, he said, which is even "the least questionable thing about a certain positivism", but, at the same time, "the structure of the institution itself depends closely on the conditions of nature". In other words, "one can either take up a challenge or not take up a challenge"; and, he added,

> if one takes up a challenge, there are many ways of doing so; however, we can only take up a challenge because that challenge is brought to us, and the way in which it is brought to us conditions to some extent the various ways in which we can take up the challenge.

Thus, contrary to what some jusnaturalists maintain, nature does not dictate any precise solution, but must nevertheless be taken into consideration in the development of rules. The law is addressed to human beings, and it cannot ignore this fact. In other words what "ought to be" does not mechanically follow from what "is", but it cannot ignore the being to whom it is addressed.

This does not mean, however, that dignity can be given a precise and immutable content. A historical and geographical look shows that the definition of dignity varies according to time and place.[20] However, it is possible to define a hard core of dignity. While it is easily accepted that dignity requires not treating a human being as a thing or an animal (or as a reservoir of biological material or spare parts), it is less clear that, conversely, it implies not forgetting that a human being is not a pure spirit, and therefore has needs that must be met if dignity is to be respected. It was in this context that dignity appeared in international texts after the Second World War, in particular in the 1948 Universal Declaration of Human Rights.[21]

---

19 J-L. Gardies, *L'erreur de Hume*, PUF, Paris 1987, pp. 118–19.

20 See C. McCrudden, above n. 3, 655 *et seq.*

21 Apart from the preamble and Art. 1, where dignity is invoked in a general sense, it appears twice with the idea of basic human needs, once in Art. 22 (Everyone "is entitled to the satisfaction of the economic, social and cultural rights indispensable for his or her dignity".),

Once again, it is probably the Germans who understand the meaning best. The famous *Hartz IV* decision of 9 February 2010, which establishes the right to a minimum standard of living in accordance with human dignity ("*menschenwürdiges Existenzminimum*"), and speaks of granting every human being "the material conditions indispensable for his or her physical existence and for his or her minimum participation in social, cultural and political life", can be cited in this sense. Even more recently, the Bundesverfassungsgericht ruled, on 5 November 2019, that the sanctions imposed on the long-term unemployed, including cuts in their monthly allowances, must not exceed 30 per cent of the stipulated minimum, otherwise they would be incompatible with respect for their dignity.

In conclusion, it could be recalled that the fundamental question of law is that of its legitimacy. Even in Kelsen's case, the presupposed norm, although purely formal, nevertheless also reflects this need for recognition, by those subject to the law, of the binding nature of the norms of the pyramid. Of course, in totalitarian systems, the use of force may be used to impose obedience to the laws, but it is possible to think that adherence to the values affirmed and staged by the legal system is a condition of its sustainability.

In any case, in contemporary democratic societies, the equal dignity of human beings is part of the legitimacy of the law. Of course, it has not always been recognised and valued in all places. It can even be historically dated, because it is part of a humanist[22] way of thinking, in which man is valued,[23] and even, with the weakening of faith, placed at the centre.[24]

This period will, undoubtedly, come to an end, and it is perhaps the most striking contemporary regression to see that, once again, and in new forms (evil never returns where it was expected), the equal dignity of human beings is no longer self-evident or an absolute necessity. Paradoxically, this is the worrying aspect of the contemporary omnipresence of the notion of dignity: when we talk about it so much, it is because it is no longer self-evident, since it no longer goes without saying. Will we have to experience once again the dramatic consequences to which the contempt of human beings leads?

---

and once in Art. 23 ("Everyone who works has the right to just and favourable remuneration ensuring for himself or herself and his or her family an existence worthy of human dignity.").

22 See E. Bloch, *Droit naturel et dignité humaine*, original ed., Suhrkamp Verlag, 1961 (French translation in Payot, 1976).

23 Even if Michel Villey noted that "respect for the human person, not in the letter but in substance, was not the invention of Kant, nor even a Christian invention. No virtue was more exalted in Rome than humanitas, which is both the duty to perfect human nature in oneself and to respect it in others.": M. Villey, *Le droit et les droits de l'homme*, 2nd ed., PUF, 1990, p. 87.

24 Rémi Brague also reminds us that, "in antiquity, the adjective 'human', where it was not purely descriptive, often referred to a weakness", and that it is only with modernity that it became a quality: R. Brague, *Le règne de l'homme: Genèse et échec du projet moderne*, Gallimard, L'Esprit de la cité, Paris 2015, p. 113.

EQUALITY BETWEEN EFFICIENCY AND DISTRIBUTION

A Law and Economics Reconceptualisation of a Principle of Justice

Andreas ENGERT

1. INTRODUCTION

Much of the intellectual allure of economics – including for lawyers – lies in its reductionism. Reductionist theories find richness in parsimony. They trace diverse phenomena back to a few basic principles, preferably a single one. If successful, they uncover commonality in difference, and hidden association between the seemingly unrelated. The more the central principle proves itself through explaining existing regularities, the more it also becomes a benchmark for identifying and critiquing deviations.

For all their possible benefits, reductionist approaches come at a cost. Much received wisdom can no longer be taken for granted, but must be painstakingly deduced from a limited set of principles. Equality in economic theory provides an example. For lawyers and philosophers, it is itself a fundamental principle of justice that neither requires nor lends itself to further justification, and competes only with liberty for precedence. By contrast, equality does not count among the first principles of normative (law and) economics. One might be tempted to conclude that equality of form or substance has no significance for law and economics.

This chapter aims to dispel this perception. To demonstrate that law and economics has a concept of equality, one first has to locate equality within the system of normative economics. Lawyers and philosophers traditionally assign equality to distributive justice (*iustitia distributiva*).[1] This suggests that equality should be classified as a problem of distribution also in economics. However, it will become apparent that the economic concept of distribution is narrower than the traditional understanding of distributive justice, because it relates only to the distribution of monetary wealth. It follows that, from an economic point of view, many equality concerns present themselves as issues of efficiency, not distribution. It is here that the advantage of a reductionist approach best shows itself: reconstructing duties of equal treatment from an overarching goal of economic efficiency provides a justification – rather than a mere assertion – of the imposition of such duties and their limitations.

The chapter begins by recalling the economic distinction between the two normative dimensions of efficiency and distribution (section 2). The focus will then shift to efficiency justifications for two types of equal treatment rules.[2] Tying these obligations to an efficiency rationale likely offers the greatest intellectual gain from a law and economics account of equality (section 3). However, the issue of distribution also deserves attention, not least because one can ask whether the economic focus on monetary wealth is too narrow compared with traditional views in law and philosophy (section 4).

2. THE DISTINCTION BETWEEN DISTRIBUTION AND EFFICIENCY

In normative economics, the distinction between efficiency and distribution remains of fundamental importance. Its role is to carve out a set of issues from

---

1 For the legal perspective, see, e.g. C-W. Canaris, *Die Bedeutung der iustitia distributiva im deutschen Vertragsrecht*, Verlag der Bayerischen Akademie der Wissenschaften, München 1997, p. 36; for the philosophical perspective, see S. Gosepath, 'Equality' in E. Zalta (ed), *Stanford Encyclopedia of Philosophy*, Stanford 2021, s. 3, available at <https://plato.stanford.edu/archives/sum2021/entries/equality>.

2 For the derivation of a third group of equal treatment duties, see A. Engert, 'Gleichbehandlungsgebote als Vertragshilfe' in G. Bachmann et al (eds), *Festschrift für Christine Windbichler*, De Gruyter, Berlin 2020, p. 51.

the greater problem of social justice that, firstly, is more amenable to universal agreement and, secondly, can be addressed independently of the remaining problems.[3] That distinct set of questions is efficiency. Distributive justice, on the other hand, is said to lack an equally compelling normative yardstick.[4]

Universal acceptability is ingrained into efficiency because it constitutes its primary guidance: a social state is said to be "Pareto superior" to another state if it makes at least one person better off – according to her own assessment – without impairing the position of any other person.[5] Accordingly, a social state is "Pareto efficient" if no other state is Pareto superior, i.e. if no other state is preferred by at least one person while leaving everybody else at least equally well off. Thus, Pareto efficiency is defined by possible agreement over changes. Since everyone's potential consent is needed, it reflects the formal equality of all members of society. A distinctive feature is that consent need only be constructive. If everyone is in a position to agree without suffering a loss or disadvantage, objecting to change can hardly be justified. Withholding consent would seem unconscionable and equivalent to inflicting harm on the potential beneficiaries. The epitome of a Pareto improvement is a contract that requires the actual consent only of the contracting parties. If *A* and *B* agree on an exchange of their goods, *C* should not be able to block the transaction. The core of Pareto efficiency is a denial of the grant of veto power to unaffected parties.

This is not a trivial proposition. In fact, *C* might have a plausible reason to oppose the exchange between *A* and *B*. While she suffers no loss, *A* and *B* gain from the transaction, so that their position improves not only relative to the status quo, but also in comparison to *C*. This raises the question how the increased wealth should be divided not just between *A* and *B*, but also in regard to *C*. Blocking the exchange would afford *C* the power of forcing *A* and *B* to share some of their surplus. If this seems an odd argument from the angle of contract law, imagine *C* is the government representing all fellow citizens of *A* and *B*. The power to tax *A* and *B*'s transaction amounts to granting consent, under the condition that they share part of their surplus with the government. Refusing veto power to outsiders becomes a compelling requirement only after bracketing off the problem of distributive justice.

Whether, and to what extent, *A* and *B* should have to share the surplus with other members of society is, by experience, a far more contentious issue than deciding whether the exchange should take place at all. Separating the two

---

3 Properly understood, economic efficiency analysis constitutes a (partial) theory of justice: F. Rödl, *Gerechtigkeit unter freien Gleichen*, Nomos, Baden-Baden 2015, pp. 78, 84. Many view it, however, as separate from justice: see, e.g. D. Miller, 'Justice' in E. Zalta (ed.), *Stanford Encyclopedia of Philosophy*, Stanford 2021, s. 4, available at <https://plato.stanford.edu/archives/fall2021/entries/justice>.

4 See section 4 below.

5 This is the "weak" Pareto criterion.

questions, therefore, greatly simplifies answering the second question. One can think of the separation as a temporal sequence: society first agrees on distributive justice by determining initial endowments. In the second step, Pareto superior changes are effected to realise gains from trade. Given that distribution has been settled beforehand, no one has reason to object. If needed, the process can be repeated: the initial distribution could be founded on certain assumptions about the final distribution after Pareto improvements during the second phase. If these expectations prove incorrect, or if conditions change, the question of just distribution can be raised anew – leaving aside that it will hardly ever be possible to reach consensus on what constitutes a just (initial) distribution. All that matters for separating distribution and efficiency is that no conceivable position on distributive matters gives reason to prevent Pareto improvements, based on the initial distribution. Those who consider the final distribution unfair must challenge the initial endowments.[6]

A valid objection to Pareto efficiency is that it provides little guidance for the law. In fact, true Pareto improvements are hardly ever seriously contested in debates over law and policy,[7] arguably because the injustice of doing so would be manifest. To gain practical significance, the Pareto criterion must be relaxed towards the less demanding (and more controversial) Kaldor–Hicks criterion.[8] The consensus required by this test becomes even more hypothetical: instead of requiring that a change does not harm anybody, it is now deemed sufficient that those who gain from a change are willing – but do not have to – make up for any losses inflicted on others. If full compensation actually took place, the change would pass the Pareto test. But the Kaldor–Hicks criterion allows compensation to remain a mere possibility, making the losers anything but indifferent to the change. All the test requires is that the gains of the winners outweigh the shortfalls of the losers.

---

6 The claim is that justice never demands thwarting Pareto gains. It is a different matter whether it can be justified to prevent or jeopardise Pareto improvements in political and economic struggles for a distributive cause.

7 See R. Posner, 'The Ethical and Political Basis of the Efficiency Norm in Common Law Adjudication' (1980) 8 *Hofstra Law Review* 487, 489 ("Pareto-superiority is useless for most policy questions"); A. Polinsky, 'Probabilistic Compensation Criteria' (1972) 86 *Quarterly Journal of Economics* 407, 407 ("crippling as a criterion for undertaking public policies"). This is true even for interventions in the freedom of contract. For example, a minimum wage can reduce employment because reservation prices of potential employers can be below the minimum wage. Nevertheless, abolishing the minimum wage would not constitute a Pareto improvement because it would leave all those employees who achieve higher earnings because of the intervention worse off. To qualify as a Pareto improvement, the reform would need to exclude only those contracts from minimum wage regulation that otherwise would not be entered into.

8 N. Kaldor, 'Welfare Propositions of Economics and Interpersonal Comparisons of Utility' (1939) 49 *Economic Journal* 549, 550 *et seq.*; J. Hicks, 'The Foundations of Welfare Economics' (1939) 49 *Economic Journal* 696, 706.

Evidently, imposing a loss because it could be – but is not – fully compensated is much harder to justify than the Pareto criterion. Only the gist of the relevant arguments can be given here. First of all, there is no compelling reason to put the onus on the beneficiaries of a "change" and in favour of "vested" interests. Instead, it can be conceived of as a selection between two equally possible, symmetric options, such as in the initial assignment of an entitlement to one of two contenders. Viewed from this angle, the Kaldor–Hicks criterion amounts to auctioning the entitlement to the highest bidder.[9] With this reformulation, the Kaldor–Hicks criterion avoids the criticism of taking rights without compensation; who should be entitled to a right in the first place is what the criterion seeks to determine.

What remains to be done is to provide an affirmative justification as to why rights or benefits should be awarded to the highest bidder. One approach is to relate the idea of consensus not to the individual rights and benefits, but to the adoption of the Kaldor–Hicks criterion as a general rule. Bundling the allocation of different rights is already implied in the use of the Pareto criterion: a typical contract is Pareto superior only if the mutual obligations are viewed as a package; payment of a price is acceptable to the buyer only in combination with the seller's delivery of the good. In the same vein, one can argue that the consistent application of the Kaldor–Hicks criterion is Pareto superior to the use of other criteria and, therefore, justified by the more innocuous hypothetical consent required for the Pareto criterion. The claim is that comprehensive adherence to Kaldor–Hicks efficiency makes (almost) all members of society better off, or at least not worse off, even without administering actual compensation payments.[10] The underlying assumption is that gains and losses are distributed randomly and independently across the entire population. Since, by definition under the Kaldor–Hicks criterion, benefits exceed losses for every change, the law of large numbers ensures a net gain for each individual. Unfortunately, it seems impossible to test this claim empirically. Even a plausibility assessment is difficult, not least because one would have to determine a competing allocation of rights and benefits against which the Kaldor–Hicks efficiency would be measured. The alternative arrangement would be a counterfactual if the status

---

9 On the equivalence of Kaldor–Hicks efficiency and an auction rule, see J. Coleman, 'Efficiency, Exchange, and Auction: Philosophic Aspects of the Economic Approach to Law' (1980) 68 *California Law Review* 221, 241 *et seq*. Accordingly, for a "wealth maximisation rule", see R. Posner, 'The Value of Wealth: A Comment on Dworkin and Kronman' (1980) 9 *Journal of Legal Studies* 243, 244.

10 For both an intuitive argument and a rigorous analysis, see A. Polinsky, 'Probabilistic Compensation Criteria', above n. 7 ("quasi-Paretian compensation criterion"); see also Y.K. Ng, 'Quasi-Pareto Social Improvements' (1984) 74 *American Economic Review* 1033. The argument is embraced for law and economics by R. Posner, 'Ethical and Political Basis', above n. 7, 491 *et seq*. A recent and more critical assessment can be found in Z. Liscow, 'Is Efficiency Biased?' (2018) 85 *University of Chicago Law Review* 1649.

quo, as many adherents of law and economics argue, already largely reflects the demands of Kaldor–Hicks efficiency.[11]

The empirical and conceptual difficulties can be avoided by introducing a normative consideration. For that, one has to return to the issue of distribution. The compensation of losses caused by the Kaldor–Hicks criterion is the equivalent of a subsequent redistribution of net gains from the "change". This suggests the following procedure: apply the Kaldor–Hicks criterion consistently and tally the hypothetical compensation payments; use a person's gains to offset her hypothetical compensation claims; and, in the last step, close any remaining balances through taxes or social transfers.[12] Admittedly, it will not be possible to calculate exact balances from concrete Kaldor–Hicks changes, because of uncertainties in facts and the lack of a benchmark status quo. Without such a reference point, just distribution can be assessed on its own terms, invoking the separation logic developed above for the Pareto criterion. A practical guideline could be to maintain a stable relative distribution of the societal wealth[13] that is constantly being increased by Kaldor–Hicks efficiency. Insofar as the distribution of wealth can be regulated separately, there is no longer a convincing justice reason to oppose an increase in the total wealth available for distribution.[14]

3. EQUALITY AS AN IMPLICATION OF EFFICIENCY

Most normative work in (law and) economics pursues the implications of Kaldor–Hicks efficiency for specific issues of law and policy. The approach is strictly reductionist: after the question of just distribution has been relegated to a separate debate, any prescriptions must be derived from efficiency as the sole remaining objective. Unlike in doctrinal legal scholarship, pre-existing rules or widespread notions of justice have no independent weight.[15] One attraction of

---

11 For the (controversial) idea that judge-made common law tends towards efficiency, see T. Zywicki and E. Stringham, 'Common Law and Economic Efficiency' in F. PARISI (ed.), *Production of Legal Rules, Encyclopedia of Law and Economics*, Edward Elgar Publishing, Cheltenham 2011, p. 107.

12 More on taxes and transfers in section 4.2 below.

13 For example, the Gini coefficient of income and wealth distribution. For implementation through the tax and transfer system, see the text accompanying nn. 51 and 52.

14 This is at least true if principles of justice pay no regard to the strategies needed to assert them in political power struggles (see n. 6 above). If, instead, one incorporates these strategic considerations, justice may well require to pursue distributional goals in inefficient ways. For a nuanced justification of this approach, see L. Fennell and R. McAdams, 'The Distributive Deficit in Law and Economics' (2015) 100 *Minnesota Law Review* 1051, 1083 *et seq.* (arguing that inertia and other deficiencies of the legislative process in tax law justify consideration of distributional issues in other areas of the law).

15 But they can serve as a heuristic. One might presume that especially long-standing legal rules rarely turn out to be inefficient.

this radical restriction of admissible arguments is that it encourages a precise and imaginative analysis of effects and interdependencies. Seemingly self-evident postulates of justice – such as the rule against theft – often pose astonishing difficulties when they have to be derived from efficiency, but solving such riddles often stimulates thinking about other issues.[16]

In the following subsections, this approach will be brought to bear on rules of equal treatment. To do so, one must abandon the assumption that equality relates to a distribution problem. Instead, duties of equal treatment must be shown to be an outgrowth of Kaldor–Hicks efficiency; that is, a means of maximising wealth across all members of society. On the one hand, equal treatment can be thought of as an incentive scheme for agents to align their behaviour with efficiency (section 3.1). On the other hand, it will be argued that anti-discrimination rules – a special type of equal treatment duties – can encourage efficient investment in human capital, such as through education and the formation of skills and attitudes. This line of reasoning also showcases that normative economics can account for particularly sensitive issues of social justice (section 3.2).[17]

3.1. EQUAL TREATMENT AS AN INCENTIVE SCHEME

From an economic perspective, legal rules for controlling behaviour can be classified as incentive schemes. In this regard, interesting problems arise if actions of an "agent" cannot directly be rewarded or punished, particularly because important circumstances are known only to the agent but not the "principal": the person affected by, or charged with, guiding his or her behaviour (such as a regulator or court). The claim to be made in this subsection is that equal treatment rules, in view of this information asymmetry, can serve as the best incentive scheme available, and are adopted for this reason, not because of any distributional effects.[18]

3.1.1. *Key Idea*

The key idea is the following: an equal treatment requirement forces the agent to extend his or her decision, in a given instance, to all other cases that resemble it in a relevant aspect. This is akin to the Kantian test of whether one is willing to

16 See R. Hasen and R. McAdams, 'The Surprisingly Complex Case Against Theft' (1997) 17 *International Review of Law & Economics* 367.

17 Other equal treatment rules in contract, employment and competition law are considered in A. Engert, 'Gleichbehandlungsgebote als Vertragshilfe', above n. 2.

18 A similar efficiency rationale for equal treatment rules in public law is offered by P. von Randow, 'Equal Treatment Rules and Rent Seeking' in H. Siekmann et al. (eds.), *Festschrift für Baums*, Mohr Siebeck, Tübingen 2017, p. 931.

accept the maxim of one's actions as "general law".[19] The duty of equal treatment transforms this thought experiment into an incentive scheme for the decision-maker: the maxim of his or her initial decision actually becomes the binding law for his or her future actions, and he or she must live with its consequences. This enhances his or her incentives if he or she has a general interest in acting efficiently, but can be tempted, in certain cases, to sacrifice value maximisation for his or her own private advantage. A prime example of this efficiency rationale is equal treatment of shareholders in company law.[20] In fact, legal scholars have acknowledged that, here, the link to distributive justice is especially tenuous.[21]

3.1.2. *Full Argument*

To develop the argument, start from a simple model: assume an agent *A*, who is entrusted with managing the affairs of an entity *E*, and owns a share of θ (with $0 < \theta < 1$) in *E*, for example as a partner or manager with performance-based pay. In relation to outsiders, *A*'s share of θ incentivises him or her to enter only into transactions that are profitable for *E*. However, a conflict of interest arises if *A* can derive advantages for him or herself from a transaction. For instance, if *A* consummates a transaction between *E* and him or herself as counterparty,[22] this may result in a return of π to *A*, and a corresponding return of γ for *E*. The transaction is efficient if $\pi + \gamma > 0$. However, *A* will accept it if $\pi + \theta\gamma > 0$. The conflict of interest can cause *A* to inflict a loss on *E*, and to deviate from efficiency if, for example, *A* has a 10 per cent stake in *E* ($\theta = 0.1$), his or her immediate benefit from the transaction is €10 ($\pi = 10$), and *E* loses €20 ($\gamma = -20$).[23]

Avoiding this outcome would be straightforward if the law were able to prohibit inefficient transactions outright.[24] However, there are good reasons against enacting a legal duty to "only make profitable business decisions", or to enter only into efficient transactions.[25] While courts can attempt to evaluate business decisions, there is a considerable risk of error. As a consequence,

19 See. I. Kant, *Grundlegung zur Metaphysik der Sitten*, J. Hartknoch, Riga 1786, p. 52 ("act only according to that maxim by which you can at the same time wish it to become a general law"). English translation available at <https://groundlaying.appspot.com>.

20 See, e.g. Art. 85 Directive (EU) 2017/1132 relating to certain aspects of company law.

21 See D. Verse, *Der Gleichbehandlungsgrundsatz im Recht der Kapitalgesellschaften*, Mohr Siebeck, Tübingen 2006, p. 77 *et seq.*; C-W. Canaris, above n. 1, p. 36.

22 Self-dealing is the most straightforward example. An analogous analysis applies to a case where *A* receives a benefit from the counterparty, or is otherwise under its influence.

23 *A*'s profit from the transaction is $10 + 0.1(-20) = 8$, while the efficiency outcome is $10 - 20 = -10$.

24 Or if the law were to force *A* to act exclusively in *E*'s interest, so that she would only carry out transactions with positive γ. Such a rule would also prevent *A* from making inefficient decisions.

25 Cf. S. Myers, 'Determinants of Corporate Borrowing' (1977) 5 *Journal of Financial Economics* 147, 157 ("No sane lawyer attempts to write a contract requiring management to 'abstain from suboptimal decisions'".).

a transaction that was profitable and efficient when initiated could well be condemned as a breach of duty if it happens to turn out badly. Holding agents liable for violation of such an error-prone standard can result in excessive litigation or distortion of incentives, particularly towards risk avoidance.[26]

An equal treatment rule can be less costly and more effective. In terms of the simple model, it would require *A* to offer the same transaction to all others who are in a sufficiently similar position. The effect on *A*'s incentives depends on the number and size of other counterparties that can claim equal treatment. Assume that the additional parameter $\lambda > 1$ captures the factor by which total transaction volume increases if *A* must make the transaction opportunity available to additional parties; simply put, it is the number of additional cases that are equal to *A*'s own transaction. This changes *A*'s incentives: whereas his or her benefit from concluding the transaction used to be $\pi + \theta y$, it now becomes $\pi + \lambda\theta y$. The effect of *A*'s decision on *E* increases by the factor λ, which can fully or partially offset *A*'s weak incentives from sharing only $\theta < 1$ in *E*'s gains and losses. In the example above, *A* would refrain from the harmful transaction if λ were greater than 5.[27]

An example from company law can illustrate the incentive effect. *A* could be a shareholder with a stake of θ in the corporation. Consider a transaction with substantial private benefits π with no consideration from the recipients, such as the payment of a dividend. Because of the significant benefits, all other shareholders will insist on equal treatment and claim a transaction of the same size for themselves: hence $\lambda = \frac{1}{\theta}$. With an equal treatment rule in place, *A*'s outcome from carrying out the transaction amounts to $\pi + \lambda\theta y = \pi + \frac{\theta}{\theta} y = \pi + y$. The transaction is efficient if $\lambda(\pi + y) > 0$. It follows that *A* consummates the transaction if and only if it is efficient. The dividend example also demonstrates why the equal treatment rule can be superior to attempting to prescribe a specific decision: a dividend to shareholders is efficient if the amount distributed is worth more in the hands of shareholders than for the corporation; that is, if $\lambda y < \lambda\pi$. In order to administer a rule that dividends be paid only when it is efficient, a court would have to evaluate whether the investment opportunities of the corporation are more valuable than investments or consumption by its shareholders. The equal treatment rule spares courts this intricate judgement by ensuring efficient incentives of the shareholder majority.

---

26 These shortcomings have motivated a broad exemption from liability for corporate managers, known as the business judgment rule: see H. Spamann, 'Monetary Liability for Breach of the Duty of Care?' (2016) 8 *Journal of Legal Analysis* 337; A. Engert and S. Goldlücke, 'Why Agents Need Discretion: The Business Judgment Rule as Optimal Standard of Care' (2017) 13 *Review of Law & Economics* 1; A. Engert, 'Why manager liability fails at controlling systemic risk' in B. Lomfeld, A. Somma and P. Zumbansen (eds), *Reshaping Markets*, CUP, Cambridge 2016, p. 161.

27 With $\lambda = 6$, *A*'s total gain would no longer be 8, as in n. 23 above, but $10 + 6 \times 0.1(-20) = -2$.

However, the analysis also reveals the perils of equal treatment as an incentive scheme. Equal treatment magnifies the consequences of the decision in the single case. This can, but need not, neutralise potential incentives to act inefficiently. If *A*'s share θ multiplied by the expansion factor λ remains too small, a harmful, self-interested transaction may still be worthwhile for *A*.[28] The equal treatment rule, then, not only fails to correct *A*'s incentives, but also increases the efficiency loss by the factor λ.[29] Given the circumstances, some may consider this at least to be a fair outcome, because the opportunity to loot *E* is not reserved exclusively for *A*. Yet "equal treatment in value destruction" increases the loss of social wealth. As an incentive scheme, equal treatment can only be justified if it succeeds in pushing *A*'s behaviour towards efficiency. Settings with high private benefits π and little incentive alignment through θ are particularly risky. The effect of the factor λ is ambiguous: it improves incentives but also magnifies the potential losses.

The dividend example offered particularly favourable conditions for an equal treatment rule: for the corporation, the value of money paid to shareholders does not depend on the recipient. Conversely, a given dividend is worth approximately the same to different shareholders. It follows that γ and π barely differ across transaction partners: all of the latter are "materially equal" for the purposes of applying the equal treatment rule. The simplicity of this assessment compares favourably with any attempt at regulating dividend payments directly, which would require courts to evaluate the corporation's available investment opportunities. The advantage of equal treatment rules is less stark in other instances, especially when determining equality poses greater difficulty. By highlighting incentive alignment as the relevant purpose, efficiency analysis helps to identify what constitutes equality, namely business opportunities that have the same or a similar effect on *E*.

3.2. EQUAL TREATMENT AS AN INVESTMENT INCENTIVE

Explaining equal treatment of shareholders under company law as a way of restraining self-dealing and other conflicts of interest may still have intuitive appeal for many lawyers. By contrast, a wealth maximisation account of other equal treatment rules will appear more far-fetched. Perhaps this is particularly true for anti-discrimination rules in private law, which are often justified by invoking fundamental human rights. This has little in common with a careful balancing of costs and benefits. Nevertheless, economists have not shied away

28 An example is $\pi = 10$, $\theta = 0.01$, $\gamma = -20$ and $\lambda = 10$. For *A*, the transaction remains privately profitable despite the equal treatment requirement: $10 + 0.01 \times 10(-20) = 8$.

29 In the example from n. 28, the efficiency outcome deteriorates from $10 - 20 = -10$ without the equal treatment rule to $10(10 - 20) = -100$ with the rule.

from applying their analytical toolkit to discrimination.[30] A good starting point for exploring the efficiency foundations of anti-discrimination law is found in incentives to invest,[31] especially in human capital.[32] The potential reward from an economic approach lies, again, in offering a more specific justification that lends itself to deriving more differentiated normative conclusions. In addition, efficiency arguments rest on claims about real-world effects and interdependencies, for example regarding the causes of unequal treatment of different groups. All of this can open up new perspectives for the discourse about anti-discrimination law and policy.

3.2.1. Key Idea

The efficiency case made here against discrimination is based on preventing a pernicious equilibrium where human abilities and talents lie idle instead of contributing to social wealth. In this account, discrimination results not from dislike, or even hatred, of the disadvantaged group but from rational use of information: because the statistical distribution of certain characteristics differs across groups, membership of a group can make a person appear less suitable for a given transaction. As members of the group are less likely to be considered for the type of transaction, a self-fulfilling prophecy can arise. If sought-for characteristics increase market opportunities less for members of the group than for others, cultivating them carries less reward. Anti-discrimination rules seek to unsettle this equilibrium by providing equal market opportunities to the group, and thus the incentive to develop the relevant skills and qualities.

3.2.2. Full Argument

Economists have pursued various explanations for group disadvantages.[33] The argument sketched in the previous paragraph builds on the notion of

---

[30] See the literature overviews by K. Lang and J.-Y. Lehmann, 'Racial Discrimination in the Labor Market: Theory and Empirics' (2012) 50 *Journal of Economic Literature* 959; K. Arrow, 'What Has Economics to Say About Racial Discrimination?' (1998) 12 *Journal of Economic Perspectives* 91.

[31] While investment incentives also guide behaviour, their analysis belongs to a different strand of economic models from the incentive schemes in section 3.1.

[32] The following analysis overlaps in part with A. Engert, 'Allied by Surprise? The Economic Case for an Anti-Discrimination Statute' (2003) 4 *German Law Journal* 685, 689 *et seq.* and 693 *et seq.*

[33] The earliest account explains discrimination with preferences directed against the group (taste-based discrimination): see G. Becker, *The Economics of Discrimination*, University of Chicago Press, Chicago 1957 (usually cited from the 2nd ed., 1971). For a summary of this approach in the labour markets, see K. Lang and J-Y. Lehmann, above n. 30, 970 *et seq.* More recently, systematic differences in behaviour between groups have received greater attention, such as gender differences in competitive behaviour: see U. Gneezy, K. Leonard and J. List, 'Gender Differences in Competition: Evidence from a Matrilineal and a Patriarchal Society' (2009) 77 *Econometrica* 1637.

"statistical discrimination" as a cause of discrimination.[34] It starts from the general problem of information asymmetries: markets often suffer from the fact that essential characteristics of persons, goods or services remain unknown to potential counterparties. Information asymmetry entails adverse selection: poor quality displaces good quality and, as a consequence, valuable opportunities for cooperation remain unused ("lemon market"). To alleviate this problem, market participants strive for information indicative of quality. This can lead employers or landlords to rely on association with a group as a cue to the expected characteristics of a potential employee or tenant. Relying on such prejudice can be rational at the individual level. For historical or other reasons, the relevant characteristic may be more or less prevalent in different groups. This can make group membership an imprecise but still useful piece of information. At the same time, even after exploiting alternative sources of information, important characteristics remain hard to assess. For instance, a job applicant's CV, educational achievements and reference letters provide only an incomplete view of their professional capabilities. It is even more difficult to evaluate creditworthiness or personal qualities such as integrity, conscientiousness or commitment, which are of obvious importance to employers or landlords.

Two recent empirical studies underscore the relevance of these aspects. The first concerns the professional success of female and male lawyers in US law firms during the 2000s. It starts out with the familiar finding of a highly significant gender gap in both income and career advancement. When educational background, work experience, family responsibilities and other observable characteristics were incorporated, the gap diminished, but continued to remain significant.[35] Yet, after performance measures – to wit, billable hours with clients and volume of business generated – were included, the differences in income and career success became insignificant.[36] Law firms seemed to reward performance irrespective of gender. More important for the above argument is that gender differences in measured performance largely disappeared if the lawyers' self-reported intensity of career aspirations were included.[37] This suggests, on the one hand, that individual commitment drives performance and, as a result, differences in income and promotion. On the other hand, strong career aspirations seemed more prevalent among male lawyers. This implies that gender provides an (imperfect) indication of the degree of commitment.[38]

---

34 Seminally, E. Phelps, 'The Statistical Theory of Racism and Sexism' (1972) 62 *American Economic Review* 659; K. Arrow, 'The Theory of Discrimination' in O. Aschenfelter and A. Rees (eds), *Discrimination in Labor Markets*, Princeton University Press, Princeton 1973, p. 3.

35 G. Azmat and R. Ferrer, 'Gender Gaps in Performance: Evidence from Young Lawyers' (2017) 125 *Journal of Political Economy* 1306, 1345 *et seq.*

36 Ibid., 1347 *et seq.*

37 Ibid., 1334 *et seq.*

38 The study did not investigate whether law firms' hiring decisions differed on the basis of gender.

The second study relates directly to statistical discrimination. It examines the effects of "ban the box" policies that prevent employers in the US from asking applicants about criminal records prior to an interview. From an employer's perspective, criminal records can point to undesirable traits, ranging from lack of work ethics to violent behaviour. However, according to the study, the aim to better integrate former offenders into the labour market backfired: introduction of the rules appeared to impair the hiring prospects of black Americans, who have a higher incidence of criminal records.[39] This is strong evidence of statistical discrimination: the use of a group characteristic as an indication of hidden characteristics.

Statistical discrimination can be inefficient if the forgone transaction gains for the group outweigh the selection benefits for the discriminating side.[40] However, it is particularly harmful if it makes the acquisition of productive characteristics less attractive to the disadvantaged group. If statistical discrimination reduces the prospect of obtaining an attractive position or suitable housing, it becomes less worthwhile to develop the attributes desired by employers and landlords. The returns on human capital investments diminishes for the respective group.[41] For instance, the lower career ambitions of female lawyers in the study summarised above, possibly complemented by a stronger orientation towards family tasks, could result from law firms having this very expectation and, therefore, limiting the career opportunities of women.[42] The goal of breaking such a self-fulfilling prophecy aligns well with the fairness notion that immutable attributes should not affect the opportunities of individuals or groups if they are unrelated to the pertinent task or transaction.

The final judgement on the efficiency of statistical discrimination, however, depends on the losses suffered by the group from statistical discrimination and, conversely, losses by the opposite market side from banning statistical discrimination and coping with a greater share of less suitable candidates.[43] Even if statistical discrimination discourages the group from developing the asked-for characteristics, the efficiency balancing depends on the size of the various effects.[44] An additional consideration is how well (or how poorly)

---

39 J. Doleac and B. Hansen, 'The Unintended Consequences of "Ban the Box": Statistical Discrimination and Employment Outcomes When Criminal Histories Are Hidden' (2020) 38 *Journal of Labor Economics* 321.

40 See A. Engert, 'Allied by Surprise?', above n. 32, 694 *et seq.*

41 See the formal model in A. Moro and P. Norman, 'A general equilibrium model of statistical discrimination' (2004) 114 *Journal of Economic Theory* 1.

42 As mentioned above, the study produced no evidence of statistical discrimination in this particular instance, as it found no significant differences between genders in how measured performance was rewarded.

43 Cf. A. Engert, 'Allied by Surprise?', above n. 32, 694 *et seq.* (offering a sketchy assessment, without the aspect of a self-fulfilling prophecy).

44 See the broad analysis in P. Norman, 'Statistical Discrimination and Efficiency' (2003) 70 *Review of Economic Studies* 615.

anti-discrimination laws can be enforced. If statistical discrimination is difficult to prove, they can lead to costly and frustrating litigation without effectively improving the position of the group. The failure of efficiency analysis to offer a clear-cut conclusion may seem disappointing. For law and economics researchers, it is an invitation to investigate the relevant variables, and to establish at least their orders of magnitude. The efficiency criterion provides and structures a research agenda, rather than producing a definitive precept.

4. EQUALITY AS A PRINCIPLE OF DISTRIBUTIVE JUSTICE

Equal treatment can, in certain instances – perhaps surprisingly – be a corollary of efficiency. It has also been mentioned, in passing, that efficiency itself reflects an assumption of formal equality: in maximising wealth across all members of society, an increase in value has equal weight regardless of whom it benefits: "one euro is one euro". Yet the normative economics of equality do not end with efficiency. Equality inevitably plays a central role in the just distribution of income and wealth. It has been discussed extensively whether normative economics has anything to say about distributive justice (section 4.1). If one answers the question in the affirmative, a closer look at equality in distribution again leads back to the possibility of separating distribution from efficiency (section 4.2).

4.1. *DE DISTRIBUTIONE EST DISPUTANDUM*

Since the 1940s, the prevailing view in economics – in contrast to classical Benthamian utilitarianism – had been that issues of distribution defy scientific analysis, and must be left to political struggle. The bedrock of this belief was the doctrine that no rational method existed for "interpersonal comparisons of utility"; that is, for weighting preferences across individuals. This does not affect efficiency, because it maximises monetary value as a common denominator. The verdict applies, however, to the goals that individuals pursue with their wealth and other resources. The contention is that there is no way of determining, with any degree of scientific objectivity, whether one euro is worth more in the hands of the wealthy or the poor, the educated or the uneducated, the selfish or the compassionate, etc. An English economist from the 1930s gives a remarkable account of the respect for individual autonomy and divergent cultural values that motivates this belief:

> I had the strongest bias in favour of utilitarian analysis. … I was powerfully attracted by the proposition … that recent developments of the theory of value could be

> invoked to demonstrate the desirability of the mitigation of inequality. When I look back on that frame of mind, I find it easy to understand the belief of Bentham and his followers that they had found the open sesame to problems of social policy.
>
> But, as time went on, things occurred which began to shake my belief … I am not clear how these doubts first suggested themselves; but I well remember how they were brought to a head by my reading somewhere … the story of how an Indian official had attempted to explain to a high caste Brahmin the sanctions of the Benthamite system. "But that," said the Brahmin, "cannot possibly be right. I am ten times as capable of happiness as that untouchable over there." I had no sympathy with the Brahmin. But I could not escape the conviction that … the difference between us was not one which could be resolved by the same methods of demonstration as were available in other fields of social judgement.[45]

To the academic researcher, it might seem prudent to abstain from claiming scientific truth in questions of distribution. Yet, society and politics cannot avoid the demands for distributive justice. Leaving this call unanswered does not sit well with the normative ambitions of economics. In addition, while efficiency and distribution can be analysed separately, redistribution feeds back into efficiency: The Kaldor–Hicks criterion operates on reservation prices for entitlements; they, in turn, depend on individual income and wealth. Efficient allocation, thus, varies with the distribution of income and wealth.

This interaction alone does not necessitate a unified approach. Efficiency analysis can take distribution as a given, and maximise wealth on that basis.[46] There is, however, a trade-off between distribution and efficiency that requires balancing in a common framework. The reason is that redistribution itself is costly, in the sense of reducing total wealth. This is not because monetary value changes when it is transferred from one person to another; a mere payment does not affect efficiency. But a government bureaucracy is needed to administer any redistributive scheme, which is costly. Even more consequential is that redistribution impacts on incentives and behaviour. It dampens activities that trigger payment obligations under the scheme – for example, the generation of taxable income – and it encourages activities or characteristics that are used to identify the beneficiaries.[47] The conclusion is that, to provide one euro to the recipient of a transfer, much more than one euro must be taken from the burdened party.[48]

---

45 L. Robbins, 'Interpersonal Comparisons of Utility: A Comment' (1938) 48 *Economic Journal* 635, 635 *et seq.*

46 Several successive steps could be needed, e.g. because efficiency leads to uneven wealth increases, distribution is adjusted and triggers new reallocations for efficiency reasons.

47 In addition to this substitution effect, income effects can work in the opposite direction. The crucial point is that distribution rules never only transfer wealth, but also bring about behavioural changes.

48 For the US tax system, it has been estimated that the transfer of $1 from the highest to the lowest income earner causes a burden of $1.77: N. Hendren, 'Measuring economic efficiency using inverse-optimum weights' (2020) 187 *Journal of Public Economics* 104198, 9.

The efficiency loss does not imply that economics were opposed to redistribution. Since efficiency has been justified by bracketing off distribution, it has no bearing on distributive justice. Therefore, if economics confines itself to efficiency, it can do no more than to quantify the costs of redistribution. It has to refrain from balancing the conflicting goals, or at the very least from providing an analytical framework for that purpose. This seems unsatisfactory. Therefore, economists are increasingly setting aside their reservations against interpersonal utility comparisons and have begun to construct non-monetary measures of aggregate social welfare. Numerous possibilities have been explored to translate individual preference satisfaction into measures of utility, and to combine them in a "social welfare function".[49] Aggregating welfare across individuals enables economics to state a rationale for redistribution, based on the diminishing marginal utility of money: for the less well off, an additional euro provides more satisfaction than for the affluent.[50] A social welfare function, then, provides the analytical tool to trade off the (decreasing) welfare gains from redistribution against its (increasing) efficiency costs and, on this basis, to determine the optimal level of equalising income and wealth.

4.2. THE CRITERIA OF DISTRIBUTIVE JUSTICE: THE SEPARATION OF EFFICIENCY AND DISTRIBUTION REVISITED

With an interpersonal summation of utility and the diminishing marginal utility of money, the market-like "formal" equality of the efficiency goal – one euro is one euro, no matter who owns it – can be balanced against the "substantive" equality in the satisfaction of needs. Surprisingly, the edifice of efficiency analysis can remain largely untouched if, and to the extent that, efficiency and distribution remain separable not only analytically, but also practically. This animates the proposition, mentioned earlier, that redistribution should be accomplished through taxes and social transfers, while all other areas of law and government should aim exclusively at efficiency. This claim seems well founded, at least at the outset: the guiding principle of tax and social transfer laws is to attribute burdens and benefits on the basis of individual capability

---

[49] For a very accessible introduction, see M. ADLER, *Measuring Social Welfare*, OUP, Oxford 2019, p. 20 *et seq*. See also L. KAPLOW and S. SHAVELL, *Fairness versus Welfare*, Harvard University Press, Cambridge 2002, p. 24 *et seq*.; L. KAPLOW, *The Theory of Taxation and Public Economics*, Princeton University Press, Princeton 2008, p. 41 *et seq*.

[50] From an empirical perspective, see, e.g. D. KAHNEMAN and A. DEATON, 'High income improves evaluation of life but not emotional well-being' (2010) 107 *Proceedings of the National Academy of Sciences of the United States of America* 16489.

and need. The tax and social transfer regimes are unique in their comprehensive coverage of an individual's income and wealth, and their ability to target differences in the marginal utility of money.[51] Other areas of law can achieve need-based redistribution (far) less precisely. They would have to make rough assumptions as to whether, for example, shareholders are "typically" wealthier than employees (although shareholders are often employees, and vice versa). Redistribution by means other than taxes and social transfers, therefore, are likely to cause a twofold efficiency loss: firstly, because – as has been pointed out – any redistribution inevitably reduces wealth; and, secondly, because they operate not on income and wealth, but regulate specific activities, which become less efficient if the rules are tweaked towards distributive goals.[52]

An important objection to the separability claim is that distributive justice depends not only on needs; that is, on the marginal utility of money.[53] Besides equal preference satisfaction, a just distribution of income and wealth could also consider subjective effort and, in this sense, moral "merit". This would suggest that taxes and transfers also depend on the recipient's exertion of effort, such as through labour, or other contributions to the good of other individuals or the community. Because tax law does not contemplate the amount of effort, one might infer that, for instance, employment law should be harnessed to ensure a just distribution of income.

To respond to this critique, one first needs to clarify that much of what other theories of justice call "merit" is already reflected in efficiency analysis. Efficiency requires that efforts be "rewarded" to the extent that the cost of effort provision exceeds the benefits. Crucially, efficiency is not equivalent to market outcomes. For instance, if existing labour markets fail to put a person's labour to productive use, such involuntary unemployment is an efficiency loss. The resulting inefficiency includes forgone benefits from social integration in a work environment, and from job satisfaction; they enter the efficiency calculus insofar as employees would be prepared to pay for them (or require compensation to agree to give them up).[54] In addition, market prices fully recognise the value of labour

---

51 Certain aspects of family, employment or insurance law come close, but these institutions are better explained by mutual insurance and efficient risk allocation than by redistributive goals.

52 This "double distortion" argument goes back to L. Kaplow and S. Shavell, 'Why the Legal System is Less Efficient than the Income Tax in Redistributing Income' (1994) 23 *Journal of Legal Studies* 667. For the critique, see n. 14 above.

53 A related objection is based on specific in-kind needs, such as in the regulation of health risks with different vulnerabilities: see M. Adler, above n. 49, p. 225 *et seq*.

54 For the non-pecuniary consequences of job losses, see D. Sullivan and T. von Wachter, 'Job Displacement and Mortality: An Analysis Using Administrative Data' (2009) 124 *Quarterly Journal of Economics* 1265 (documenting a long-term increase in mortality among laid-off workers). When determining the reservation prices of workers for non-monetary benefits, an efficiency analysis would also have to correct for incomplete information and deviations from rationality.

only if there are property rights in the product. Therefore, market incentives for labour effort are often (far) too weak, particularly for the production of public goods. In response to these often-severe market imperfections, economists turn their attention to additional institutions – including laws – that come as close as possible to full efficiency, in light of the real-world constraints.

Competing theories of justice likewise have to grapple with an obstinate reality that fails to fully reward individual "merit". To compare such theories with efficiency on an equal footing, one can conduct a thought experiment and strip away the real-world constraints impeding the implementation of any normative conception. The relevant question then becomes whether "merit" deserves greater reward than what efficient incentives require, in such a frictionless world. For example, consider the case of a person who suffers from such severe illness or disability that her labour product and possible work satisfaction – properly valued in money – would sum to a negative amount, for instance because her labour would depend on very costly assistance, or would be intensely agonising to her. To induce the person to work anyway, compensation would have to exceed the total economic value of the service rendered. In labour relations, both parties would want to terminate such an employment. Under conditions like these, it would seem unreasonable, and almost perverse,[55] to encourage work effort as "merit". The example suggests that efficiency analysis absorbs much, if not all, of merit-based distributive justice.

5. CONCLUSION

The reductionism of economics was introduced as part attraction, part irritation to lawyers and philosophers. The manifold ways to derive equality from the first principles of economics reveal yet another remarkable feature: lawyers and philosophers tend to expect an economic analysis to deliver unambiguous value judgements and policy advice. This is unfair, insofar as jurisprudence and social philosophy, for their part, hardly ever offer unanimous conclusions on any issue of law and justice. Nonetheless, the complaint points to another particularity: normative (law and) economics is founded on the concepts and theories of positive economics. In consequence, it is open to, and indeed depends on, empirical findings to test its claims and derive more specific prescriptions. In this sense, normative economic analysis is less a "system" of justice than an

55 The provocative language is borrowed from L. Kaplow and S. Shavell, 'Fairness versus Welfare: Notes on the Pareto Principle, Preferences and Distributive' (2003) 32 *Journal of Legal Studies* 331, 335 ("pursuit of notions of fairness results in needless and, at root, perverse reduction in individuals' well-being").

ongoing research programme. Relying on assumptions and empirical findings that remain subject to revision, it scarcely comes to definitive conclusions. For a theory of justice, openness to real-world effects and changing assessments need not be a disadvantage. Law itself, on the other hand, requires greater stability. As with other theories of justice, normative economics provides an outside vantage point for critical reflection of the law, not a substitute for legal rules and legal doctrine.

DIMENSIONS OF EQUALITY IN PRIVATE LAW

Translating between Law, Society and Technology

Dan WIELSCH

1. INTRODUCTION

The bearing of the principle of equality between private actors is yet to be adequately determined. Like the concept of justice itself, it must be separated from the dichotomy of *iustitia distributiva* and *iustitia commutativa*, which reflects the distinction between the State and society; between public and private relationships.

However, this reference to a dichotomy itself misses the point. Not only is a categorical division of the spheres of justice at odds with the actual structure of society and its proliferation into multiple subsystems, but it also reduces the right to equality to a mere instrument for the allocation of goods, to and between persons, across the board. Both the idea of an equal distribution of rights (in citizens' relationships with each other), and the idea of an equal distribution of what is actually required to exercise such rights (a citizens' claim against the State), miss the guarantee of freedom implied by these rights in general, and by the right to equality in particular.[1] Both instances are based on an understanding of law that assimilates rights as possessions. From a procedural concept of law, this approach tends to "misunderstand the legal constitution of freedom as 'distribution' and to assimilate it to the model of the equal distribution of acquired or allocated goods".[2] This characterisation implies a positivism of rights, legal entities, and rules of distribution, treating them all as pre-existing. The view of rights as an inventory of possessions and abilities ("property"), implies a far-reaching positivism, treating the individual, their goods, and the rules that apply to them as a given. This, almost inevitably, results in categorisation of rights in the relationship between private individuals as being rights of ownership or dominion, or exclusion rights; while the relationship between individuals and the State is framed as being characterised by rights of protection, or negative rights. But how can this be, if the individual cannot be assumed to be pre-existent? What, then, when options for action and communication do not yet exist, and must first be generated?

Then, the law, including the right to equality, would have to be set to accommodate a potential mutual constitution of rights, personal identity, and social practice. Law would have to be geared towards the becoming of the positive, to foster participation in the generation of rules for social institutions which *then* produce social individuals and cultural works. Thus, freed from merely marking out physical, objective freedoms, rights related to the shaping of social institutions become participation rights.[3]

The following sections will examine the potential of equality rights in shaping non-State rules. In particular, digitalisation creates conditions in which the protection of freedoms guaranteed by (constitutional) law are not covered by the State, but must be provided by decentralised social institutions shaped by private rights. Under these conditions, the rights to equality advance to first-rate rights of political participation.

---

1 Generally, the equal distribution of rights is underlined by a formal legal paradigm, while equal opportunity to exercise said rights is accented by a material legal paradigm.

2 J. Habermas, *Between Facts and Norms* (W. Rehg, tr.), MIT Press, Cambridge, MA 1996, p. 419.

3 On the reconstruction of private rights as rights to participate in the establishment of social institutions, see D. Wielsch, 'Medienregulierung durch Persönlichkeits- und Datenschutzrechte' (2020) *JuristenZeitung* 105, 113 *et seq.*

2. SOCIETY AND LAW: FROM STRUCTURES TO FUNCTIONS

Tradition has viewed equality through a divisional pattern, particularly with the help of the law. Until the nineteenth century, society was interpreted as a whole being made up of parts. The basic concept of society was founded in the *koinonía* (*communitas, societas*), which presupposed generic equality of the basic state of humankind essentially, by contrasting it with animals: "As equals, and by virtue of their equality, people have common affairs. Equality is the basis of this commonality".[4] This line of argument from the social sciences corresponds with an ontological concept of the world, which tries to comprehend the world as a wholeness of being, by focusing on the internal relations of the whole, taking the truth of one evident starting position (elements, atoms) and transferring it to the next entity in order to explain it.[5]

This is, however, like trying to understand time by disassembling a clock. By allocating each part its own place in the world, philosophical concepts of justice neutralise and harmonise real-world inequality, and the ethical obligation inherent in proportional equality is silent on distribution criteria.[6] But the "natural" order inherent in this structured division makes it clear that nature not only determines the parts, in the form of individual persons, but also the further division of the whole from which societal duties and positions arise.[7] Equality is measured in how well this is observed ("*suum cuique*").

Differentiating between a whole and its parts shifts the gaze to the internal relationships within the whole,[8] directing attention to the internal order – the "structure" – whose rationale is guaranteed by substance. Little focus is given to relationships with the "environment": everything is viewed from within, and not from the perspective of an external observer who sees both sides of every boundary.[9] As such, the opportunity to thematise specific differences, and to investigate the meaning of their fundamental structures, is lost. The durability of this divisional model is owed to its elasticity, and this is the reason why the idea of the world as a uniform whole did not ebb until the twentieth century. Under changing historical circumstances, the focus of the argument (the "nature") may begin with the whole (pantheism) or the part (atomism); with

---

4 N. Luhmann, 'Die Weltgesellschaft' (1971) 57 *Archiv für Rechts- und Sozialphilosophie* 1, 2.

5 N. Luhmann, *Zweckbegriff und Systemrationalität*, Mohr, Tübingen 1968, p. 174; N. Luhmann, 'Soziologie als Theorie sozialer Systeme' in *Soziologische Aufklärung: Band 1*, Westdeutscher Verlag, Opladen 1970, p. 113 (p. 115 with fn. 4).

6 Aristotle, *The Nicomachean Ethics, vol. 6* (D. Ross, tr.), 2nd ed., OUP, Oxford 2009, pp. 1131a 28–1131b 8.

7 N. Luhmann, *Theory of Society, vol. 2* (R. Barrett, tr.), Stanford University Press, Stanford 2013, p. 197.

8 Ibid.

9 Ibid.

the ends (the teleology of ancient ethicists) or the means (deontology of modern ethicists); from above ("high" society/nobility) or below (bourgeois or socialist revolutions) and vary the opposing side accordingly.[10]

Social theory suggests that fundamentally new perspectives can only open up when the world view shifts from a whole/part dichotomy to a system/environment model. Instead of being confined to structures, this approach takes the view that systems are not merely differentiated sums of their parts, but are themselves part of an environment in which their structures and identity are constituted only through creating and maintaining a stable difference between the internal and the external.[11] The internal can only be explained by co-considering the external. Following Luhmann's concept of meaning, we see that the most general function of systemic (expectation) structures is to reduce the complexity of the "world". This then makes it possible to take a functional approach to system structures, without having to take on their fixed perspective and internal constraints.[12] Instead, the divisional model and its focus on structure is reversed, prioritising function above structure. As a variety of structures serve equally well to reduce complexity, a system can reproduce itself as easily through changing its structures as it can by maintaining them.[13] Now we can interrogate the functions of specific structures for interpreting the world, for example the use of hierarchical models to interpret the relationship of a whole with its parts. It also suggests an understanding of the internal division of society, i.e. the inequality between individuals, as a secondary phenomenon produced by the primary differentiation of social systems interacting with their environments.[14]

In contrast to social theory, which is limited to observation, shifting to analysis of system/environment relationships brings normative significance for the law, because it reveals the conditions under which freedoms of the individual can take the form of rights. The exercise of subjective rights must not compromise the integrity of those institutions and social systems in which the conditions for autonomous action are created.

---

10 N. Luhmann, 'Gesellschaft' in *Soziologische Aufklärung: Band 1*, Westdeutscher Verlag, Opladen 1970, p. 139.

11 N. Luhmann, '*Zweckbegriff und Systemrationalität*', above n. 5, p. 175. System differentiation, therefore, does not mean that the whole will be broken into parts, but is no more than recursive system creation, in which the system creation is consistently repeated in the system through new differentiations between the systems and environments in the systems. Every subsystem reconstructs the overarching system to which it belongs, and in which it participates with its own (subsystem-specific) differentiation between system and environment. The potential to enhance the structural richness of social theory, arising from a shift to the system/environment structure, is significant. See N. Luhmann, '*Theory of Society, vol. 2*', above n. 7, p. 131 *et seq.*

12 N. Luhmann, '*Zweckbegriff und Systemrationalität*', above n. 5, p. 114.

13 W.L. Schneider, *Grundlagen der soziologischen Theorie: Band 2*, 3rd ed., Springer VS, Wiesbaden 2009, p. 272.

14 G. Teubner, 'The Anonymous Matrix: Human Rights Violations by "Private" Transnational Actors' (2006) 69 *Modern Law Review* 327, 333.

Thus, contract law must not only determine the "will" of the parties, but, rather, has to prove that a "contractual programme" can govern the interaction between the parties, while being compatible with the requirements of other instances of constituting meaning in the social environment. In terms of social references, sociological jurisprudence distinguishes between systems of interaction, systems of organisation, and social systems.[15] A programme agreed by the parties may conflict with the morality of interaction (for example, informal expectations based on the specific conduct of the parties), with the institutional requirements of markets (for example, unfair commercial practices), or organisations (for example, corporate codes), as well as with the self-normativity of social systems, such as requirements imposed by religion, politics or economic measures. According to this approach, non-consensual elements, such as the obligation to perform in good faith found in §242 of the German Civil Code, are nothing more than compliance of the contract with such environmental requirements.[16]

Thus, broadening our gaze to incorporate the social dimensions of subjective rights is not an end in itself. Social institutions are consolidated by the actions of individuals, acting freely. As social institutions, in turn, determine the actual conditions for autonomous action, the effect of exercising rights on these institutions becomes a normative problem that inherently concerns the law. This also reveals the political dimension of private rights: they permit the operation of social institutions, whose effects extend to a large number of (uninvolved) people.[17] The substance of individual rights can, therefore, only be determined in the context of their functions for social institutions.

However, the claim that "the central determinate of private law lies in the discretion of the individual" ignores these connections.[18] The law's restraint with regard to social institutions, reflected in that assertion, reaches as far as constitutional law, with liberal constitutionalism deliberately not seeking to extend the idea of the constitution to social subsystems ("constitution of civil society through its non-constitution", as it were).[19] According to this, legal protection only extends to individuals and their goods. The model simply assumes the conditions exist for the exercise of subjective rights. Social order

15 G. Teubner, *Law as an Autopoietic System* (A. Bankowska and R. Adler, trs.), Blackwell, Oxford 1993, p. 118, following the differentiation of N. Luhmann, 'Interaction, Organisation, and Society' (S. Holmes and C. Larmore, trs.) in *The Differentiation of Society*, Columbia University Press, New York 1982, p. 71.

16 D. Wielsch, 'Iustitia mediatrix: Zur Methode einer soziologischen Jurisprudenz' in G.-P. Calliess, A. Fischer-Lescano, D. Wielsch and P. Zumbansen (eds), *Soziologische Jurisprudenz – Festschrift für Gunther Teubner*, De Gruyter Recht, Berlin 2009, p. 401.

17 On the exact development of this thought, see D. Wielsch, 'Gesellschaftliche Transformation durch subjektive Rechte' in A. Fischer-Lescano, H. Franzki and J. Horst (eds), *Gegenrechte – Recht jenseits des Subjekts*, Mohr Siebeck, Tübingen 2018, p. 154 *et seq.*

18 For this argument, see H.C. Grigoleit, 'Anforderungen des Privatrechts an die Rechtstheorie' in M. Jestaedt and O. Lepsius (eds), *Rechtswissenschaftstheorie*, Mohr Siebeck, Tübingen 2008, p. 77.

19 G. Teubner, *Constitutional Fragments*, (G. Norbury, tr.), OUP, Oxford 2012, p. 16.

should come about by itself, as a result of civil liberties; thus, order becomes a consequence, rather than a precondition, of equal freedoms.[20] The social effects of rights are not addressed in law.

3. RELATIONAL REFORMULATION OF THE PRINCIPLE OF EQUALITY

Shifting attention to the relation between rights and social institutions has consequences, not least for understanding the principle of equality. The orthodox focus of legal doctrine on the individual seems to render the equality principle inapplicable to the operation of social institutions. It reduces the general right to equality, so strenuously fought for in bourgeois revolutions, to a prohibition on treating individuals in comparable situations differently without objective justification. It does not consider the extent to which the law treats social rationalities differently, and thus changes the conditions of the situations in which individuals later find themselves, without the ability to take legal action against those conditions – at least not before a court with a formalistic understanding of the law. The social functions of legal forms are disregarded. However, should these functions gain social dominance, they merge into the forms and make up their particularistic content. Still appealing to the unchanging, timeless function of legal forms to guarantee freedom and equality, then, actually benefits that specific legal content at the expense of other modes of social practice.[21] Critical legal thinking must reveal the bias inherent in specific legal forms, and their inability to expand "across the board", and expose the extent that structure structurally excludes, or discriminates against, social activities. (see section 3.1 below).

The social reductionism of its methods also means the law does not see the effect of technological systems on communication and the formation of social structures. The problem here is not that the law is capturing this social normativity unequally. Rather, the problem lies further back in the chain: the functionality of technological systems that do not operate on the basis of meaning must first be translated into social normativity. This translation is achieved with the help of the legal form. Here we do not have to turn to a social critique of the legal form, but instead have to use the legal form as a prerequisite to critique technologically regulated social interaction. It is not possible to judge the permissibility of unequal treatment without first revealing the normative

20 R. Wiethölter, *Rechtswissenschaft*, Fischer Funkkolleg, Frankfurt am Main 1968, p. 165. On Wiethölter's programme to make the conditions for freedom obtainable through law, see T. Sheplyakova, 'Recht Schrägstrich Freiheit und umgekehrt' (2019) *Kritische Justiz* 558, 566.

21 See R. Wiethölter, 'Zur politischen Funktion des Rechts am eingerichteten und ausgeübten Gewerbebetrieb' (1970) *Kritische Justiz* 121, 139.

relevance of the technological processes. In a way, the right to equal treatment must be able to create the conditions for its own application (see section 3.2 below).

3.1. EQUAL RESPONSIVENESS TO SOCIAL NORMATIVITY

It is from the imperative of justice to issue impartial practical judgements that the law receives a responsibility to consider the interdependent relationships between autonomies in a functionally differentiated social world, when interpreting its own legal forms. However, this requires that legal thinking has to be freed from the orthodox focus on the interactions between individuals. According to a subject-centred reading of the *ius suum cuinque* principle, an action can only be termed "just" if it takes all the rights of the person affected by it into account.[22] But since social systems are essential for individuals to act autonomously, this concept of justice must be opened up and supplemented with normative social perspectives.[23] In methodological terms, this means private law must also reconstruct the social autonomies arising from the right to equal treatment to have a complete perspective. The reconstruction must consider the conflicting rationalities of action arising from social interaction, and resolve these conflicts with equal consideration of all sources with normative meaning. In contrast to the normativity of social practice, the law is required to be reflexive in the forms it uses to represent these normativities. This reflexivity of its forms distinguishes the law from other social systems: it cannot externalise this normative demand on its own normativity, as it is driven by justice.[24]

A jurisprudence proceeding according to this method can be described as "relational", as it must first clarify the connection between the individual rights being exercised and the social autonomies concerned; and, secondly, it must consider that each system constitutes the environmental conditions for the other. An *initial relational reformulation of the principle of equality* (R_1) can, therefore, be stated thus: in the first instance, the law must adequately represent *all* social institutions and systems affected by the exercise of a right internally, and must respond *equally* to all of them. When partisan structures are identified, the legal

22 G. VLASTOS, 'Justice and Equality' in J. WALDRON (ed), *Theories of Rights*, OUP, Oxford 1984, p. 60: "an action is *just* if, and only if, it is prescribed exclusively by regard for the rights of all whom it affects substantially".

23 D. WIELSCH, 'Grundrechte als Rechtfertigungsgebote' (2013) 213 *Archiv für civilistische Praxis* 718, 750; D. WIELSCH, 'Relationales Urheberrecht' (2013) *Zeitschrift für Geistiges Eigentum* 274, 298.

24 Law has a special role: unlike other systems, it cannot call upon itself to move from merely constituting its medial autonomy to constitutionalising it. If (as according to G. TEUBNER, '*Constitutional Fragments*', above n. 19, p. 103) one can speak only of "social constitutions", where the reflexivity of a social system is juridified (via legal processes that are themselves reflexive), this opportunity is obviously lacking for the law itself.

forms and instruments must be restructured in such a way as to adequately represent the social normativities in question.

This multilateral reconstruction of ordinary law is made binding by the fundamental rights *de lege lata*.[25] As all fundamental rights have equal status in practice,[26] the conditions of all competing freedoms must also be taken into account. In contrast to the application of ordinary law, the legal system cannot avoid the social multilateralism of rights after their inclusion in a catalogue of fundamental rights. A fundamental right neither comes, nor stands, alone.[27] Private law positions and the companion doctrines which can be viewed as the expression of self-normativities of social functions thus remain anchored in a whole-of-society context.

However, fundamental rights themselves can be subjected to a relational reading. By viewing the fundamental rights as a social institution, Luhmann consistently reversed the limitation of fundamental rights to the protection of the individual. According to this argument, fundamental rights *primarily* protect the differentiation of society (into various social systems with different requirements of rationality), particularly against attempts to use excessive political control to undo or limit this differentiation.[28] In contrast, a traditional reading shows this protection of society occurring through statutory restrictions of fundamental rights.[29] This institutional interpretation turns the traditional concept of fundamental rights on its head: they are no longer directed at the protection of predetermined spheres of individual freedom, but protect the fragile *preconditions* of individual freedom, which then automatically lose the status of precondition, and become something which has to be generated.

This change in perspective is essential for making plausible the existence of specific individual rights. These rights reflect the different requirements for the generalisation of communication within the different spheres of society. As such, it would be mistaken to derive them from human dignity (as expressed in Article 1 of the German Constitution), and to interpret them merely from the interests of the individuals involved. As argued elsewhere, "an unbiased analysis of the human personality, its structure, problems, and needs, experience and potential to process such experience, would never result in the catalogue

---

25 D. Wielsch, 'Grundrechte als Rechtfertigungsgebote', above n. 23, 751 and 753.

26 Most recently, see the explicit findings of the Constitutional Court of the Federal Republic of Germany, Order of 6.11.2019 – 1 BvR 276/17, ECLI:DE:BVerfG:2019:rs20191106.1bvr027617, para. 141, on the consistency of this principle with the law of the European Court of Justice (ECJ) and the European Court of Human Rights.

27 D. Wielsch, 'Gesellschaftliche Transformation' above n. 17, p. 157.

28 N. Luhmann, *Grundrechte als Institution*, Drucker & Humblot, Berlin 1965, pp. 23, 71 *et seq.* and 96.

29 According to this alternative reading, the legal reservations serve, inter alia, the function of preventing self-blockades of the protected systems (see K-H. Ladeur, *Kritik der Abwägung in der Grundrechtsdogmatik*, Mohr Siebeck, Tübingen 2004, p. 60).

of fundamental rights with its categories and accentuations".[30] Fundamental rights "do not listen to the *natura humana*, but correspond with the problem constellation that results from social differentiation".[31]

To be sure, this does not dismiss an individualistic reading of fundamental rights. It simply means that fundamental rights are not only safeguards for individual self-expression, but also figure as protective institutions for social expectations formed outside of the political realm.[32] If fundamental rights are removed from the context of the political system, and are assigned horizontal effects between private actors, the protection they offer will extend further on all sides, and can be formulated accordingly: fundamental rights protect differentiation processes in social systems from a "disproportionate" expansion of other sub-rationalities.[33]

3.2. EXTENSION INTO THE SYNTACTIC WORLD: DIGITAL REGULATION'S RIGHT TO JUSTIFICATION

The fundamental right under Article 11 Charter of Fundamental Rights of the EU (CFR-EU)/Article 5 German Constitution (GG) is particularly important for social differentiation, as freedom of expression determines the opportunities for structural coupling between individual consciousness and communication, and thus the potential for confusion and variability in social systems. Freedom of communication, as formulated in the well-known *Lüth* judgment, is to be regarded as "the matrix, the indispensable condition of nearly every other form of freedom (Cardozo)", beyond even the functional connection with the democratic State that featured in that case.[34] Article 5 GG ensures the freedom to choose the topics, recipients and media for communication. This freedom ensures that complementary expectations of behaviour are largely formed according to social processes, without being steered or restricted by politics. Thus, "norms, roles, and institutions can be formed and tried out casually and in colourful, contradictory abundance".[35] Functionally specific differentiation requires a certain degree of freedom in how expectations for communication are formed, and becomes institutionalised when the individual has full control

30 N. Luhmann, '*Grundrechte als Institution*', above n. 28, p. 80.
31 Ibid., p. 97.
32 Ibid., p. 98.
33 For more on this lateral effect, especially derived from Art. 3(1) GG, see section 4.2.1 below.
34 Constitutional Court of the Federal Republic of Germany, Judgment of 15.01.1958 – 1 BvR 400/15, ECLI:DE:BVerfG:1951:rs19580115.1bvr040051, para. 31.
35 Original wording in German: "zwanglos und in bunter, widerspruchsreicher Fülle Normen, Rollen und Institutionen gebildet und ausprobiert werden" (N. Luhmann, 'Grundrechte als Institution', above n. 28, p. 102).

over their self-expression. The differentiation of modern society requires that communication be released from overly narrow standards of expression.[36]

Precisely this issue becomes problematic in the face of digitised communication. In pre-modern society, forms of expression, participants, and topics were closely guided, if not bound, by the contextual specification of close personal relations, and standardised through group-specific and hierarchical conventions. Today, communication is channelled by the codes and algorithms of digital intermediaries. This has the effect that these private internet intermediaries, the very actors behind the technological revolution, are the main threat to the openness and potential differentiation of communication. Internet Service Providers (ISP)s regulate access according to their own rules, which they can also enforce themselves, as a result of their control over the logical architecture of media functions. As a consequence, the normativity of the digital world is independent from the rules that apply in and to the analogue world.

However, this does not yet capture just how radical the influence of digital media has been for communication. At first glance, data and communication rules prescribed by digital intermediaries seem only to bind individual speech, or acts of speaking, to certain forms, and thus limit their ability to structurally couple social communication to individual consciousness. The fundamental effects of digitisation on communication, however, go much further, creating a novel structure that couples social communication to autonomous digital systems using data, and its transmission in digital networks. Thus, for the first time, we are faced with the evolution of the social system partly detached from human consciousness. Just when it seemed that society could not get any more complex, having exhausted the potential to link human consciousness with globalised functional systems and a global society fed by maximum inclusion in social systems, society created a new environment to stimulate further development.[37] Now algorithms are taking over, increasing complexity and raising it into a new dimension. As a result, society is now orthogonally linked on two sides; simultaneously to consciousness *and* to digital systems.[38]

Data-driven communication installs its own selectivity, based on a syntax of data processing independent of meaning.[39] This operational independence does not mean that the non-symbolic processing of data has no effect on society.

---

36 Ibid., pp. 21–23.

37 For N. Luhmann, *Theory of Society*, above n. 7, vol. 1, p. 321, this is related to the marking of forms, which allows for rich differentiation and classification without being bound to the functional system codes.

38 M. Amstutz, 'Dateneigentum: Funktion und Form' (2018) 218 *Archiv für civilistische Praxis* 439, 514.

39 Ibid., pp. 451 and 486 rightly emphasised a *"Doppelcodierung von Daten"*, which involves two syntaxes: the digital syntax, which allows data to become a medium able to perform the functions of processing, storing, and transmitting; and the semiotic, which serves to code the information contained in the data.

On the contrary, data-driven applications may *drive* social interaction, particularly because they influence the images of persons constructed by social systems.

In a functionally differentiated society, the individual is functionally fragmented. It is split up into several 'selves', in order to be able to meet the requirements of different social environments and cope with the diversity of requirements.[40] Society's various functional systems have different roles for, or concepts of, persons. These are standardised collages of expectations which, depending on the social context, prescribe different behaviour as appropriate. *Homo economicus*, *homo politicus* and *homo scientificus* all separate and coexist, each with their own measured stride: "the individual is defined by divisibility".[41]

However, digitisation removes the semantics of these social constructions of persons. In contrast to consciousness and communication systems, digital systems operate outside of the context of meaning. Using mass collection of (behavioural) data, algorithms determine correlations between persons and events, and make predictions about their future behaviour. Certainly, it is not so much the accuracy of the predictions that matters, but rather their use to pre-empt possible courses of action that can guide the further operation of social systems. Autonomous digital systems undermine the function of understanding,[42] and, as the possible courses of action are technically enforced, the algorithmically constructed digital world validates itself. Thus, how individuals perceive themselves in social systems begins to form along the lines of an algorithmic rationality: "Who we are ... is also a declaration by our data as interpreted by algorithms. We are ourselves, plus layers upon layers of ... algorithmic identities".[43] This paves the way for an "algorithmic governmentality", in which behaviour is not controlled according to social norms that express certain expectations. These expectations, preferably formed previously in deliberative processes, have given way to electronic architectures that anticipate all possible courses of action derived from inductive computational processes.[44] This control system is operated, not by the State, but by the private operators of these algorithmic systems, where they have

---

40 N. Luhmann, 'Individuum, Individualität, Individualismus' in *Gesellschaftsstruktur und Semantik: Band 3*, Suhrkamp, Frankfurt am Main 1993, p. 223.

41 Ibid.

42 M. Amstutz, above n. 38, 515. Attributing actions to individuals in the process of communication is no longer possible (behavioural data are aggregated into clusters), and also no longer necessary (as it is no longer a matter of interpreting and understanding actions, but rather of anticipating potential actions and their technical implementation).

43 J. Cheney-Lippold, *We Are Data*, New York University Press, New York 2017, p. 5.

44 A. Rouvroy, 'Governing Without Norms: Algorithmic Governmentality' (2018) 32 *Psychoanalytical Notebooks* 99 describes the peculiarity of this form of control: "the 'profiles/scores/matches' through which individuals are classed, assessed, recomposed or sanctioned, and through which the merits, needs, opportunities or dangers contained in life forms are assessed, are based on the numerical signals arising from trajectories, relations and interactions of individuals rather than on norms resulting from prior deliberative processes".

not already handed over control to an unsupervised learning algorithm. The new *dispositif* of control, therefore, is primarily civil in character.[45]

From this, a *second relational reformulation of the principle of equality* (R_2) can be inferred: the principle of equality must be extended from the analogue (semantic) world into the digital (syntactic) world. This is because the latter influences how, and to what extent, societal structures form, and thus in turn the preconditions of individual freedom. To extend the principle of equality from the analogue to the digital, the law must first (R_{2a}) determine the potential for autonomous digital systems to impact on the formation of social structures, and present the inherent normativity of digital selections. The principle of equality can only be effective in the context of digital regulation if it can translate machine normativity (the digital regulatory scheme, or how selections are made) into positive norms, as this is the only way to reveal potential unequal treatment. Subsequently (R_{2b}), the law must render machine normativity contestable. Normativity must be decoded, making it no longer automated – adding the level of lawmaking, so to speak. Both of these require the principle of equality to be binding on private actors. The second relational reformulation, therefore, targets the *preconditions for the principle of equality to apply*. The applicability of the principle of equality must first be created, if it is to apply to the digital environment of society.

4. EQUALITY RIGHTS AND THE CHANGE OF SOCIAL PRACTICE

4.1. THE PRINCIPLE OF EQUALITY AS REFLEXIVE LAW

4.1.1. Social Normativity

Were justice to plead with the law, according to this first relational reformulation, it would ask it to respond to changes in social practice. In practical terms, this would require a loosening of its fixation on the autonomy of persons, turning instead to the perspective of social normativities as a supplement. More precisely, the law should provide for two elements: (1) forms and methods that can recognise and process social change that has already occurred; and (2) forms and methods that are suitable for initiating change in social practice.

Under conditions of positive law, the principle of impartiality (R_1) is operationalised by fundamental rights, which act as procedural requirements for any form – State as well as private – of lawmaking.[46] The validity of law is

45 M. Amstutz, above n. 38, p. 517.

46 D. Wielsch, 'Grundrechte als Rechtfertigungsgebote', above n. 23, 753.

not determined by its content or the values it represents, but by the way it is formed, with consideration of specific normative perspectives. These are initially formulated in civil liberties, whose various areas of protection, as mentioned above, provide rights that represent the normative integrity of specific social functions that require consistent updating to reflect changing contexts.

Above all, however, the general principle of equality (Art. 20 CFR-EU/ Art. 3(1) GG) continuously forces the law to deal with the exercise of rights under *changed conditions*. With unrelenting consistency, it calls for a review of legal rules in the face of changing environments. The principle of equality thus makes the law ask itself whether a *new social practice* (this is decisive: the person whose treatment is in question must be seen as the representative of a social practice!) can really be treated legally in the same way as an old one. Where this is not the case, it then demands the establishment of a *new rule* appropriate to the new social practice. The principle of equality is the thorn in the flesh of positive law: it alone makes pure self-inspection *legally* impermissible for the law. It is, therefore, in this regard, a unique *legal innovation machine*.

However, having a machine and making it work are two different things. The "principle of personal equality" is a particularly effective driver, requiring justification, in general, of any unequal treatment of relations between private individuals.[47] It is drawn from the common principles of specific equal treatment obligations in current private law.[48] Adding a requirement for equal treatment between private parties results in a highly responsive instrument of the law for registering unequal treatment in its environment. The law must then validate its results by examining whether there is any justification for this unequal treatment. This creates a "burden of justification", which serves to "structure the contexts of the specific social conflict in such a way that the individual effects of the unequal treatment on the interests of the unequally treated person become visible and can thereby be addressed".[49]

Equal treatment obligations can, therefore, be read as a political right to ask for justification for private measures, and to contest them. Reformulating equal treatment obligations as a principle of personal equality extends their scope of application beyond the realm of State decisions. This, in turn, paves the way for individuals to also ask why they are affected differently by social institutions. These obligations, therefore, appear to be a necessary supplement to civil liberties, particularly where the regulation of social institutions is beyond

47 M. Grünberger, 'Grundstrukturen (allgemeine Strukturmerkmale) von Gleichheitssätzen' in S. Kempny and P. Reimer (eds), *Gleichheitssatzdogmatik heute*, Mohr Siebeck, Tübingen 2017, p. 7.

48 Detailed analysis in M. Grünberger, *Personale Gleichheit*, Nomos, Baden-Baden 2013, p. 315 *et seq*.

49 Ibid., p. 1049.

the control of the State, or deliberately kept out of its reach, for example as with the self-regulation of media.

4.1.2. Digital Normativity

Providers of digital services can use technology to directly enforce contractual claims and other conditions. This ability to enforce (alleged) rights, without requiring prior assessment by the courts, stands in stark contrast to what "normally" happens in the analogue world. The smart contracts and upload filters in use with many smart devices, and with social platforms in particular, limit the "ability to (mis)behave".[50] Any form of alternative behaviour, unlawful or otherwise, is not possible: the setting, application and enforcement of standards have merged. This then allows the dominant rationale of the service – in the case of social networks, the reconstruction of social interaction for the purpose of maximising economic exploitation – to unfold unchecked. There is a lack of corrective measures in the interests of the whole of society which could compensate for a failure to consider other perspectives: in the analogue world, these would arise, at the latest, on the level of enforcement of a contract or other legal act.

Insofar as the content of terms of use, or code-regulated data processing, are concerned, judicial proceedings can provide an additional level of reflection in the social rule-making processes existing on the periphery of the legal system. This, of course, requires that statutory fairness tests can identify the specific dangers emanating from autonomous digital communication structures. By its nature, this then becomes constitutional review of non-legislative law.[51]

It should be noted that the standard of such societal-constitutional control is not simply an identical copy of the guarantees contained in State constitutions that the political process will not infringe on other autonomies. It must be developed specifically for media constitution in the era of digitalised communication.[52]

However, as we know from the world of State-made law, substantive standards cannot sufficiently determine the application and enforcement of rights.

---

50 M. Becker, 'Von der Freiheit, rechtswidrig handeln zu können' (2019) *Zeitschrift für Urheber- und Medienrecht* 636, 647.

51 See G. Teubner, *Societal Constitutionalism: Alternatives to State-centred Constitutional Theory* (I.L. Fraser, tr.), OUP, Oxford 2003, p. 20: "One ought not to be deceived by the antiquated private law review formulas of 'good morals', 'good faith', that the ordinary courts use as to the fact that here, substantively, it is 'ordre public', i.e. the fit between 'private' norms and constitutional norms, especially human rights, that is being decided. Yet a closer look shows that they are being measured not by the political constitution of the state but a constitution of their own. The resolve is simultaneously a judicial liberation and a judicial constraint on the dynamics of a system-specific rationality."

52 D. Wielsch, 'Private Law Regulation of Digital Intermediaries' (2019) 27 *European Review of Private Law* 197, 205.

When looking at statements made by users in social networks, for example, the context of the communication must be taken into account. So far, so straightforward; but, for example, where intermediaries are obligated to take measures to protect third-party copyrights, court orders must consider the possibility of different variants of technological protection, and the civil liberties of the service provider itself, in particular its entrepreneurial freedom, as well as the interests of third-party users of the medium to access information.

To enable correction of actions exploiting the leeway that private actors inevitably retain, some laws have established complaint and redress procedures for digital intermediaries. For example, Article 17(9) of the Directive 2019/790 on Copyright in the Digital Single Market (DSM Directive) provides that platform operators who are required to take technical measures to protect against copyright infringements are also obliged to establish procedures to review their measures. It explicitly requires that decisions to block or remove user-generated content be "subject to human review". In addition, out-of-court redress procedures should "enable disputes to be settled impartially". For social media platforms, a comparable obligation is contained in section 3(1) of the German Network Enforcement Act (Netzwerkdurchsetzungsgesetz, or NetzDG), which requires the establishment of effective and transparent procedures for dealing with complaints about illegal content. At the international level, the Manila Principles on Intermediary Liability (2015) and the Santa Clara Principles on Transparency and Accountability in Content Moderation (2018) require intermediaries to establish appropriate complaint procedures for the benefit of users. Facebook has gone beyond internal review procedures, by setting up the Facebook "Oversight Board", as an independent body whose rulings are transparent and binding on the company, to review removal decisions.[53]

Simply establishing such a body is not sufficient, however: the decisions of this body in particular, and the network's own procedures in general, must treat cases equally if they are to meet the basic requirements of procedural fairness. Thus, we have a self-imposed obligation on the intermediary to comply with its own earlier decisions.[54] A duty to justify every instance of unequal treatment requires an arms-length perspective, and a special kind of decision autonomy. Direct decision-making must be disciplined in such a way that it is detached from the entanglements of the specific case, and can remain consistent.[55]

---

53 See <https://www.oversightboard.com/governance/>. On the motivation for its creation, see M. Zuckerberg, 'A Blueprint for Content Governance and Enforcement' (*Facebook*, 15.11.2018) <https://tinyurl.com/y2ry5cj3>. They also mention a "Supreme Court of Facebook". On this, see K. Klonick and T. Kadri, '*Facebook v. Sullivan*: Building Constitutional Law for Online Speech' (2019) 93 *Southern California Law Review* 37, 95 *et seq*.

54 C. Gusy, 'Richterrecht und Grundgesetz' (1992) *Die öffentliche Verwaltung* 461, 469; M. Payandeh, *Judikative Rechtserzeugung*, Mohr Siebeck, Tübingen 2017, p. 175.

55 N. Luhmann, '*Grundrechte als Institution*', above n. 28, pp. 174 and 176.

Thus, the principle of equality can gain traction as soon as the intermediaries' fusion of rule-setting and technological rule-enforcement is disentangled by the interposition of obligatory proceedings. As in the case of the separation of powers, the very fact that a social network has to review its own measures results in the creation of standards, and thus increases the level of reflection.[56] The principle of equality thus proves to be an essential component of the *self-constitution* of autonomous digital media.

4.2. EQUALITY RIGHTS AS PARTICIPATION RIGHTS IN DIGITAL REGULATION

4.2.1. Rights to Justification of Private Access Regulation

The principle of equality gains relevance for legal relationships between private actors where they determine the conditions of access to the public sphere, and thus the prerequisites for the exercise of fundamental freedoms, in particular the freedom of communication. This also applies to the extent that intermediaries are called upon to mediate effective legal protection on the Internet. Both aspects are interrelated.

The conditions of the public sphere are increasingly determined by private actors operating the infrastructure for communication (whether digital or analogue).[57] Such actors enable public access to protected works and personal information alike, and they structure public communication (social networks). Thus, normatively (drawing on decisions based on their terms of use), and definitely, as a result of their control of the technology, these actors have the ability to selectively control access to the medium and exclude individual users and content from the public sphere.

Justification for denying access is often based on the fact that the excluded party has infringed, or is infringing on, the rights of third parties, meaning that service providers are acting to protect the rights of third parties. Under digital

---

56 On the indirect effect of the specific controls provided by a functional distribution of State power, see B. Grzeszick, in T. Maunz and G. Dürig (founders), *Grundgesetz-Kommentar*, 82nd ed., C.H. Beck, Munich 2018, Art. 20, para. 38.

57 See Constitutional Court of the Federal Republic of Germany, Order of 18.07.2015 – 1 BvQ 25/15, ECLI:DE:BVerfG:2015:qk20150718.1bvq002515: "*Wenn heute die Kommunikationsfunktion der öffentlichen Straßen, Wege und Plätze zunehmend durch weitere Foren wie Einkaufszentren, Ladenpassagen oder durch private Investoren geschaffene und betriebene Plätze als Orte des Verweilens, der Begegnung, des Flanierens, des Konsums und der Freizeitgestaltung ergänzt wird … Der beabsichtigte Ort der Versammlung steht zwar im Eigentum einer Privaten, ist zugleich aber für den Publikumsverkehr offen und schafft nach den Feststellungen des* LG *einen Raum des Flanierens, des Verweilens und der Begegnung, der dem* Leitbild des öffentlichen Forums *entspricht.*"

conditions, the essential link between a legal claim and its enforcement by the State is lost. Thus, in the context of digital networks, effective legal protection for intellectual property and personal rights can often only be ensured with the assistance of intermediaries. The idea that a guarantee of private rights also implies their enforcement – as held by the German Constitutional Court[58] – becomes precarious.

Entities under the EU liability regime for intermediaries have a multilateral responsibility to provide effective legal protection against illegal actions of third parties. However, in contrast to the injunctive relief against the perpetrator in cases of copyright infringement, injunctions requiring platform operators to take protective measures concern more than a bilateral legal relationship, and must consider a multipolar relationship between the copyright holder, the perpetrator, the intermediary and its users. According to European Court of Justice (ECJ) case law, the intermediary's responsibility to implement appropriate measures therefore includes considering the fundamental rights of all those affected, including the freedom of information of internet users, and ensuring that these rights can be exercised effectively.[59] Against this background, the aforementioned provision in Article 17(9) of the DSM Directive was enacted. In the same vein, the *"Google Spain"* judgment obliged search engines to ensure that privacy rights are respected in the services offered. As this may require published search results to be removed, the interests of Internet users in access to information must be considered before any such deletion can take place,[60] as must the interests of the person uploading the content.[61] Search engine operators are, therefore, required to weigh up their decisions about media functions against the fundamental rights of those who would be affected. To meet this responsibility, Google not only established an "Advisory Council on the Right to be Forgotten", made up of external experts to formulate criteria and guidelines for balancing future decisions, but also set up a procedure for reporting and reviewing removal requests.

---

58 Constitutional Court of the Federal Republic of Germany, Order of 19.10.1993 – 1 BvR 567/89, ECLI:DE:BVerfG:2005:rs20051206.1bvr19, para. 52 *et seq.*

59 Laying the foundations, ECJ, Judgment of 27.03.2014 – Case C-314/12, *UPC Telekabel Wien GmbH v. Constantin Film Verleih GmbH and Wega Filmproduktionsgesellschaft mbH*, ECLI:EU:C:2014:192, para. 55 *et seq* (*"UPC Telekabel"*).

60 See ECJ, Judgment of 13.05.2014 – Case C-131/12, *Google Spain SL and Google Inc. v. Agencia Española de Protección de Datos (AEPD) and Mario Costeja González*, ECLI:EU:C:2014:192, para. 81 (*"Google Spain"*), where, admittedly, the fundamental rights of the data subject are generally assumed to prevail. In cases where Internet intermediaries are involved in communications, the German Federal Court of Justice speaks of an "overall balancing" between the right of personality of the person concerned, on the one hand, and the interests of the users and intermediaries themselves, on the other: see German Federal Court, Judgment of 23.6.2009 – VI ZR 196/08, ECLI:DE:BGH:2011:251011UVIZR93.10.0, para. 43.

61 On the analysis of the ECJ *"Google Spain"* judgment, see B.P. Paal, 'Online-Suchmaschinen – Persönlichkeitsrechts- und Datenschutz' (2016) *Zeitschrift für Europäisches Privatrecht* 591, 610.

The protection of copyright and privacy rights on the Internet may, thus, require digital intermediaries to set up self-regulatory procedures for the protection of third parties. According to this, State law would, under conditions of increased uncertainty, exercise its own responsibility to guarantee fundamental rights, specifically by making them normatively binding on powerful private actors.[62] The State's responsibility to protect rights in general, and fundamental rights in particular, has always followed from its power to enforce the law. To the extent that all or part of this enforcement shifts from the State to private actors, the responsibility borne by both the State and the private actor also change. Here it becomes clear that the future focus will be on the mode of fundamental rights effect known in Germany as "protecting fundamental rights through procedure".

The aforementioned case law on intermediaries' duties of care usually deals with actions brought against intermediaries by right-holders. But what applies for cases in which users want to defend themselves against the measures taken by intermediaries? Generally, this starts with the contractual relationship between the intermediary and its user who allegedly infringed the rights of others. Further procedural requirements for access regulation that affects contractual performance may arise if the intermediaries are bound by the principle of equal treatment under Article 20 CFR-EU/Article 3(1) GG.

The German Constitutional Court's "stadium ban" decision sets new standards here. The court held that, although private contractual relationships are generally not subject to the justification requirements of the equal treatment requirement, it is different when a person is refused access to a public event on the basis of unilateral decision-making power, where this exclusion has a considerable impact on the ability of the person concerned to participate in social life.[63] In this case, the decision to refuse access made by a private entity had a social impact because it resulted in a nationwide 'stadium ban' based on the German football association guidelines, which means – and this is often overlooked – it was part of the access regulation of an entire social sector. In such cases, the power to exclude is tied to the existence of an objective reason for the exclusion. Therefore, the court stated procedural requirements:

> In particular, stadium operators must make reasonable efforts to clarify the facts of the case. This includes, at least in principle, that the persons concerned be given a hearing prior to the imposition of a stadium ban. Reasons must also be provided for the decision upon request in order to enable the persons concerned to assert their right to seek legal recourse.[64]

---

62 See also D. Wielsch, 'Die Haftung des Mediums' in B. Lomfeld (ed), *Die Fälle der Gesellschaft: Eine neue Praxis soziologischer Jurisprudenz*, Mohr Siebeck, Tübingen 2017, p. 142.

63 Constitutional Court of the Federal Republic of Germany, Order of 11.4.2018 – 1 BvR 3080/09, ECLI:DE:BVerfG:2018:rs20180411.1bvr308009, para. 41.

64 Ibid., para. 46.

An objective reason for refusing access could be that the petitioner posed a threat to the rights of third parties (*in casu* a football fan prone to violence). Like the digital intermediaries, the stadium operator also has the responsibility for a public space. Recognising this responsibility does not mean that private parties are performing State tasks, nor does it constitute a "privatisation of the state's exercise of power".[65] It is not a matter of co-opting private actors for State purposes, but of social sectors forming under self-constitutionalisation, which holds especially true for media that develop independently from any State action. However, every organiser of a major event has a duty of care linked to the dangers typical of such an event. In the case of digital intermediaries, the establishment of a duty of care can be linked to the fact that they are providing decentralised access to the legally protected interests of third parties (rendering intermediaries subject to a kind of "functional liability").[66] If self-regulation is not already in place (as is the case as in Facebook's "community standards"), it will become necessary in order to meet these duties of care.

If we line up a measure restricting access and, incidentally, the entire private regime of access regulation, against Article 20 CFR-EU/Article 3(1) GG, a private party is indeed bound by the right of another party to a fair trial.[67] In substance, this is a publification of the exercise of private power. Directly binding private access regulation concerning the principle of equality is considered problematic in some cases, because the affirmation of a constitutional right of access would then apply in other cases, even where exclusion is permissible under the statutory provisions of the General Equal Treatment Act (AGG), or under the rules of competition law.[68]

However, this ignores the fact that the German Constitutional Court is concerned precisely with the procedural safeguards required by Article 3 GG that play no role in competition law or the AGG, which is concerned with violations of substantive principles of competition, or discrimination on the basis of proscribed characteristics, respectively. Here, too, the reverse is true, in that simple statutory law, were it to allow barriers to access for the public without precautions for a fair procedure, would in turn have to be assessed in the light of Art. 3 GG.

The principle of equality thus acts as a kind of "constitutionalisation anchor" with regard to private access regimes, in that it urges them to adopt procedural safeguards for the interests affected by their decisions on whether to grant or deny

---

65 This is, however, claimed by A. Hellgardt, 'Wer hat Angst vor der unmittelbaren Drittwirkung?' (2019) *JuristenZeitung* 901, 909.

66 D. Wielsch, 'Funktion und Verantwortung. Zur Haftung im Netzwerk' (2019) *Rechtswissenschaft* 84, 107 *et seq*.

67 Correctly seen in A. Hellgardt, n. 65, 908, with reference to BVerfGE (official reports of the German Constitutional Court) 101, 397 (p. 404 *et seq*.).

68 Hellgardt (ibid.) complains that, in this regard, private law effectively has its hands tied.

access, unless the establishment of such procedures has already been ordered by the law. The principle of equality induces, as it were, a constitutionalisation of access regimes "from within". Guaranteed in Article 3 GG as a subjective right, not just a norm, it can be mobilised under certain conditions by the individual petitioning for access, and provides a right to justification of private access regulation. The principle of equality provides scope for participation in the design of private access rules by those who are affected.

4.2.2. *Rights to Justification of Syntactic Normativity*

4.2.2.1. Normativity of Network Protocols

However, equal treatment requirements can "open up" the regulation of digital communications by intermediaries, beyond merely the basic fair procedure requirements used to restrain political power in State constitutional law. Rather, equal treatment imperatives can also directly bind how syntactic structures are constructed. Regardless of their doctrinal source, they operate as media constitution law in that they both constitute the autonomy of the digital medium and limit its effect on other autonomies. This echoes the way that the State's constitution links the creation of society's capacity for political self-impact with protecting social autonomies from this very impact, if unproportionate.

Article 3(3), subparagraph 1, of Regulation (EU) 2015/2120 on measures for access to the open Internet (EU Net Neutrality Regulation) provides a *statutory requirement for equal treatment* at the level of protocols and standards of data transmission on the Internet. In principle, it requires "providers of internet access services [to] treat all traffic equally, when providing internet access services, without discrimination, restriction or interference, and irrespective of the sender and receiver, the content accessed or distributed, the applications or services used or provided, or the terminal equipment used". This can be regarded as an expression of "net neutrality", as envisioned and enshrined in the early stages of Internet development by the consistent implementation of the "end-to-end" principle in network protocol construction.[69] This principle has decentralised decision-making authority for the use of the Internet and thereby constituted the new medium as a common good.[70] As such, users need only comply with the specifications of the Internet Protocol, not the will or technical specifications of a network operator.[71] Separating ownership (over the physical layer of network infrastructure) and control (over possibilities of actions on

---

69 B. van Schewick, *Internet Architecture and Innovation*, MIT Press, Cambridge, MA 2010, p. 90 *et seq.*

70 D. Wielsch, *Zugangsregeln*, Mohr Siebeck, Tübingen 2008, p. 243.

71 On increasing development independence and enabling autonomous innovation under a broad end-to-end principle, see B. van Schewick, above n. 69, p. 204 *et seq.*

the logical layer) ensures the medium's receptivity to development, and has contributed to an enormous variety of network-based applications. This access rule, implemented by means of technology, is, however, being placed under increasing pressure by new network technologies that allow access providers to treat specific data (from anywhere in the global network) differently once it has entered the subnetwork they operate, differentiating by characteristics of origin or content.[72] In contrast, Article 3 of the EU Net Neutrality Regulation requires equal treatment in data transport.[73]

The obligation to ensure equal treatment in the transmission of data cannot be waived through contractual agreements, in a bilateral relationship between an Internet access provider and its end user. This explains why the courts confirmed the official prohibition of a mobile phone plan which specifically limited bandwidth for video streaming.[74] The equal treatment requirement is an objective requirement, which protects the functional principles of the Internet for the benefit of all end users: its waiver (by users of a specific service provider) would, in fact, be equivalent to a contract to the detriment of third parties.[75] While users may agree to exercise their access rights under Article 3(1) in accordance with the provisions of Article 3(2) of the Net Neutrality Regulation, and agree upon technical conditions for access (concerning, for instance, data volume or speed), these agreements must however be "application neutral", and may not differentiate between different categories of data.[76] In addition to protecting end users, the equal treatment requirement is, therefore, an independent institutional safeguard, as the purpose of the regulation is "to guarantee the continued functioning of the internet ecosystem as an engine of innovation".[77] This freedom to develop higher-level applications, and thus

---

72 For related developments, see J.H. Klement, 'Netzneutralität: der Europäische Verwaltungsverbund als Legislative' (2017) *Euoparecht* 532, 534.

73 More specifically, Art. 3(1) EU Net Neutrality Regulation on access-related net neutrality, and Art. 3(3) on transmission-related net neutrality.

74 High Administrative Court (Oberverwaltungsgericht, OVG) Münster, Judgment of 12.07.2019 – 13 B 1734/18, ECLI:DE:OVGNRW:2019:0712.13B1734.18.00; previously, Administrative Court (Verwaltungsgericht, VG) Köln, 2019, 197. In the main proceedings (VG Köln, Judgment of 20.01.2020 – 9 K 4632/18, ECLI:DE:VGK:2020:0120.9K4632.18.00), the question was referred to the ECJ of whether agreements within the meaning of Art. 3(2) Net Neutrality Regulation on features of Internet access services such as price, data volumes or speed, agreed between providers and end-users of internet access services, must satisfy the requirements of Art. 3(3) Net Neutrality Regulation, and the principle of equal treatment that it contains.

75 OVG Münster, above n. 74, para. 18.

76 Ibid., para. 24.

77 See Recital 1 and Art. 1 of Regulation (EU) 2015/2120 of the European Parliament and of the Council of 25 November 2015 laying down measures concerning open internet access and amending Directive 2002/22/EC on universal service and users' rights relating to electronic communications networks and services and Regulation (EU) 531/2012 on roaming on public mobile communications networks within the Union [2015].

maintain the autonomy of the medium, is preserved by binding the syntax of network protocols to an equal treatment requirement. The law requires all data be treated equally at the transmission level, to protect the fundamental freedoms of the user population as a whole.

4.2.2.2. Algorithmic Normativity

It seems obvious, then, to also bring the principle of equality and prohibitions on discrimination to bear in the context of algorithmic regulation and decision-making based on machine learning, in order to prevent discriminatory output from an automated system.

However, there are two considerations that must be taken into account here. Firstly, it is not possible to eliminate all bias from the training data used for machine learning systems. While this goal is understandable, in the hope of establishing an algorithm which has learned only from non-discriminatory and representative training data, discriminatory attributes often correlate with other, non-discriminatory attributes, which then act as "proxies".[78] Prohibiting the use of discriminatory training data would not, therefore, result in an objective, neutral algorithm, but only serve to better mask the discrimination it produces. Secondly, bias is inherent in machine learning, as it is prerequisite for inductive inferences.[79]

It may be helpful here to compare this with the way human understanding operates, as described by philosophical hermeneutics. Bias, according to hermeneutical thought, is not a disturbance, but a productive condition for understanding meaning. Even though this gives us bias as a constitutive element, it is, of course, presumed that it can be corrected.[80] True hermeneutic consciousness is only opened up to the claim of cultural tradition if it has an ability to experience the tentative application of prejudice to what is to be understood, and correct it accordingly. Instead of obtaining conclusive knowledge, the "truth of experience always contains the reference to new experience", where

78 M. Hildebrandt, 'Privacy as Protection of the Incomputable Self: From Agnostic to Agonistic Machine Learning' (2019) 20 *Theoretical Inquiries in Law* 83, 102.

79 T. Mitchell, *Machine Learning*, MIT Press/McGraw-Hill, Cambridge, MA 1997, p. 42, speaks of an "inductive bias", and notes that, "a learner that makes no a priori assumptions regarding the identity of the target concept has no rational basis for classifying any unseen instances".

80 According to H-G. Gadamer, *Truth and Method* (J. Weinsheimer and D.G. Marshall, trs.), 3rd ed., Continuum, London 2004, p. 238 *et seq.*, the process of understanding meaning depends precisely on the constant revision of preliminary drafts. Accordingly, hermeneutic consciousness demands a fundamental readiness for openness and the fact that one's own standards can be questioned (ibid., p. 334 *et seq.*).

"false generalisations are constantly refuted by experience, what is held to be typical is, as it were, de-typified".[81]

Openness to having one's own standards questioned may, for historical understanding, merely be a question of appropriateness, but it becomes obligatory for machine learning systems, to the extent that decisions affect the rights and freedoms of the individuals involved. The idea of external correction for technological systems is not new; it is familiar from both open innovation networks ("peer production"), and through the involvement of users in the production of new technologies ("prosumers"). Ultimately, it underpins the very goal of developing robust technological systems. Once these technological systems become autonomous, and assume regulatory functions, the idea assumes a normative quality.

Machine learning plays a particular role when processes become too complicated to describe analytically, but there is sufficient training data available. This allows predictions or decisions to be made without any predefined rules,[82] and greatly increases the need for co-determination in the development of those rules.

The consequence of the fact that algorithms start from a "ground truth" is, therefore, not that machine learning should be treated as a threat and intensively regulated from the outset, but that data-driven algorithms should be designed around opportunities for co-determination by those affected. The same normative claim is discussed under many labels, whether we are discussing the institutionalisation of dissent as an expression of the rule of law,[83] as a central element of the democratic principle,[84] or as a generalisation and re-specification of political autonomy that should also be made effective for decentralised rule formation beyond State legislation.[85] In each case, the issue is that machine architectures can be tested, and in the event of doubt, submitted to revision. Such "agnostic machine learning" would be based on the possibility that those affected by change to their environment caused by data-driven algorithms can raise objections to the "ground truth", and the initial design of the data

---

81 Ibid., p. 325 *et seq.*

82 Fraunhofer-Institut IAIS, *Vertrauenswürdiger Einsatz von Künstlicher Intelligenz*, Fraunhofer-Institut IAIS, Sankt Augustin 2019, p. 10.

83 M. Hildebrandt, 'Privacy as Protection of the Incomputable Self', above n. 78, 107 with relevant notation, speaks of binding to "the adversarial core of the Rule of Law", but founds her position predominantly by referring to democratic theories, particularly Mouffe's agnostic model.

84 On institutionalised dissent as a core element of the principle of democracy (in addition to consensus building), see G. Teubner, 'Quod Omnes Tangit: Transnational Constitutions Without Democracy?' (2018) 45 *Journal of Law and Society* S5, S11.

85 D. Wielsch, 'Medienregulierung durch Persönlichkeits- und Datenschutzrechte', above n. 3, 114.

processing. Those responsible for the design must then consider alternatives[86] that will establish experimental and reversible data architectures, so that technological regulation will be treated as something to be generated, and not as something prescribed. Thus, digital normativity is "positivised", and able to be changed, instead of remaining in its "natural" condition. In other words, decentralised normative learning can occur in digital systems. To the extent that affected persons can influence the design of the algorithms, digital technological architecture is taking on the form of "social" architecture: decentralisation according to the principle of democracy allows digital normativity to be positivised.

In the first instance, data protection law is called upon to implement such normative learning in automated data processing. It imposes specific information obligations on the data controller with regard to the data subject. According to Articles 13 (2)(f) and 14(2)(g) of the General Data Protection Regulation 2016/679 (GDPR), the controller must provide "meaningful information" about the existence of automated decision-making, the logic involved, and the scope and effects of processing. These obligations are supplemented with the rights of access (Art. 15 (1)(h) GDPR) and rights of objection to the processing of personal data (Art. 21 (1)(2) GDPR).[87] Most importantly, Article 22(3) of the GDPR only permits fully automated decision-making under the additional condition that the controller takes "suitable measures" to protect the individual(s) concerned, who have "at least the right to obtain human intervention on the part of the controller, to express his or her point of view and to contest the decision".[88] These rights can be reconstructed as procedural requirements for algorithmic regulation, as an expression of the protection of fundamental rights through procedure.[89] They are intended to ensure that algorithmic decision-making is transparent and fair,[90] effectively placing some controls on what is otherwise a unilaterally determined

86 M. Hildebrandt, 'Privacy as Protection of the Incomputable Self', above n. 78, 109.

87 On the GDPR body of regulations with regard to automated processes, see M. Martini, in B.P. Paal and D.A. Pauly, *DS-GVO*, 2nd ed., C.H. Beck, Munich 2018, Art. 22, para. 4.

88 The German literature overwhelmingly sees Art. 22(1) GDPR as a fundamental prohibition of automated individual decisions, with exceptions in para. 2 and additional caveats in para. 3: see P. Scholz, in S. Simitis, G. Hornung and I. Spiecker (eds), *Datenschutzrecht*, Nomos, Frankfurt am Main 2019, Art. 22, para. 16, with relevant notations. For an alternative reading regarding proactively exercising the right to object, see S. Wachter, B. Mittelstadt and L. Floridi, 'Why a Right to Explanation of Automated Decision-Making Does Not Exist in the General Data Protection Regulation' (2017) 7 *International Data Privacy Law* 76, 94 *et seq.*

89 Explicitly on the guarantee of fundamental rights protection through procedures in the form of the minimum guarantees of Art. 22(3) GDPR, see M. Martini, above n. 87, para. 39.

90 B. Buchner, in J. Kühling and B. Buchner (eds.), *DS-GVO/BDSG*, 2nd ed., C.H. Beck, Munich 2018, Art. 22, para. 34; P. Scholz, above n. 88, Art. 22, para. 56.

technological normativity. Those affected should be able to protect themselves against significant disadvantage from the algorithm, specifically by uncovering unequal treatment or discrimination and, where necessary, contesting this treatment using other legal instruments.[91] These minimum guarantees also bind private controllers to rule-of-law standards: the "right of appeal" is autonomously interpreted under EU law as a right to have a decision reviewed, for which there is not yet a civil law equivalent.[92]

These requirements are intended for, and limited to, enabling review with human involvement for previously made automated decisions. The review must be open-ended, and bring in the point of view of the person affected.[93] To this end, the data subject must be in a position to question the decision, and raise substantiated objections, whereby the provision of information about the abstract functionality of the algorithm and the essential decision-making criteria is sufficient to meet the transparency obligations.[94] Thus, there is no requirement for an exact explanation of the personal data evaluated by the algorithm in the individual case, as discussed in terms of the expanded catalogue of minimum guarantees in the recitals of the GDPR, stating that it should include the right "to obtain an explanation" (cf. Recital 71 GDPR).[95] A summary of the rights provided in Article 22(3) of the GDPR reveals that the law recognises the opacity associated with the operational autonomy of a technical system, and in fact forces a transition of (automated) decision-making into "justification mode".[96] Regardless of actual technical barriers or objections based on confidentiality and protecting trade secrets against detailed disclosure of the machine decision-making processes, an explanation of how a machine decision came about is not equivalent to its justification.[97]

The ability to verify machine-generated normativity is also a leading consideration, even beyond the scope of the GDPR. Article 22 of the GDPR

---

91 According to recital 71, subpara. 2 of the GDPR, controllers are to undertake appropriate mathematical or statistical measures to prevent outcomes which may have "discriminatory effects on natural persons on the basis of racial or ethnic origin, political opinion, religion or beliefs, trade union membership, genetic or health status or sexual orientation, or that result in measures having such an effect".

92 K. von Lewinski, in S. Brink and H.A. Wolff (eds), *BeckOK Datenschutzrecht*, 32nd ed., Art. 22 DSGVO, paras. 50 and 52.

93 P. Scholz, above n. 88, Art. 22, para. 59.

94 L.K. Kumkar and D. Roth-Isigkeit, 'Erklärungspflichten bei automatisierten Datenverarbeitungen' (2020) *JuristenZeitung* 277, 285.

95 See, firstly, B. Goodman and S. Flaxman, 'European Union regulations on algorithmic decision-making and "a right to explanation"' (2017) 38(3) *AI Magazine* <https://arxiv.org/abs/1606.08813>. For further discussion, see S. Wachter, B. Mittelstadt and L. Floridi, above n. 88, 76, with other references.

96 L.K. Kumkar and D. Roth-Isigkeit, above n. 94, 284 and 286.

97 M. Hildebrandt, 'Algorithmic regulation and the rule of law' (2018) 376(2128) *Philosophical Transactions of the Royal Society* 1, 3.

only prohibits purely automated individual decision-making, and does not cover the sensitive and much more common constellations where algorithms prepare information for, or substantially guide, a decision made by a human.[98] In fields determined by technology, such as medicine, duties of care under tort law are dependent on the state of the art in science, which is itself determined by the developmental level of machine learning models, where their diagnosis and prognosis capacities exceed those of human experts. That said, the performance of machine models does not determine legal duties of care. Rather, additional consideration must be given to whether the algorithm is intelligible, as this is the only way to enable critical scientific discussion, and subject the decision to review for potential false negative or false positive predictions.[99] The need for algorithms to be intelligible, even outside of fully automated decision-making, is therefore not established by data protection law. Instead, it results from the regulatory function of the algorithm in the case at hand, which must be considered by contract and tort law when formalising due diligence requirements. It is not only in the medical context that the questions of whether a machine model can be contested are central to measuring explanatory obligations. Once again, as far as decisions are made on the basis of digital regulation, in the absence of specific statutory procedural rules, a procedural minimum standard can be derived from national and European fundamental rights,[100] and then implemented through general contract and tort law.

The reverse problem can also arise where differentiated, unequal treatment is required, for example when digital platforms rely on algorithms to apply their policies on the publication of user-generated content. Facebook's community standards consider whether the subject of the information is a "public figure" or a private individual, when deciding whether or not to remove content. In making this decision, Facebook's community standards, in turn, consult Google News, despite the fact that this external reference cannot really be called legitimate, given that a person's prominence on Facebook is itself a grounds for being identified as a "public person", thus creating a feedback loop. Moreover, Google algorithms' automated evaluation of messages cannot take advantage of the filtering function of editorial media, whereby a public interest in the person is signalled through the media coverage.[101] In the spirit

---

98 M. Martini, above n. 87, para. 46; P. Scholz, above n. 88, Art. 22, para. 11.

99 P. Hacker et al., 'Explainable AI under contract and tort law: legal incentives and technical challenges' (2020) 28 *Artificial Intelligence and Law* 415.

100 On the procedural requirements that the ECtHR takes from the fundamental right to respect for private and family life in Article 8 of the ECHR, see B. van der Sloot, 'Decisional privacy 2.0: the procedural requirements implicit in Article 8 ECHR and its potential impact on profiling' (2017) 7 *International Data Privacy Law* 190, 201.

101 K. Klonick and T. Kadri, above n. 53, 77.

of the European Court of Human Rights' *"Caroline"* ruling, the definition of the public interest cannot be purely demand-driven, which, in the case of digital media, is precisely what occurs when algorithms aggregate information indiscriminately.[102]

In this constellation, it is not a matter of unequal treatment due to a hidden normativity generated by algorithm, but the reverse, so to speak, as the algorithm treats all information equally, without the differentiation that may arise from adequately taking the semantic context into account, or considering it at all. Thus, the algorithm-based normativity must be supplemented with appropriate semantic criteria, and the decision about the public person status of an individual must be made based on an interpretation of information that has been contextually interpreted and understood.[103] Also, in this constellation, syntactic normativity must be able to be contested from outside by those affected, and effectively pressured into justifying itself.

5. THE RIGHT OF EQUALITY AND ITS FUNCTION IN PRIVATE REGULATION

By focusing solely on the role of the principle of equality in the political system, the potential of the principle to play a role in constitutionalising social institutions is overlooked. Usually, application of the equality principle presumes positive law, and that State power is divided, itself a fundamental step in constitutionalising political power that is already implemented. These existing structures, however, turn to castles in the air in the face of non-political, horizontal regulation, and particularly in the case of technological regulation. In these types of private governance, the task of formalising normativities in the first place then falls to the right of equality. During this relational reformulation (see section 3 above),

102 ECHR, Judgment of 24.6.2004 – Case 59320/00, *Von Hannover v. Germany*, ECLI:CE:ECHR:2004:0624JUD005932000, para. 63 *et seq*.

103 ECJ, Judgment of 3.10.2019 – Case C-18/18, *Glawischnig-Piesczek v. Facebook Ireland Ltd.*, ECLI:EU:C:2019:821, para. 45 *et seq.* draws narrow limits to an automated evaluation of statements with content that violates personality rights, as the obligation to block access to a specific statement previously declared unlawful by the court only extends to formulations that are similar in meaning if the intermediary can "resort to automated techniques and means of investigation", and does not have to make an "autonomous assessment". This "autonomous assessment" would be tantamount to forcing the intermediary to perform a general monitoring obligation that is inadmissible within the meaning of Art. 15(1) of Directive 2000/31. Accordingly, the automated filtering of communications is to be limited by the intermediary to "slightly differently formulated[ed]" (ibid., para. 41) utterances, while larger deviations, which force consideration of the semantic context, are not to be assessed by the machine.

the equality right has to be adjusted to the semantic and syntactic regulation of communication via digital media; to regulation of the coupling between communication and consciousness, and to regulation of the coupling between communication and autonomous digital systems.

Some statutory provisions already exist at the first, semantic, level, which require intermediaries to set up procedures to protect the rights of third parties. Here, the fusion of norm and technical enforcement in private regulation is disentangled, and its self-constitution is triggered (see section 4.1.2 above). Thus, the prerequisites for applying the principle of equality are met, as the network's own procedures must satisfy the basic requirements of procedural fairness. The requirement for equal treatment of cases involving similar situations forces the formation of general standards, and raises the level of reflection in the private regime with regard to environmental concerns. The standards by which protection measures are made – particularly decisions to block or exclude content – are now subject to justification, and may be openly politicised. For cases involving the regulation of private access, in which no statutory duty has (yet) been set to bind protective measures to due process, a procedural minimum standard in favour of users petitioning for access can be derived from Article 3 GG (see section 4.2.1 above). The fundamental right to equality serves as an individual right to a justification for private access regulation.

In the second, syntactic, level, requirements for equal treatment may already bind the construction of syntactic normativity, as formed through network protocols for data transmission. This fundamental decision on media regulation, which affects a deeper layer of the modularised architecture of the Internet, is intended to ensure the same opportunities for access and use on the upper application layer (see section 4.2.2 above). In contrast, it does not seem appropriate to narrow the construction of autonomous algorithms in the same way from the outset. However, insofar as algorithms take on regulatory functions, the use of procedure to protect fundamental rights requires that algorithmic normativity is able to be reviewed and corrected. This process shifts technologically coded digital standards to positive normativity, while also rendering them subject to change. Thus, the relevant fundamental rights, particularly equality rights, operate in their procedural capacity, as rights to justification of syntactic normativity (see section 4.2.2.2 above).

Under private regulation conditions, rights to equality thus convey the ability to participate in the setting of the rules which grant access (to goods, works, information or data). While those affected can participate in State-based norm-setting, through subjective voting rights (see Article 38 GG), in private relationships equality rights can serve as participation rights. This function of equality rights is particularly significant for transnational or cross-border matters because rights of equality are recognised ubiquitously, and form part of every constitutional order – as with private autonomy, used for the creation of transnational private regulation. Increasingly, German and European fundamental rights of equality are being used for constitutionalising private legal relationships, in the absence of statutory rules.[104] To keep pace with the new forces of social evolution, the political potential of equality rights will also have to develop further.

---

104 Particularly with regard to the prohibition of discrimination provided in Art. 21(1) CFR-EU, the ECJ has also recently affirmed direct effects of private transactions: ECJ, Judgment of 17.4.2018 – Case C-414/16, *Vera Egenberger v. Evangelisches Werk für Diakonie und Entwicklung e.V.*, ECLI:EU:C:2018:257, para. 76 *et seq.*, confirmed in ECJ, Judgment of 22.1.2019 – Case C-193/17, *Cresco Investigation GmbH v. Markus Achatzi*, ECLI:EU:C:2019:43, para. 76. In many member states, the recognition of the direct effects of fundamental rights among private parties is far advanced: see M. Borowsky, in J. Meyer and S. Hölscheidt (eds), *Charta der Grundrechte der Europäischen Union*, 5th ed., Nomos, Frankfurt am Main 2019, Art. 1 GR-Ch, para. 43, with reference to the country reports in L. Burgorgue-Larsen (ed), *La Charte des droits fondamentaux saisie par les juges en Europe*, Pedone, Paris 2017.

INDEX

EUROPEAN CONTRACT LAW AND THEORY SERIES

1. *Rules and Principles in European Contract Law*, Jacobien Rutgers and Pietro Sirena (eds.)
2. *European Contract Law and the Charter of Fundamental Rights*, Hugh Collins (ed.)
3. *European Contract Law in the Digital Age*, Stefan Grundmann (ed.)
4. *European Contract Law in the Banking and Financial Union*, Stefan Grundmann and Pietro Sirena (eds.)
5. *European Contract Law and the Creation of Norms*, Stefan Grundmann and Mateusz Grochowski (eds.)

www.ingramcontent.com/pod-product-compliance
Ingram Content Group UK Ltd.
Pitfield, Milton Keynes, MK11 3LW, UK
UKHW051928100926
8556IPUK00022B/1430

9 781839 702778